Catholics in Colonial Days

CATHOLICS
IN
COLONIAL
DAYS

BY

THE REV. THOMAS P. PHELAN, M.A., LITT.D., LL.D.

PROFESSOR OF ANCIENT, MODERN AND
ECCLESIASTICAL HISTORY AT THE CATHOLIC
FOREIGN MISSION SEMINARY, MARYKNOLL,
N. Y.

GRYPHON BOOKS
ANN ARBOR, MICHIGAN · 1971

This is a facsimile reprint of the
1935 edition published in New York
by P.J. Kenedy & Sons.

Library of Congress Catalog Card Number 74-145706

To the faculty and students of the Catholic Foreign Mission Seminary, Maryknoll, N. Y., past and present, priests, brothers, sisters, at home and in the Field Afar, before whom these lectures were delivered during two decades, this volume is affectionately inscribed.

Preface

THE story of Catholic achievement in the thirteen colonies during colonial days has received scant treatment at the hands of our leading historians. True, the first century after the discovery by the Genoese mariner has been treated *in extenso,*—to omit these details would make the early chapters unintelligible,—but with little or no reference to the religion of the hardy discoverers and explorers who followed in the footsteps of the pathfinder, although shrines and chapels were reared, on its soil, the Holy Mass celebrated a quarter century before the arch-heresiarch burned the Papal Bull before the gates of Wittenberg. Calvert's noble experiment in civil and religious toleration evoked much praise and admiration from the premier historian of the United States in the first editions of his mammoth work, but in later reprints, the fulsome encomiums were diluted, the well merited approbation omitted. In the opinion of many writers, Catholics were a negligible quantity in American national life until the late forties of the last century, when political agitation and economic depression drove thousands of German and Irish exiles to the hospitable shores of the modern Utopia. Many Catholics, deceived by the suppression of the true facts, hold similar opinions in regard to the emigration of their religious brethren to America. As a natural sequence, the deeds of the Catholic pioneers, discoverers, explorers, missionaries, settlers, diplomats, soldiers, scholars and leaders, are unknown, their heroic record unsung. Catholics are regarded as new-comers in the Republic, aliens in race, aliens in country, aliens in religion, with no colonial traditions or glories, their only claim to citizenship and freedom, the bravery of their newly arrived ancestors who fought so valiantly to preserve the integrity of the Union, during the fraternal strife of the last century. That Catholics played a prominent role in the winning of independence, the foundation of the nation, seems unbelievable, even to the descendants of the Catholic heroes. Charles Carroll of Carrollton, signer of the Declaration of Independence, Commissioner to secure the alliance or the neutrality of the Canadians, the friend and councillor of Washington, is occasionally mentioned. John Barry, the Father of the Navy, receives some praise; the others who gave their mite to the cause of freedom are seldom recorded, never with any reference to their religion nor their nationality. Even the scions of distinctively Irish and Catholic families are disguised under a modern title, in an endeavor to signify that they had deserted the faith of their ancestors. The English, French, Germans, Indians, Italians, Scotch, Swiss and the other lesser members of the Old Church are enumerated in such an impersonal manner that their religious affiliations are concealed from the casual reader.

More than three decades ago, the Columbian Assembly,—the pioneer Fourth Degree Organization of the Knights of Columbus, the patriotic degree of the Order,—proposed to enlighten its members and the mass of lay Catholics on the record of their brethren in colonial and Federal days. A Lecture Bureau was formed, suitable subjects selected, speakers assigned gratis to all councils, schools, societies anxious to learn the true story of Catholic achievement during the colonial period and the formative years of the national life. The compiler of this volume served on the staff for more than a score of years, delivering historical addresses and lectures at the Catholic Summer School of America, Cliff Haven, N. Y., St. Joseph's Seminary, Dunwoodie, Manhattan College, and before more than three hundred educational, literary, and fraternal organizations in New York, New Jersey, Connecticut, Massachusetts, and Pennsylvania, in widely scattered Western centers, in the Southland and in Canada. During the author's two decades of teaching at the Catholic Foreign Mission College and Seminary, Maryknoll, the material was utilized in the American and Church History courses.

The book, however, is not a slavish reprint of these popular addresses and Seminary lectures, as much new matter has been added, additional chapters written, to insure the unity and cogency of the story, and the entire work recast into a series of essays. It was planned, not as a reference work, nor a manual for trained historians, but a popular treatise on Catholic heroism in the early days, written in simple style, eliminating everything that might puzzle or retard the humblest reader. There is no claim to originality, the writer merely dug and delved into the works of the leading historians of every shade of religion, quoting their exact words, giving the sources of his statements, especially in disputed and controverted questions. It is not a definitive history,—as some callow critics are wont to assert in reviews,—nor produced under the aegis of some great seat of learning and the guidance of its historical faculty, rather it is the fruit of more than forty years of research, reading, reflection in High School, College, Seminary and two leading Universities, culling from the pages of leading American authors, Catholic essayists and historians, historiographers of the different dioceses, who have labored so faithfully to preserve the traditions of the colonial past. To break the ground, that future writers might complete the task with more grace and perfection; "to glean up the scattered ashes into history's golden urn"; to supply the Catholic laity with authenticated data; to eliminate the many myths and legends which invariably creep into the pages of history; to assist his brother priests with neither leisure nor aptitude for extensive research or study; to instill in the minds of the young apostles carrying the Gospel truths to the field afar, the true story of Catholic achievement in their native land, stripped of all fiction and exaggeration, was the sole reason for the publication of this work. The treatment is necessarily brief, as tomes might be written on every chapter. It is merely an epitome of facts for the busy Catholic, to assist the seeker after truth, the student plodding along the early stretches of his journey. It is neither comprehensive nor extensive, in matter or authorities, as more learned and abstruse arguments might be furnished, more famous authors cited, but the compiler preferred to recommend books and authors found in the ordinary reference libraries. Many pamphlets, innumerable brochures have been scrutinized, their contents noted, their accuracy tested, but to recommend the multitudinous magazine articles, to quote from the many theses presented in partial requirement for the reception of college or university degrees, would be a herculean task for the writer, and of doubtful advantage to the reader. To impart the true Catholic flavor to the story, to insure correctness of statement, he has quoted and referred to the diocesan histories, compiled by the distinguished clerics of the years gone by.

The author feels that this little compendium may aid students in Catholic High Schools and Colleges, supplementing the ordinary text books, supplying accidental omissions, correcting needless errors or idle legends which creep into the pages of history. For teachers of the lower and even the higher grades he hopes it may be a *vademecum*, suggesting new phases, spurring them on to consult new sources of information, drawing their own conclusions, imparting correct knowledge to the little ones confided to their care. He has been moved to publish this work by the kindly urge of former auditors or students, who have heard these addresses or lectures, and are loath to have the labors of three decades lost. The Pastoral Letter of the Fathers of the Council of Baltimore, December seventh, 1884, has been his chief inspiration in preparing and publishing this manual: "That the history of the United States should be carefully taught in all our Catholic schools, and have directed that it be especially dwelt on in the education of the young ecclesiastical students of our preparatory seminaries; so also, we desire, that it form a part of the home library and home reading. We must keep firm and solid the liberties of our country by keeping fresh the noble memories of the past, and thus sending forth from our Catholic homes into the arena of public life, not partisans but patriots." To thus aid Catholic students, to supply correct information to writers or speakers, to inform the Catholic laity of the glorious record of their forebears in the faith, is the sole reason for sending forth this book.

The many unjust and intolerant laws, both civil and religious, framed in England during the penal days, adopted and augmented by the various colonial assemblies have been frankly and clearly explained, not to arouse sectarian hatred, or to revive bitter memories, but to show the many disabilities under which the Catholic minority groaned during the colonial period, thus emphasizing their loyalty during the struggle for freedom. "We remember, but we forgive," was the slogan of Charles Carroll of Carrollton and the downtrodden and disfranchised Catholics of Maryland, as they threw themselves wholeheartedly into the fray. So the Catholic student, understanding the trials and sufferings of his ancestors in the faith, may appreciate and value more fully the religious and civil liberty he now enjoys, thus making him a better Catholic and a better American.

Mindful of the motto of the Sage of Monticello, "to correct errors of fact before they become inveterate by repetition," the writer has attempted to separate the wheat from the chaff, to root up the cockle without destroying the good seed. But life is short, man's intellect finite, the demesne of history endless in its extent. Perhaps in correcting the errors of others he has fallen into equally egregious blunders. Yet his sin is material not formal. His guide has been the favorite apothegm of Pope Leo XIII: "The first law of history is not to dare to tell a lie; the second, not to fear to tell the truth; besides, let the historian be beyond all suspicion of favoring or hating anyone whomsoever." If errors of commission or omission have crept into the text, the author craves the charity of the critics: "Which if I have done well and as becometh the history is what I desired; but if not so perfectly it must be pardoned me." (II Mach. XV-39.)

The author owes a deep debt of gratitude to His Excellency, Most Rev. James A. Walsh, D.D., M. Ap., Father General and cofounder of the Catholic Foreign Mission Society of America and to the faculty and students of the Seminary at Maryknoll for their kindly encouragement and universal courtesy during the two decades he has filled the chair of history at that institution; to the memory of Martin I. J. Griffin, the Philadelphia historian who for years urged him to gather up the scattered fragments of Catholic American History into one compact volume; to the late John G. Coyle, M.D., LL.D., the devoted physician, Catholic gentleman, valiant knight, acute historian, sincere Christian, loyal friend, whose countless words of encouragement and keen discernment were his guide and his inspiration in his formative years. To all who aided him by advice or correction, or who stimulated him in his research work, he returns his sincere thanks.

Feast of SS. Peter and Paul.
June 29th, 1934.

CONTENTS

xv

Introduction

THE Egyptians of the Old Kingdom were the first ship builders, constructing rude vessels for commerce or pleasure, to ply along the Nile or the Red Sea.[1] Later, their war ships patrolled the Great River as a protection against enemies or harassed the Syrian coasts for plunder. The Egyptians were timid sailors, surpassed in valor by their neighbors, the Phoenicians, the pioneer seafarers. "Centuries before Rome was founded, or Greece heard of in history, when Egypt was bound up in herself, whilst the Hebrews were yet in the house of bondage, and neither Assyria nor Babylon had given signs of greatness, the ships of these extraordinary people were sailing far and wide."[2] To obtain raw materials for their many manufactures, they visited Cyprus for copper, Spain for tin, and as some authors aver, passed through the Pillars of Hercules and traded in the British Isles.[3] They visited or colonized the shores of Greece and Asia Minor, the islands of the Aegean, Sicily, Sardinia, Northern Africa, and founded the city of Gades (Cadiz) eleven centuries before the

[1] Breasted, Hist. of Egypt, 95.
[2] Souttar, Hist. of Ancient Peoples, 280.
[3] *Ibid.*, Hist. of Ancient Peoples, 231.

Christian era. Phoenician colonies were planted at Carthage and Utica, and their hardy mariners penetrated to Britain and the German Ocean, discovered the Canary Islands, probably visited the Cape Verde and Madeira groups and according to Herodotus, circumnavigated Africa in a three years' voyage. The Greeks were inferior to the Phoenicians, although Colaeus passed through the Pillars of Hercules, penetrated to Britain and the German Ocean, or as far west as the Saragossa Sea. The Romans made few discoveries although many voyages were made to the Arabian Gulf and thence to India, but her sailors were principally the conquered Phoenicians.

As geographers usually represented the world as a plain, stretching from the Aegean Sea to the fabled River Oceanus, beyond which began the realms of darkness and mystery, the home of the demons where Heaven and Tartarus met, voyages beyond the Straits of Gibraltar were feared by the ancient navigators. Homer styles this region a land of death and danger, Pindar maintains that only a God could penetrate west of Gades, and even the historians and geographers had vague notions of the extent of the ocean and the size and shape of the world. Pythagoras in the sixth century taught the sphericity of the earth and Plato made the theory popular. Cicero, Virgil, Ovid, confirmed these opinions. From the earliest ages, popular fancy and historical traditions dotted the broad expanse of waters with numerous islands and fabled nations. Homer sings of the Elysian Fields, situated on the outer frontier of the world, peopled by immortal heroes. Hesiod calls them "The Islands," Pindar, "The Isles of the Blessed." These legendary islands are frequently mentioned in historical and geographical writings, even after the discoveries of Columbus. Pliny relates that King Juba sent an expedition to the Fortunate Islands,—probably the Canaries,—visited by the Phoenicians at an earlier date. Plato, in "The Republic," tells of the famous Atalantis, a tale ascribed to Sais, an Egyptian priest, of prehistoric times. "It lay west of the Pillars of Hercules, and was larger than Asia and Africa combined." [4] After conquering the nations, "even Libya to the gates of Egypt, and Europe as far as Tyrrhenia," [5] it was shaken by a mighty earthquake, engulfed by great floods, and sank beneath the waves. The islands of the Atlantic are pictured as the loftiest peaks of this submerged continent. Other islands and countries are enumerated by the ancient writers; Antilla, or the Seven Cities, was discovered and settled by an Archbishop and six bishops, who had fled from Spain at the beginning of the Moorish persecutions. St. Brendan's, St. Malo's, Brazil, are frequently mentioned in the chronicles of the Middle Ages. To explain the origin of these legends, many fantastic theories have been advanced, but undoubtedly they may

[4] De Costa, Pre-Col. Discoveries, XIII.
[5] Winsor, Aboriginal Am., I-16.

be traced to the expeditions of the Phoenicians to the Canaries, Cape Verde and Madeira islands. Their memory lingered long in popular fancy, and even in the fifteenth and sixteenth centuries these names appear on maps and charts and several expeditions were dispatched to locate the mysterious lands.

The Catholic Church preserved and extended the knowledge of the ancients, through the industry and perseverance of the monks. The works of Aristotle were studied, the sphericity of the earth acknowledged by all except the few who still clung to the old traditions. Saint Bede, the Venerable, Anglo-Saxon monk of the eighth century, taught the entire system of ancient geography in his book, "De Natura Rerum"; Isidore, Archbishop of Seville, composed a treatise on astronomy and cosmography; Pope Sylvester II, the famous Gerbert, mathematician and monk, encouraged the study of the classical authors; Virgilius, Celtic monk and saint, Bishop of Salzburg, proved the rotundity of the earth, and the existence of the antipodes and by his rare mathematical skill prepared the way for later discoveries. The Universities and the Schoolmen made Aristotle popular, and his geographical theories were taught and perfected by these great masters. Saint Albertus Magnus, Universal Doctor, was an indefatigable student of science and formulated proofs of the sphericity of the earth, which won the praise of Humboldt, and are still quoted; his pupil, Saint Thomas

Aquinas, the Angelic Doctor, expresses many original views on geography and the configuration of the earth; his fellow Dominican, Vincent of Beauvais, in "Speculum Naturale," furnishes the student with a wealth of scientific facts; Roger Bacon, the Franciscan, another pupil of Saint Albertus Magnus, maintained in his work, "Opus Majus," that by sailing westward land would be found, and that the distance from Europe to India was inconsiderable. Cardinal Nicholas of Cusa, a Rhinelander, wrote many works on the size and shape of the earth; Cardinal Peter D'Ailly, Bishop of Cambrai, composed a narrative which aided Columbus materially; Paul Toscanelli, the Florentine cosmographer, was an authority on geography and navigation.

The Crusades brought the Western World into close relations with the Orient, as the capture of Jerusalem and the acquisition of the maritime ports of ancient Phoenicia enabled the Italian merchants to trade with the near Eastern lands, the republics of Genoa, Pisa and Venice becoming rich and powerful through this lucrative trade. The fall of the Holy City, and the subsequent expulsion of the Christians from the seaboard towns, closed these markets, so merchants and mariners sought a water way to bring them to the rich marts of Cipango and Cathay. The conquests of Genghis Khan (1206-1227), opened up Central Asia, and various priests, travelers and merchants entered these mysterious lands. In 1245, Pope Innocent IV sent John of Carpini, a

Franciscan Friar, to Tartary, who visited Mongolia and brought back a message from the great monarch, who styled himself "the scourge of God for Christians," and republished an account of his travels, "Liber Tartarorum." In 1316, another Franciscan, Odoric of Pordenone, visited India, sailed to China via Java and Sumatra, where his order had founded a monastery at Peking, and an Archbishop reigned. He wrote an account of his experiences, still preserved in Italian, French and Latin manuscripts. St. Louis IX of France sent another Franciscan, William of Rubrouck, to introduce Christianity in Tartary, but the mission was a failure although his book was interesting. The most distinguished and best known traveler was Marco Polo, who visited China with his two uncles, remaining there and in Mongolia for twenty years, composing the volume which made him famous, "The Travels of Marco Polo, the Venetian." These narratives inspired merchants and mariners to brave the terrors of the unknown seas to share in the riches of the East.

The pioneer in promoting those voyages was Prince Henry of Portugal, surnamed the Navigator, the fourth son of King John. He established an observatory at Cape St. Vincent, gathered around him a distinguished coterie of geographers and navigators, devoting himself to study and observation, sending out expeditions to explore and colonize the Azores, Canaries, and Cape Verde groups, and to visit the African coasts. In 1488,

Bartholomew Diaz rounded the Cape of Good Hope, and in 1497, Vasco de Gama reached the Indies. The compass was now in general use, the astrolabe for computing the sun's altitude and calculating the latitude and longitude had been invented, and maps and charts more or less accurate had been drawn. The Sea of Darkness still had terrors for the unwary mariners, but the mists were clearing and the voyage of the Genoese mariner was to solve the problems of centuries.

Catholics in Colonial Days

CHAPTER ONE

Pre-Columbian Discoveries

WAS Columbus the first navigator to sight the shores of America? Various peoples and individuals dispute his claim. "There is not a race of eastern Asia,—Siberian, Tartar, Chinese, Japanese, Malay,—with the Polynesians,—which has not been claimed as discoverers, intending or accidental, of American shores, or as progenitors, more or less perfect or remote, of American peoples; and there is no good reason why any of them may not have done all that is claimed." [1] Some writers aver that the Aleutian islands, the narrow Behring's straits, furnished a convenient pathway from the eastern to the western continent, others that the numerous islands dotting the Pacific Ocean were a ready means of communication for daring mariners, as occasionally, Chinese or Japanese junks, driven by stress of storm westward, were stranded on the beaches of California or farther north. While all these conjectures seem possible, there is no conclusive testimony that they are probable.

In the fifth century, Buddhist priests from China are

[1] Winsor, Aboriginal Am., I-59.

3

said to have journeyed from Kamchatka across the Aleutian islands and Behring's straits and settled in Mexico which they called "Fusang," although later historians identify "Fusang" with Japan rather than Mexico.[2] Las Casas and other Spanish writers advance a theory that the Ten Lost Tribes of Israel settled in America, a statement corroborated by various New England divines, notably, John Elliot and Cotton Mather.[3] The migration of African or Egyptian tribes to Central or South America was a favorite theory of Peter Martyr, as the Caribs have many racial characteristics of the Africans.[4] Lord Kingsborough claimed that Saint Thomas the Apostle and after him Saint Columba visited the Western Hemisphere and that other Christian missionaries came to evangelize the aborigines journeying as far south as Peru.[5] Certain popular traditions among the tribesmen and a great respect for the cross as a symbol were the main reasons for this assertion.

In 1170, Prince Madoc, a Welsh chieftain, driven from home by persecutions, set sail for the west, where he found a new land. After establishing a colony, he returned to Wales, and having equipped ten small vessels, returned to the infant settlement. His subsequent career is shrouded in mystery. The story is related at

[2] Fiske, Dis. of Am., I-171.
[3] Winsor, Aboriginal Am., I-115.
[4] *Ibid.*, Aboriginal Am., I-117.
[5] Kingsborough, Mex. Antiquities, VI-285.

length in the Welsh annals, and some philologists claim
that traces of the Celtic language are found in the
speech of several aboriginal tribes. Robert Southey's
poem, *Madoc*, commemorates his achievements. Other
writers assert that the Basques, hardy sailors from the
Bay of Biscay, frequented the American waters in quest
of whales years before the discovery of Columbus and
that the traditions of these early fishermen gave the
Genoese navigator the first impulse for western discovery. Under the leadership of John Vas Costa Corte-
real the Dutch visited Newfoundland and fished off
the banks in 1463-64 although the theory is highly improbable. In 1476, John Skolnow, a Pole, in the service
of Christian I of Denmark, made a voyage to Greenland and charted the coast of Labrador. In 1488, Jean
Cousin of Dieppe, while sailing along the coast of
Africa, was driven westward by a violent storm and
landed in Brazil. All these discoveries have found defenders among geographers and historians. Some voyagers may have found their way to the new continent
but the evidence adduced by their admirers is not supported by properly authenticated testimony and the
claims are rejected by critical historians.

Three claims however deserve serious consideration,
those of the Zeno brothers, the Irish and the Northmen.
In 1558, a narrative was published at Venice, purport-
ing to relate the adventures of two brothers, Nicolo and
Antonio Zeno, Venetians, who in the latter years of the

fourteenth century, were wrecked in the North Atlantic and lived for some years at "Frislanda." Here they met a sailor, shipwrecked in a strange land to the west where he was marooned for twenty-six years in a civilized country which he called, "Estotiland." To the south was "Drogio," inhabited by cannibals, farther south, another territory, filled with great towns and magnificent temples.[6] This account was sent to another brother in Venice with a map of the regions, where it remained forgotten for more than two centuries until a younger Nicolo, great-grand-grand-grandson of the writer deciphered the ancient manuscript and reproduced the old chart.[7] The names of the places and the individuals mentioned in the narrative have puzzled the historians yet the mystery may be explained. The Scandinavian names, harsh to southern ears were softened by the Italian translator, the Faroe Islands became "Frislanda," and Shetland, "Estland." The Lord of the Isles, called Zichmni by the brothers was, in reality, Henry Sinclair, Earl of the Orkneys, a well-known figure in the history of that period.[8] As the original manuscripts were never produced, the story lacks confirmation in many details. Some writers maintain its veracity, claiming the discrepancies are due to the faded, obscure writing of the old reports and the inability of the transcriber to properly understand the names of the persons and the places.

[6] Winsor, Aboriginal Am., I-72.
[7] Fiske, Dis. of Am., I-267.
[8] *Ibid.*, Dis. of Am., I-270.

One geographer calls it: "one of the most puzzling in the whole circle of literature." [9] Another sums up the controversy: "Without hazarding anything like a positive opinion, it would seem to me likely enough that this voyage of the Scandinavian fisherman to the Coast of North America in the fourteenth century may have happened." [10] Undoubtedly the brothers made a voyage to Greenland and to another country, possibly America, although some historians assert it was to the coast of Iceland.

A tradition prevailed among the American Indians from Hudson's Bay to the Gulf of Mexico, that white men appeared among them at an early period and preached a new religion. It is claimed by some writers that these visitors were Irish monks and as some assert, St. Patrick or St. Columba came to America or sent priests to convert the aborigines.[11] In the Landnama Bok, one of the Norse Sagas, there is a significant reference to the voyage of Are Marson to Ireland—it—milka, or Greater Ireland where white men dwelt near Vinland the Good.[12] Another mariner was wrecked on a distant shore where the people spoke a language resembling Irish.[13] Geographers and historians have endeavored to locate this region, placing it in Canada,

[9] Pinkerton, Hist. of Scotland, I-261.
[10] Fiske, Dis. of Am., I-291.
[11] De Costa, Pre-Col. Dis. of Am., Intro. XXIII.
[12] *Ibid.*, Pre-Col. Dis. of Am., 86-87.
[13] *Ibid.*, Pre-Col. Dis. of Am., 101.

Virginia, Carolina and Florida, and some philologists claim that certain words and sounds found in the Indian dialects are of Celtic origin. The story of the wanderings of St. Brendan, patron of Clonfert and Ardfert, was well known and universally accepted during the Middle Ages. An adventurous spirit, he visited the various Irish monasteries, crossed the sea to Wales, and came to Iona where his friend St. Columba ruled. With a party of monks, he sailed westward and after seven years came to a fair land with a delightful climate, luxuriant vegetation and fertile soil which he called "Terra Repromissionis." This region has been identified by some authors as Virginia or Florida, by others, as the Canary or Madeira islands or possibly the Fortunate Islands of Pliny. According to tradition, the Irish monk journeyed westward as far as Ohio,—some writers maintain that the mound builders were descendants of those Irish settlers. He returned to Ireland, made another voyage to the western world, although later researches show he again returned home, built a school and monastery at Clonfert and died in the monastery at Annaghdown.[14] The Island of St. Brendan is frequently mentioned in mediaeval literature, especially in the "Golden Legend" of Voraginius, the Provincial of the Dominicans and Bishop of Genoa.[15] The story of his wanderings is related in the Irish annals, and the chronicles of

[14] D'Alton, Hist. of Ireland, I-61.
[15] McGee, Irish Settlers in Am., 20-21.

England, France, Italy, Netherlands and Spain. The narrative is not improbable, as the ancient Irish were a seafaring people, closely related to the Phoenicians. In 296, they invaded Denmark and in the following century menaced England and met the Roman conquerors. They visited the northern coasts of Scotland and the Faroe and Orkney islands. In the ninth century when the Northmen came to Iceland, they found relics of the former settlers, books, bells, croziers, souvenirs of the occupation by the Irish monks and their followers. Humboldt and the Bollandists relate the voyages of St. Brendan and Professor Rafn, the Danish historian, attests: "A perusal of the forgotten or hidden manuscripts in the libraries of Europe may some day supply the conclusive proofs that the Irish monk of the sixth century discovered the continent of America."

In 860, Gardar, a Dane, of Swedish descent, landed in Iceland, and four years later, Nadodd, a pirate, was driven to its shores. In the northern annals it was styled Gardar's Island or Snowland. Towards the close of the ninth century, Ingolf founded a settlement which in the next half century attracted seventy thousand settlers to the island.[16] In the first quarter of the tenth century, Eric, the Red, exiled from Norway, for manslaughter, came to Iceland. In a quarrel, he slew another man, and fled away, sailing westward until he came to Greenland. "The Landnama Bok" shows that

[16] De Costa, Pre-Col. Dis. of Am., Intro., XXI ff.

the island had been visited by Gunnbiorn in 876.[17]
Many colonists came from Iceland to the new country
and various settlements were founded. In 986, Biarne
Heriulfson, driven by storms to the southward, descried
a strange land, and fourteen years later, Leif Ericson
sailed in quest of the new country. He found a stony
region with ice-covered mountains which he called
Helluland; farther south, sandy shores and wooded hills
which he named Markland; later he came to a pleasant
coast, abounding in grapes which he styled, Vinland.
Other voyagers followed in his wake and his brother,
Thorvald, spent three winters in the new lands. Thorfinn
Karlsefne and his wife attempted to form a settlement,
but were attacked by the hostile natives and during his
sojourn his wife gave birth to a son, Snorre. Trading
voyages are chronicled until the middle of the fourteenth century, when the story abruptly terminates. In
1342, the Eskimos invaded Greenland, a pestilence broke
out, and communication with Norway and Sweden
ceased. Until the beginning of the eighteenth century,
the fate of the once flourishing colony of Greenland
was shrouded in mystery.

When Christianity was introduced in Iceland and
Norway, missionaries came to Greenland and converted
the settlers. A bishop was consecrated, churches and
monasteries erected, and the faithful contributed to the
Crusades and paid Peter's Pence in walrus tusks. In the

[17] *Ibid.*, Pre-Col. Dis. of Am., Intro., XXV.

Vatican archives, the names of sixteen bishops who ruled over the See of Gardar are enumerated. One of these bishops, Eric Upsi, visited Vinland in 1121. The ruins of the Cathedral and several churches and monasteries are silent witnesses to the sterling Catholicity of the early Norse settlers in Greenland.

Historians and geographers have vainly tried to locate the places visited by these northern explorers. Helluland was probably situated near the Straits of Belle Isle, or in Labrador, or northern Newfoundland; Markland, in southern Newfoundland, Cape Breton or Nova Scotia; Vinland in southern Nova Scotia or New England. The descriptions are too vague to enable scholars to identify these places with any degree of certainty. The Northmen left no permanent marks of their visit, although for years the old, stone mill at Newport and the Dighton Inscription were regarded as relics of their expeditions.

The claims of the Scandinavians rest on the manuscripts contained in the old Norse Sagas. The most important is, the "Codex Flatoiensis," or "Flat Island Book," written in the period from 1387 to 1395.[18] The narratives are honest and straightforward, and have all the requirements for authenticity and veracity, while the internal evidence, descriptions and explanations favor the claims of the writers. Although absurdity and exaggeration occasionally appear, they strengthen

[18] *Ibid.*, Pre-Col. Dis. of Am., Intro., XLI.

rather than weaken the original claims. "No historical student has the slightest doubt that the Norsemen discovered America almost five hundred years before Columbus arrived at the Bahamas." [19] Their voyages however, produced no effect either on the aboriginal tribes or the European world, and were forgotten for centuries, barren of all results. "In no sense was any real contact established between the eastern and western halves of our planet until the great voyage of Columbus in 1492." [20]

[19] McCarthy, Col. and His Predecessors, 25.
[20] Fiske, Dis. of Am., I-294.

CHAPTER TWO

Columbus and His Voyages

THE fifteenth century was the Renaissance period, a famous epoch in the history of modern times. The universities of the thirteenth century had laid the foundations of scholarship and research on a broad, substantial basis, and the reintroduction of Greek ideas and ideals gave a mighty impetus to every branch of education and progress. It produced men and women of ability and energy who not only achieved great deeds, but also inspired less gifted with the spirit of enthusiasm and emulation. Architecture, literature, medicine, music, painting, and science were assiduously cultivated and the manufacture of stained glass and porcelain, and the binding and illumination of books were brought to the highest perfection. Prince Henry, the Navigator, was the pioneer in the revival of maritime discovery; Cardinal Nicholas of Cusa was the leading geographer; Leonardo da Vinci, Michelangelo and Raphael were the most distinguished architects, painters and sculptors; Aeneas Sylvius (Pope Pius II), Erasmus and Thomas More were rare scholars; St. Thomas of Aquin, St. Albertus Magnus, Saint Bonaventure, Roger Bacon were churchmen and students; William of Salicet, Guy de Chauliac, Vesalius revolutionized the study of anatomy and surgery; St. Catherine of Genoa, St. Ignatius Loyola and St. Teresa added luster to the ancient church. In every country of Europe, literary, religious and social activity reigned, and men and women were achieving success in every department of human endeavor.

Columbus lived and died during this stirring period. His contributions to its triumphs are so considerable, a well-known writer has styled the years from 1450 to 1550, "The Century of Columbus." [1] Although he wrote much concerning himself, his family, and his exploits, and his son Fernando, and his friend Las Casas were sympathetic biographers, yet his early history is obscure, the exact date of his birth uncertain, the rank and identity of his family questioned, his birth place disputed, and the site of his grave doubtful. Various dates from 1436 to 1456 have been assigned for his birth, although the period from 1436 to 1446 seems more correct and recent research gives the true date as 1446.[2] By his own testimony, he was born in Genoa.[3] Some historians have questioned the accuracy of this statement, but it is practically certain he was born in the city proper or within the boundaries of the repub-

[1] Walsh, The Cent. of Columbus, I ff.
[2] Bourne, Spain in Am., 9.
[3] Fiske, Dis. of Am., II-17.

lic.[4] Little is known of his childhood, although tradition asserts he was a student at the University of Pavia and acquired a knowledge of Latin, but modern writers deny this, saying he received only the ordinary education of a peasant boy.[5] His parents were humble artisans, woolcombers or weavers, and he worked at this simple trade. According to his own story, he began his seafaring life at the tender age of fourteen, making trips in merchant vessels and serving in naval expeditions against Naples and the Saracens. During the intervals between voyages he divided his time between labor and study, learning geography, studying astronomy and mathematics, becoming proficient in drafting maps and charts. He read the works of the most celebrated cosmographers and travelers, both ancient and modern, "The General History of Geography," by Aeneas Sylvius (Pope Pius II), "Imago Mundi," by Cardinal Peter D'Ailly, and, "The Travels of Marco Polo, The Venetian," annotated copies of which are still preserved. He read the Scriptures, especially the fourth book of Esdras, the Greek and Latin poets and geographers, and was encouraged by the views of St. Albertus Magnus, Roger Bacon, St. Thomas Aquinas and Vincent of Beauvais. The accounts of the Portuguese expeditions to the south increased his ardor for adventure, and the finding of trees, sculptured wood, and the bodies of

[4] *Ibid.*, Dis. of Am., II-17.
[5] McCarthy, Columbus and His Pre., 85.

people of an unknown race, washed ashore on the out-lying islands, confirmed his theory that the distance from Spain to India was inconsiderable. Reading and meditating on the works of the ancient and modern scholars, questioning mariners who had sailed westward, conversing and corresponding with learned men, in-creased his hopes that some day he might discover the passage to distant Cathay.

In 1470, Columbus came to Portugal, became ac-quainted with the details of the voyages to Guinea and around the Scandinavian peninsula, and participated in expeditions to Africa, the Faroe Islands, and possibly to Iceland. It is said he married the daughter or kins-woman of Bartholomew Perestrello, one of Prince Henry's mariners and the former governor of Porto Sancto, whose maps and charts he examined and studied.[7] During this period it is said he corresponded with Toscanelli, although the accuracy of this state-ment is questioned. In 1484, he petitioned King John to fit out an expedition for western research but the wily monarch listened to his plans, and then secretly sent a vessel to test his theories, but the voyage was unsuccessful. Exasperated and disgusted by the kingly duplicity, he applied, as tradition teaches, to the re-publics of Genoa and Venice and then turned his face towards Spain, the great maritime rival of the Portu-guese. The marriage of Ferdinand of Aragon to Isabella

[7] *Ibid.*, Columbus and His Pre., 88.

of Castile, united the scattered kingdoms of Spain and after centuries of occupation, the Moorish invaders were gradually expelled, until Granada, their last stronghold alone remained. While the final struggle was in progress, the Genoese pilgrim appeared before the court, where he received scant attention. However, he made many friends among the clergy and nobility, the Duke of Medina Celi, Cardinal Mendoza of Toledo, Diego de Deza, Dominican Bishop of Salamanca, Friar Antonio de Marchesa, the two priests, Santangel and Quintanilla, the treasurers of Castile and Aragon.[8] Discouraged by his apparent failure, he dispatched his brother, Bartholomew to interview King Henry VII of England while he set out for the French court. On his journey, he stopped for shelter at the Franciscan convent of La Rabida and found in the Prior, Juan Perez, a trusty friend who listened attentively to his eloquence, interested other clerics and mariners in his theories, obtained another interview with the Spanish sovereigns and opened the way to success. Although disagreements took place at the second meeting and Columbus once more set out for France, he was recalled, the King and Queen agreeing to equip an expedition, creating him High Admiral of Castile, and Viceroy and Governor General of all the lands he might discover. He was to provide one eighth of the expenses and was to receive the same ratio of profit, and his heirs were to share in

[8] Fiske, Dis. of Am., II-95.

the honors and emoluments of the voyage. His faith and perseverance had conquered and the hour of success was at hand.

On August third, 1492, three small caravels, the Santa Maria, the Nina and the Pinta sailed from the harbor of Palos. For the Admiral, it was a day of triumph, the realization of the dreams and hopes of years, for the people a time of gloom as their brethren were embarking on the Sea of Darkness, perhaps never to return. The sailors were ignorant and unfriendly, depressed by the terrors of the unknown deep, angered by the arbitrary commands of the sovereigns, that two vessels be furnished and equipped by the town as a punishment for the misdeeds of the townsfolks. Only the influence and persuasion of the Pinzon brothers quieted the fears. The fleet stopped at the Canaries for repairs and supplies and then sailed westward. Various occurrences revived the superstitions of the crew and renewed their anxiety; the vessels were becalmed, the Saragossa Sea impeded their progress, a mirage deceived them, and the variations of the compass struck terror to the boldest hearts. The Admiral, fearing to reveal the actual distance sailed each day, underestimated the progress, and explained the declination of the magnetic needle by an ingenious, astronomical interpretation. The crew murmured at the length of the voyage and the failure to reach land although the flight of birds and the green branches floating on the waves were harbingers of its proximity. On the morning of October twelfth, 1492, an island was sighted, the Admiral landed and took possession of it in the name of God and his sovereigns, reverently naming it San Salvador. He discovered Cuba and Hayti and sailed amongst the neighboring islands until his flagship was wrecked on a reef. Leaving a colony of forty men at Fort Nativity, he sailed homeward to report his discoveries. Although the natives were naked savages, the large cities and stately buildings wanting, the spices and drugs missing, Columbus believed he had found the outlying islands of the Indies, and that Cathay and Cipango were within easy sailing distance. That he had discovered a new continent was farthest from his thoughts.

His arrival in Europe was the culmination of his triumph. Driven by stress of storms to the Tagus, he was welcomed by King John of Portugal, with mingled feelings of admiration and envy. Palos greeted him with bells and illuminations, his progress from Seville to Barcelona, the march of a mighty conqueror, Ferdinand and Isabella receiving him with royal honors. The birds and animals, the golden ornaments and glittering pearls, the herbs and plants, were eagerly examined and admired. The account of the new regions was greedily read, the six natives in paint and feathers excited universal comment and applause. The sovereigns loaded the Genoese mariner with honors, the populace acclaimed him a hero.

A second expedition was planned, hundreds of nobles, soldiers and adventurers enlisting for the voyage to Golden Cathay. On September third, 1493, seventeen ships and fifteen hundred men sailed from Cadiz. Porto Rico and many small islands were visited and explored, maps and charts of the region prepared. Fort Nativity was found dismantled, the garrison missing. The cruelty of the settlers provoked the natives to hostilities, and sickness, famine and internal feuds completed the destruction of the little settlement. The city of Isabella was founded, and exploring parties sent out to seek for gold and spices. The colonists were unfitted for hard labor, preferring adventure. Discontent arose, cliques were formed, the Indians aroused, the Admiral accused of tyranny although he erred by mildness rather than severity. The exasperated aborigines planned a general massacre, but were subdued in a bloody engagement. Columbus strove to restore peace and prosperity, but his efforts were vain. In 1496, he founded San Domingo and made several trips through the islands, but weary and ill, he gave up the thankless task and returned to Spain. The King and Queen received him kindly, and showered honors upon him but only the sympathy of Isabella and a few chosen friends supported him during this period of distress.

Eager to complete his discoveries by finding Cathay and the Spice Islands, he again set sail on May thirtieth, 1498 with six ships and two hundred men. He followed the southerly course hoping to reach Cochin China and the Malaccas, but sighted land near the mouth of the Orinoco River and discovered the mainland of South America. Cruising along the Pearl Coast, he heard stories of the rich countries to the west. At San Domingo he found the infant colony disrupted by internal factions, the inhabitants discouraged and mutinous. His brothers, Bartholomew and Diego had been deposed and imprisoned and the Admiral was arrested charged with serious crimes. After many humiliations, the brothers were heavily ironed and sent home for trial and punishment. The ship captain, a humane man, wished to release the great discoverer, but he refused, saying his sovereigns alone could free him from the manacles. Popular sympathy and acclamation greeted him at Cadiz, and Isabella shed tears when she beheld his shameful plight. The charges were quashed, his honors restored, his losses reimbursed. Yet he was never reinstated in his former position as Governor of the Indies.

In 1502, he sailed from Cadiz with four small caravels and one hundred and fifty men. It was a disastrous expedition. He explored the coasts of Honduras, endeavoring to found a settlement, but the hostility of the tribesmen, the scarcity of supplies, the unseaworthiness of his vessels, prevented him from achieving success. His ships were wrecked at Jamaica and for a year he received no aid from Ovanda, the Governor. At length the survivors were shipped to Spain but the Admiral was broken by sickness and sorrow. His great patroness, Isabella, died nineteen days after his homecoming. Disease and poverty haunted the last days of his career, and on Ascension Eve, 1506, he died at Valladolid. His body was interred in the Franciscan monastery, and seven years later was transferred to Seville. In 1536, his remains and those of his son, Diego, were taken to Hispaniola and buried in the cathedral at San Domingo. In 1785, the Treaty of Basle assigned this island to France and the relics of the discoverer were borne to Havana and interred with military honors. When Cuba secured its freedom in 1898, the body was restored to Seville.[9]

The Catholic Church was ever a fond mother to Christopher Columbus. Faith was the inspiration which guided him, the solace of his disappointments and sufferings. A Catholic Queen was his patroness, a Franciscan friar his advocate, Cardinals, Bishops, Priests his supporters. "In popular allusions to Columbus, it is quite common to assume or imply that he encountered nothing but opposition from the clergy.—Without cordial support from the clergy, no such enterprise as that of Columbus could have been undertaken, in Spain at least. It is quite right we should be free thinkers; and it is also desirable that we should have some respect for facts." [10] That Jews furnished the funds for equipping

[9] Winsor, Hist. of Am., II-78.
[10] Fiske, Dis. of Am., II-95.

the initial expedition is frequently asserted. Isabella, contrary to the current tradition did not pawn her jewels. Columbus contributed one eighth of the cost, supplied or loaned probably by his friend, the Duke of Medina Celi. The crown of Castile gave seven eighths borrowed from the Santa Hermanadad or Holy Brotherhood, of which Luis de Santangel and Francisco Pinelo were joint treasurers.[11] As the former, although a converted Jew,[12] was a priest and the latter a Genoese Christian,[13] the Jewish story must be rejected as a myth. Columbus was a loyal son of Holy Mother Church, a Franciscan Tertiary, frequently wearing the habit. Before embarking on the unknown seas, he and the crew heard Mass at the little monastery of La Rabida. His flagship was the Santa Maria, the cross his standard, the Ave Maris Stella the evening hymn. The first land sighted was San Salvador, the first fort settlement, the Nativity, the first permanent city, San Domingo, the first rude edifice erected, the church of the Holy Trinity. When death came, his last words were, "into thy hands, O Lord, I commend my spirit." Every incident in his career was truly Catholic, and he considered his achievements not as a personal triumph, but rather as a dispensation of Divine Providence.

[11] McCarthy, Columbus and His Pre., 128.
[12] Fiske, Dis. of Am., II-95.
[13] McCarthy, Columbus and His Pre., 129.

Some ungenerous and biased writers picture Columbus as a fortunate adventurer who accidentally found new lands by sailing westward. This hypothesis is not only superficial but incorrect, as the Admiral was a man of genius, well skilled in the art of astronomy and navigation. The predicted eclipse of the moon, which overawed the natives and restored peace to the settlers and the explanation of the variations of the magnetic needle, are proofs of his scientific attainments.[14] He had read and considered the works of the ancient and modern geographers, had consulted the books of travel, and had based his principles on the soundest foundations. He expected to reach India by sailing westward and his contention was correct. That a new continent and another vast ocean intervened, did not vitiate his claims. Contemporary writers and voyagers believed that he had found the route to the Indies and some years elapsed before the true significance of the discovery was understood.

He was not a sordid adventurer, eager for gold and glory, rather a knight errant, a crusader for the faith. He thought himself an instrument in the hands of Divine Providence for enlarging the bounds of Christendom and rescuing the Holy Places from the infidels. In his agreement with Ferdinand and Isabella, he sought one eighth of the profits of the voyage and one tenth of all the gold and pearls which might be found and

[14] Walsh, Churchmen in Sci., II-119.

vowed "to devote every maravedi that should come to him, to the rescue of the Holy Sepulchre." [15] On his return from the first voyage he renewed this pledge, promising to equip fifty thousand foot and five thousand horse in seven years, and after another five years, to furnish a similar force. On the eve of his fourth venture he wrote the reigning pontiff, Alexander VI, in a like strain. In his journal he outlines plans for the conversion of the Pagans in the East who, in the times of Marco Polo, sought Christian missionaries. The captives brought to Spain on the first return, were baptised and sent home to convert their brethren. On the second venture, twelve priests under a Vicar Apostolic were sent out, a church established at Isabella, and plans formed to convert the natives. Although Columbus did not disdain legitimate power and moderate wealth, he valued them from a religious rather than a worldly standpoint. He was a missionary and a crusader as well as an explorer and merchant.

He was not a servile imitator who reaped the glory of earlier navigators. In his voyage to Iceland, it has been presumed by some critics, he heard the story of Vinland and had followed in the wake of the Northmen. There is no testimony to prove this ungenerous hypothesis as the true significance of the Norse discoveries was not recognized until the seventeenth century. The dreams of Columbus dealt with Cathay and

[15] Fiske, Dis. of Am., II-103.

Cipango and not with Helluland or Markland. The story of the nameless pilot, driven westward to a strange land, who died in the home of Columbus, bequeathing him his maps and charts is merely a shallow story without historical foundation as the authors of the sixteenth century question its genuineness and modern historians reject it as false. Columbus knew the teachings of the ages and adapted them to his fancy. His theory in regard to the relative position of India and Spain, proved correct, although he misunderstood the distance and thought the outlying islands of the new continent the beginnings of Asia. Yet these inaccuracies cannot deprive him of the glories of his achievement. "Nothing like it was ever done before, and nothing like it can ever be done again. No worlds are left for the future Columbus to conquer. The era of which the great Italian mariner was the most illustrious representative has closed forever." [16]

[16] Fiske, Dis. of Am., II-132.

CHAPTER THREE

Explorers and Missionaries

THE glowing descriptions of the newly discovered lands induced many Spanish navigators and adventurers to visit the new regions. Hojeda, with the daring pilot and famous map maker, Juan de la Cosa, and Americus Vespucci, Florentine merchant and literary dilettante, reached the shores of South America and explored the coasts of British Guiana and Venezuela. These visits or voyages of Vespucci, affixed his name to South America and finally to the entire continent: "His place in the history of the discoveries is the most remarkable illustration of eternal celebrity won through a happy combination of the literary gift and self-advertisement, with the coöperation of the printing press." [1] In his narratives he made no mention of the commander under whom he sailed, and the impression was established that he was the real discoverer.[2] Cordova discovered Yucatan, with its stone buildings, carved ornaments, paved streets, sculptured temples, blood-stained altars. Grijalva, his successor, guided the expedition

[1] Bourne, Sp. in Am., 84.
[2] *Ibid.*, Sp. in Am., 84.

northward to Vera Cruz, hearing vague rumors of gold and silver mines and high civilization. These stories whetted the avarice of Velasquez, the representative of Diego Colon, the Admiral's son and heir, who commissioned Hernando Cortez to seek the treasure lands. He landed in Mexico, subdued the native warriors, and added the Aztec country to the Spanish dominions. Pizarro vanquished the semi-civilized kingdom of the Incas, with its metallic treasures, Ponce de Leon discovered the peninsula of Florida, Balboa sighted the Pacific Ocean, and wading into its pellucid waters, took possession of all the territories washed by its waves, in the name of his King, Hernando De Soto crossed the Mississippi, and found his resting place in its turbulent waters. Coronado surveyed New Mexico, Arizona and the Southwest, discovered the seven cities, the Zuni pueblos, crossed the Colorado River and penetrated to the site of the present state of Oklahoma. Cabrillo explored the coasts of California; Magellan, the Portuguese, under Spanish auspices, circumnavigated the globe.

The Portuguese, ancient rivals of Spain in mercantile ventures, whose daring mariners under the leadership of Prince Henry the Navigator, and his successors, had explored the Atlantic coast, and the shores of Africa, rounded the Cape of Good Hope, and in 1497, reached the Indies under the guidance of Vasco Da Gamma. Chagrined that he had rejected the offers of Columbus,

King John summoned explorers to share in the western voyages of their hated rivals. In 1500, Gaspar Corte-Real sailed westward, reaching a land which he pronounced, "cool and with great woods," presumably Newfoundland. The next year with his brother, Miguel, he made another voyage, but his ship was lost at sea. Cabral, sailing from Lisbon for the Indies, was driven across the Atlantic, landing on the eastern shores of Brazil, just west of the line of demarcation assigned by Pope Alexander VI as the boundary between the Spanish and Portuguese possessions.

England, located on an island facing the fabled Sea of Darkness, with brave and intrepid mariners, had carried on fisheries at Iceland, and according to tradition, had visited the Cape Verde Islands and Greenland. In 1497, John Cabot, a Genoese, naturalized citizen of Venice, sailed from Bristol in a tiny caravel with a crew of eighteen men and coasted three hundred leagues along the shores of an unknown region which he named, "the land of the Gran Cham," possibly, Cape Breton, Newfoundland or Labrador. A second, and perhaps a third voyage with his son, Sebastian, has been chronicled, in which he followed the coast to the latitude of South Carolina or farther south, as various complaints were made in Spain that the English vessels had been sighted in the neighborhood of the West India Islands. Modern historians reject the claims of the younger Cabot as spurious although they admit the voyages of his father,

John. "Few characters in history owe more to modern research than John Cabot. Not a writer himself, like his great compatriot, he left his fame a legacy to his son, who instead of devoting to it a pious memorial like Ferdinand Columbus, deftly clothed himself with it and secured for over three centuries the principal credit of an expedition in which there is no direct evidence to show that he even participated." As a reward, Henry VII gave John Cabot ten pounds and in the following December, an annual pension of twenty pounds. His discoveries gave England a claim to the entire Atlantic seaboard. "He gave England a continent, and no one knows his burial place." [4]

France, likewise, was eager to share in the riches of the New World. A few years after the discovery, Norman and Breton fishermen reached the banks of Newfoundland although almost half a century elapsed before they appeared in large numbers. The treasures of Cathay and Cipango, the Indies of Marco Polo, the Golden Chersonese of the ancients, were the goals sought by the French monarchs. Da Gamma's route around the Cape of Good Hope was long and dangerous, Magellan's southern passage equally unsatisfactory, so in 1524, Giovanni da Verrazano, the rollicking Florentine, the terror of the Spanish galleons was commissioned to seek a shorter and more convenient northern passage. In his tiny caravel, the *Dauphin*, of less than

[4] Bancroft, Hist. of U. S., I-14.

a hundred tons burden, he skirted the Atlantic coast from the thirty-fourth degree, passing Chesapeake Bay, discovering New York harbor, and continuing northward to Maine. The outbreak of hostilities between England and France and the capture of Francis I at Pavia nullified his discoveries and no permanent results followed.[5] Ten years later, Jacques Cartier, a master pilot of St. Malo, was commissioned by Francis I of France to extend the boundaries of France beyond the ocean. He touched at Newfoundland, entered the Gulf, and sailed up the St. Lawrence River. The next year he again ascended the stream to the Lachine rapids, named the mountain, Mount Royal, and wintered on the rock of Quebec. The civil-religious wars retarded colonization until 1603, when Samuel de Champlain, "entered on a career which has made him perhaps the most famous figure as he certainly is the most picturesque in the romantic history of New France." [6] He planted a colony at Quebec, sustained it during long periods when the governmental aid was lacking, defying native foes and foreign plots, withstanding the forbidding climate, the unprofitable soil, the scanty crops. He went up the Saguenay and the Ottawa, journeyed to Lake Huron, searching for a water way to the Pacific Ocean, entered New York State by way of the great lake which bears his name. His successors followed

[5] Bennett, Cath. Footsteps in N. Y., 9.
[6] Thwaites, France in Am., II.

in his footsteps; "Jean Nicolet penetrated to Wisconsin; La Salle was reaching out for Louisiana; Saint Lausson visited the upper Great Lakes; Joliet and Marquette journeyed along the Father of Waters; Perrot, Duluth, and Cadillac made expeditions farther west. The lilies of France were surmounting many a log-stockaded half fort, half trading station; and on every hand it appeared likely that French overlordship had come to stay." [7]

A few months after Champlain had visited the future Empire State (1609), Henry Hudson, an Englishman, in the employ of the Dutch East India Company entered the harbor of New York, eighty-five years after Verrazano's visit. Holland had embraced the Dutch Reformed religion, Hudson was undoubtedly a member of the Established Church of England. All the other explorers were devotees of the ancient faith.

The bitter rivalry between France and England, dating from the marriage of Eleanor of Aquitania, former wife of Louis VII, to Henry Plantagenet, Duke of Anjou, afterwards Henry II of England, the long series of bloody contests for the disputed French territory, and the bigotry, racial and religious, engendered by the English reformation, the marriage of Mary to Philip of Spain, and the memories of the invincible Armada, have led many English and American historians to belittle the achievements of these two Catholic

[7] *Ibid.*, France in Am., 45.

countries in the work of discovery and colonization in the New World. The Spaniards are usually styled cruel, heartless, bloodthirsty, the French little better, bartering human life for fame and fortune. Even the missionaries, steadfast friends and defenders of the native tribes, have been maligned, their motives questioned, their actions misconstrued. True, many of the pioneer settlers were adventurers, seeking wealth and renown, practising cruelties, but this reprehensible conduct was even more pronounced in the English and Dutch settlements. Las Casas is frequently quoted as the authority for the cruelty of the colonists and clergy and crowned with laurels to the exclusion of the other priests and laymen who deserve a niche in the hall of fame. "The impetuous Las Casas, so far from standing alone is really one of the least conspicuous even in the missionary annals of his own order; and in order to convert, civilize and protect the redmen, all the religious orders rivalled each other, lavishing their blood and toil to save the Indian for time and eternity." [8] An honest comparison of the methods of the rival nations proves conclusively that the conversion, civilization, and education of the aborigines was the primary design of the French and Spaniards, their extermination seemed the sole aim of the other nations. "The tribes evangelized by French and Spaniards subsist to this day,—while it is notorious that the tribes in the territory colonized

[8] Shea, Cath. Miss. in U. S., 39.

by England have in many cases entirely disappeared and perished without ever having the gospel preached to them. The Abnakis, Caughnawagas, Kaskaskias, Miamis, Ottawas, and the New Mexico tribes remain, but where are the Pequods, Narragansetts, Mohegans, Lenlapes, Powhattans? They live only in name in the rivers and mountains of our land." [9]

Within the present limits of the republic, the Spanish missionaries roamed from Florida to New Mexico and California, from Chesapeake Bay to the Mississippi. With Narvaez's expedition came a little band of Franciscans, guided by Father John Juarez, according to the annals of the times, already consecrated Bishop of Florida. All perished through sickness, hunger or violence. The Dominican, Louis Cancer, with his companions won the martyr's crown preaching to the unruly natives. The Jesuit, Father Martinez, was slain on his arrival, his fellow missionary, Father Segura and his companions, murdered near Chesapeake Bay. Yet the blood of the martyrs was the seed of the church, flourishing missions sprang up, the converts gathered into villages, and schools were founded. The hostility of the natives, the stubbornness of the chieftains, the influence of the medicine men, the attacks and encroachments from the English colonies, their alliance with the warlike Indians, and finally the cession of Florida to England in 1763, first retarded and then utterly de-

[9] *Ibid.*, Cath. Miss. in U. S., 15.

stroyed the missions. Fired by the accounts of the survivors of Narvaez's expedition, of the existence of the
rich and powerful kingdoms of the southwest, the
Franciscan friar, Mark of Nice, with a single companion and a negro guide, toiled through the desert seeking
Cibola, the Zuni of the natives. On his return, another
friar and a lay brother returned to evangelize the inhabitants, but Father Padilla was killed by wandering
Indians. Other priests entered the field, ministering to
the fierce Texan tribes, penetrated into New Mexico
and Arizona and thence to California.

"The transmission of the heritage of European cul-
ture—was the task undertaken by the church. From
the beginning, the conversion of the natives to Christianity was a dominant motive of the Spanish policy." [10]
Every expedition had its priests, preaching, and teaching, baptizing, learning the native tongues, reducing
them to writing. Some labored in the Spanish villages,
some among the converted Indians, others followed the
wandering tribes, dwelling in the poverty and squalor
of their miserable tents. The wild aborigines were gathered into reductions, under the supervision of the
padres, taught the rudiments of education, trained to
peaceful, industrious, and religious lives.

"The earliest schools within the present limits of the
United States, were founded by the Franciscans in

[10] Bourne, Spain in Am., 302.

Florida and New Mexico." [11] The school teacher accompanied the explorer, the missionary, the soldier, the first master frequently the devoted priest or the humble brother. Some years before the opening of the Reformed Dutch School, (1633), or the Boston Latin School, (1635), there were elementary schools in New Mexico, spreading northward and westward as the conversions increased. "The early Franciscan missionaries built a school beside each church. The native languages were reduced to writing and in a few years, the Indians were learning to read and write." [12] As early as 1516, Cardinal Ximines, inspired by the saintly Las Casas, drew up a scheme for the education of the children of the settlers and those of the Indians. In Old Mexico, Pedro de Gants conducted a school for Aztec youths, and another was founded for mestizo and Spanish girls, and in 1551, Charles V gave charters to the Universities of Lima and Mexico. "Not all the institutions of learning founded in Mexico in the sixteenth century can be enumerated here, but it is not too much to say that in numbers, range of studies, and standards of attainment, by the officers, they surpassed anything existing in English America until the nineteenth century." [13] The dictionaries and grammars of the native tongues, the histories of the country and its peoples, the descriptions

---

[11] Burns, Cath. Sch. Sys. in U. S., 39.
[12] Bourne, Sp. in Am., 308.
[13] *Ibid.*, Sp. in Am., 310.

of the flora and fauna, the physical configuration of the land, the treatises on life and religion, are treasures for the historians, scientists and philologists of the present age. The cruelties of the pioneer adventurers have been exaggerated and magnified through racial hatred and rivalry, but the fact remains, that the races intermarried, the natives were converted to Christianity, educated and instructed, and regarded rather as subjects of His Majesty than implacable enemies to be annihilated. "The Spanish language will still be the common tongue of the millions who live between the Rio Grande del Norte, and the Straits of Magellan, and with the advance in knowledge, the national pride in the achievements of the Spaniards who explored a hemisphere and ineffaceably stamped upon its two continents their language, and their religion, will become an abiding inspiration." [14]

Various motives have been ascribed for the foundation of New France amidst the ice and snows of the north: the king for territorial expansion; the church to convert the heathens; the merchants to enjoy the fur trade; the adventurers to find mines of gold or silver; the soldiers to achieve glory; the people eager for adventures in the new lands.[15] The French were as eager to convert the natives as their Spanish rivals. Jacques Cartier's commission bade him explore, "in order the

[14] *Ibid.*, Sp. in Am., 318.
[15] Thwaites, France in Am., 17.

better to do what is pleasing to God, our Creator and Redeemer, and what may be for the increase of his holy and most sacred name and of our holy mother, the church." [16] Champlain brought the Recollects, the most austere branch of the Franciscan Order to the new settlement and for ten years they labored among the Indians from Tadoussac at the mouth of the Saguenay to the Nipissings on the route to Lake Huron. In 1625, at the invitation of the Recollects, the Jesuit fathers came, the two orders laboring hand in hand until the capture of Quebec in 1629. On the restoration of the French regime, the crown petitioned the Capuchins to take up the missionary duties, but they declined in favor of the Jesuits who then began the career which is the brightest page of American Catholic history.

Although they began their labors on Canadian soil, the zealous sons of Saint Ignatius followed their neophytes into territories afterwards incorporated into the new republic, ministering to the Abnakis of Maine, the Hurons of Michigan and Ohio, the Iroquois of Central New York, the Ottawas of Wisconsin, and Michigan, the Illinois of Illinois, and under another Superior, to the Louisiana tribes.[17] It was a difficult and seemingly hopeless task, the natives ignorant and immoral, cruel and superstitious, disgusting in their habits and customs, with no idea of restraint, yielding to every whim of

[16] Shea, Cath. Miss. in U. S., 123.
[17] *Ibid.*, Cath. Miss. in U. S., 27.

passion, loathing and detesting the moral teachings of Christianity. The priests were forced to paddle the frail canoes along the great rivers, portage to smaller streams, bear heavy burdens, subsist on meagre and revolting fare, live in dirty, smoky wigwams, and if famine or pestilence or hostile attack menaced the tribe, the fathers were styled sorcerers, and threatened with death. The missionaries at Mount Desert were carried prisoners to Virginia by Argall the English sea captain and pirate; Father Rahl was killed at the door of his chapel and his famous dictionary carried away as a trophy; Daniel shot down at the foot of the cross; de Brebeuf and Lallamant burned at the stake; Jogues tomahawked by a brave; Garnier stricken down while absolving a dying man; Chabanal killed by an apostate; Garreau slain from ambush; de Noue frozen amongst the ice and snows. Yet these clerical heroes never flinched. "Younger Jesuits burned with ardor to labor among the Indians of New France. Young men left camp and court to enter the order in the hope of sharing the toils of the missionaries." [18]

These apostolic men not only established missionary centers which afterwards developed into flourishing settlements, they were discoverers, voyagers, litterateurs, historians, geographers, grammarians, philologists, and agriculturists. "For the succeeding years, the illustrious triumvirate, Allouez, Dablon, Marquette,

[18] *Ibid.*, Cath. Miss. in U. S., 125.

were employed in confirming the influence of France in the vast regions that extend from Green Bay to the head of Lake Superior,—mingling happiness with suffering, and winning enduring glory by their fearless perseverance." [19] Father Marquette with Joliette discovered the Mississippi and founded flourishing settlements which later developed into a series of French outposts. His colleagues found the salt springs of New York, the copper mines of Michigan, the sulphur spring of the Senecas, the iron mines of Wisconsin. They planted wheat and introduced the plow on the prairies of Illinois, sugar cane and the silk worm in the bayous of Louisiana. To them we owe our present knowledge of the manners and customs, the languages and history, the flora and fauna of the people and the land. They reduced the dialects to writing, compiling grammars and dictionaries, translating spiritual and scientific works into the vernacular. As the aborigines had no written language, they were obliged to supply an alphabet and often to coin words and phrases to express the European ideas. They brought countless thousands to the faith of Christ and their descendants are still true to their teachings. At first the Hurons were unresponsive to their preaching and teachings, but they never lost hope, baptising infants and dying adults, patiently planting the seed in the apparently barren soil. Their deadly enemies, the Iroquois, invaded the Huron coun-

[19] Bancroft, Hist. of U. S., III-152.

try, almost annihilating the tribe, but before the fatal blow fell, thousands of converts rewarded the zeal of the missionaries. The brethren of Olier, the zealous Sulpicians, although primarily seminary priests, went on the missions, shedding their blood for the propagation of the faith. The secular priests from Bishop Laval's Seminary at Quebec labored among the Mississippi tribes, many winning the martyr's crown. "Take them by and large, in comparison with the religious of their time in other lands, and the priests and missionaries of France will not suffer in the examination, either intellectually or spiritually. Indeed the fascinating history of their remarkable and widespread missions, particularly the Jesuits,—although much might be said in praise of their less strenuous Recollects, Sulpicians and Capuchins, furnishes some of the most brilliant examples on record of self-sacrificing and heroic devotion to an exalted cause,—American history would lose much of its welcome color were there blotted from its pages the picturesque and often thrilling story of the curés and friars of Canada in the French regime." [20]

[20] Thwaites, France in Am., 137-138.

CHAPTER FOUR

Maryland

THE voyage of John Cabot, the Catholic Venetian, and the activities of Spain and Portugal in seeking
a shorter passage to the mysterious East, aroused the
sluggish and parsimonious Henry VII, and several English expeditions were dispatched westward during the
years from 1501 to 1504. According to tradition, a
priest accompanied at least one of those parties. Twenty
years later, Henry VIII sent John Rut with two vessels,
the *Sampson* and the *Mary Guilford* to find new lands,
and to seek for gold and silver. The chaplain of the
Guilford was Albert de Prato, a Canon of St. Paul's,
London, who wrote an account of the voyage for Cardinal Wolsey.[1] The religious upheaval, promoted by
Henry VIII and augmented by the ministers of the boy
king Edward VI, was partially quieted during the reign
of Mary, but the accession of Elizabeth exposed Catholics to a series of persecutions, unparalleled in religious
history. To escape the Penal Laws at home, the Catholics
began to look across the seas for a haven of refuge. In
1578, Sir Humphrey Gilbert, Sir George Peckham and

[1] Campbell, Pio. Laymen of N. A., 3.

Sir Thomas Gerard planned a colony in America, ostensibly to convert the natives and bring glory to the state, but really to provide a home for Catholic recusants. A patent was issued, but the plans failed. In 1582, a second attempt was made, and a settlement founded in Newfoundland, but Sir Humphrey Gilbert perished at sea and the site was abandoned. Twenty years later, a Mr. Winslade proposed to transfer a thousand Catholics to America but the scheme was abortive. The English ecclesiastics on the continent opposed the plan, as the government would not allow the settlers to depart and no foreign nation would allow them to sail from its ports.[2] The proposal remained in abeyance, for another twenty years until George Calvert, an Oxford graduate, and Secretary of State under James I, became a Catholic, resigned his offices, and proposed to found a colony for his persecuted brethren. He continued in the royal favor, and was created Lord Baltimore in the Irish peerage. Charles I confirmed him in his appointments, and treated him with marked kindness. In 1620, before his conversion to the ancient faith, he had acquired a site in Newfoundland which he named Avalon, intending to establish a colony where all the settlers might enjoy liberty of conscience. Catholics and Protestants emigrated to the island, priests and ministers were appointed to serve the people, but the Protestant clergy filed charges against the Proprietor for maintaining a

[2] Russell, Maryland, Land of Sanc., 27.

Popish chapel, permitting the celebration of Mass and showing favor to the Catholics. The intense cold, the long winters, the barren soil, discouraged the settlers, so Baltimore resolved to transfer his colony to a warmer climate. On the homeward voyage he visited James-town, and was tendered the odious oath of supremacy by the intolerant governor, but as he was a Catholic he refused to comply, and left the inhospitable colony. He secured from Charles I a grant south of the James River, but the opposition of the notorious Claiborne and others caused him to relinquish the claims. He then petitioned for the present site of Maryland, and the King graciously granted his request, but before the charter was granted, Lord Baltimore died, "leaving a name against which the breath of calumny has hardly whispered a reproach." [3]

His eldest son, Caecilius Calvert, was confirmed in his father's rights, and granted the charter. On the twenty-second of November, 1633, two small vessels, the *Ark* and the *Dove*, bearing a company of colonists numbering twenty gentlemen and between two and three hundred laborers and artisans, with the Jesuit fathers, White and Altham, and Brother Gervase,[4] as missionaries, sailed from the Isle of Wight, "after committing the principal parts of the ship to the protection of God especially, and of His Most Holy Mother, and

[3] Bancroft, Hist. of U. S., I-244.
[4] Browne, Maryland, 21.

St. Ignatius, and all the Guardian Angels of Maryland." [5] Leonard Calvert, brother of Lord Baltimore was placed in charge of the expedition and commissioned Governor of the new province. After a stormy voyage the little flotilla sailed up the Potomac and on the feast of the Annunciation, March 25th, 1634, landed at St. Clement's Island where Mass was celebrated, a huge cross erected, and the Litanies of the Holy Cross chanted.[6] Sailing down the stream, the Governor came to a little Indian village where he purchased, "the spase of thirtie miles of ground of them for axes, cloth and hatchets." [7] A treaty of peace was negotiated with the natives, half the settlement being assigned to the new-comers, the rest to be surrendered after the harvest. "The Indian women taught them how to use corn meal, and with the Indian men, they hunted deer and were initiated into the mysteries of woodcraft. They planted the cleared land, and in the autumn of the year were able to send a cargo of corn to New England for salt fish and other provisions. From Virginia the colonials procured swine and cattle; and within a few months after landing the settlement was enjoying a high degree of prosperity. The English race had now learned the art of colonization." [8] "To Father White and his associates was assigned a chief's cabin or hut of poles,

[5] Russell, Maryland, Land of Sanc., 75.
[6] *Ibid.*, Maryland, Land of Sanc., 77.
[7] Hughes, So. of Jesus in N. Am., I-325.
[8] Winsor, Hist. of Am., III-526.

which he consecrated as a church, and called, 'Primum Marylandiae Sacellum.' " [9] The prosperity and tranquillity of the colony for many years were due mainly to the labors of the Jesuit missionaries who instilled into the hearts of the settlers lessons of charity and justice towards the natives and so influenced the Indians by their religious teachings that war between the races was unknown and full liberty of conscience assured to every settler. "It is certain that from the time the emigrants landed at St. Mary's, religious toleration was the established custom of the province." [10] "Never was any government more indulgent to persons of all religious persuasions than that of Baltimore whilst the Roman Catholic Lords Baron of Baltimore controlled it. Lord Baltimore not only forbade persecution of Protestants, he commanded also that their religious feelings should be respected. He allowed not only freedom of worship but he gave the franchise to the poor Protestants who had been unable even to pay their expenses to Maryland. Maryland was intended from the beginning to be the land of sanctuary for the oppressed of every creed." [11] "To this land of sanctuary came the Puritans who were whipped and imprisoned in Virginia and the Prelatists who were persecuted in New England." [12] In the vast desert of intolerance extending from Georgia

[9] Browne, Maryland, 25.
[10] Winsor, Hist. of Am., III-530.
[11] Russell, Maryland, Land of Sanc., 122.
[12] Winsor, Hist. of Am., III-531.

Cromwell and the Parliamentary Party, brought troubles to the Catholics of Maryland. Many Protestant Redemptioners had served their allotted time and were entitled to vote. The Puritans, outlawed by the Anglicans, came from Virginia at the invitation of Governor Stone and settled to the number of three hundred on the Severn River. Other non-Conformists likewise sought homes in the Land of Sanctuary, Catholics dwindled to a minority, and a Protestant Governor and Councilors were chosen. These refugees planned to overcome those who had welcomed them to the colony, and Commissioners were chosen, "to reduce all the plantations within the Bay of the Chesapeake." Claiborne, the old enemy, Bennett, a refugee from Virginia, invaded Maryland, deposed the Governor and placed Fuller, a Puritan from Providence and a Board of Directors in charge of the Province. No Catholic could vote or hold office, and the Toleration Law was repealed. "None who professed the Popish, (commonly called the Roman Catholic), religion, could be protected in the province." Governor Stone mustered a force of one hundred and thirty men, attacked the usurpers but was defeated and captured. Ten prisoners were sentenced to death, four executed, the others were spared by the prayers of the women and the petitions of the soldiers.[18] Calvert took legal steps to recover his charter rights but was unsuccessful. The exiled Charles II proclaimed Bal-

[18] Russell, Maryland, Land of Sanc., 237.

timore a rebel, and appointed Sir William Davenant, the poet, Governor, although he never reached the province. On the other hand, the Commissioners planned to invalidate the charter granted to Cecilius Calvert, to consolidate the settlements of Maryland and Virginia, and to restore Kent Island to Claiborne. Opposed by both King and Parliament, the non-Catholic settlers in open revolt, the colony seemed lost to the Proprietor.

In 1656, the Commissioners of Plantation having decided in Baltimore's favor, his rights were restored, and his authority reëstablished by order of the Protector. Fendall, the new Governor began a course of intrigue against the Calverts, the Constitution was overthrown, and their authority was again swept away. Baltimore, however, dismissed the recreant official and named his brother, Philip, as Governor. The conspirators were tried, found guilty of treason, and sentenced to banishment and forfeiture of their estates,—a sentence later mitigated to a fine and perpetual disfranchisement. Quakers driven from the other colonies, came to Maryland in large numbers, and enjoyed religious and civil freedom during the administration of Fendall. Presbyterians also migrated to the religious haven although they early displayed a disposition to rebel against the laws and regulations of the Province.[19] Labadists arrived 1684, securing a large tract at Bohemia Manor. Even Jews were welcomed to the Land of Sanctuary.

[19] *Ibid.*, Maryland, Land of Sanc., 237.

The Toleration Act of 1649 seemed to debar them from all privileges, yet the records show that full citizenship was conferred on Jacob Lumbrozo.[20]

Cecil Calvert died in 1675, and was succeeded by his son, Charles, who had governed the province for fourteen years. Although his relations with the settlers were cordial, various annoyances disturbed the tranquillity of the Province. John Yeo, a parson writing to the Archbishop of Canterbury describes the colony as "a Sodom of uncleanness and a Pest House of iniquity," and prays for the establishment of a Protestant clergy, to offset the efforts of "so many professed enemies as the Popish priests and Jesuits who are encouraged and provided for." [21] The Bishop of London presented this petition to the Committee of Plantations but Charles Calvert, in a dignified paper, refuted the false charges. Claiborne petitioned His Majesty to restore Kent Island. The cry against Popery raised in England was re-echoed in Maryland and Catholics were accused of conspiring with the Indians to massacre the Protestant settlers. Although the Catholics numbered only one twelfth of the population, James II listened to these charges of disloyalty and directed the Attorney General in 1687, to issue a writ against the Charter.[22]

In 1688, William of Orange landed at Torbay and

[20] *Ibid.*, Maryland, Land of Sanc., 272.
[21] *Ibid.*, Maryland, Land of Sanc., 325-6.
[22] *Ibid.*, Maryland, Land of Sanc., 334.

James II fled to France. When the news reached Maryland, "an Association in arms for the defence of the Protestant Religion and for asserting the Right of King William and Queen Mary to the Province of Maryland and all the English Dominions" was formed under the leadership of John Coode, an unfrocked minister, convicted of blasphemy, sedition, theft and enormous crimes in Maryland, indicted in Virginia,—where he had taken refuge to escape the punishment of his misdeeds at the hands of his fellow settlers,—for drunkenness and disturbance of divine service. St. Mary's, the capital, was seized, a declaration issued accusing the Papists of plotting to massacre the Protestants with the aid of the Indians, although Catholics were few in numbers.[23] Many prominent Protestants stamped these charges as unjust and frivolous, but were threatened with fine or imprisonment for their interference.[24] However the recommendation of the Committe of Trade and Transportation was accepted by William of Orange, Lord Baltimore was deprived of his Province, and Sir Lionel Copley was appointed Royal Governor. An Assembly was summoned which proclaimed the Protestant Episcopal Church the established religion of the colony, and every inhabitant was taxed forty pounds of tobacco for its support, although the Anglicans constituted only a small minority of the

[23] Browne, Maryland, 151-2.
[24] Russell, Maryland, Land of Sanc., 347.

population.[25] The King vetoed these acts, but in 1702, they were reintroduced and passed, and received the royal assent. New oaths were devised, prohibiting Catholics from holding office, and in 1704, a statute, preventing them from practising their religion, debarring priests from their sacred functions, forbidding the teaching of children. But Queen Ann, less unjust than her Anglican subjects, in Maryland, allowed Catholic priests to officiate in private families. Hence arose the custom in colonial days of having a chapel annexed to a house. The Catholic chapels were usually called, "Priests' Mass Houses." [26] The chapel at St. Mary's was closed by the Sheriff and Catholics excluded from the first church erected in Maryland. Priests were obliged to subscribe to the Oath of Allegiance, Abhorrency, and Abjuration, composed of blasphemies against the most sacred tenets of their religion. Catholics were excused or excluded from serving in the militia and were compelled to pay double taxes for this enforced exemption. "It was made a cause punishable with fines and imprisonment for a priest to say Mass or exercise any priestly functions; and any member of the church of Rome who should teach or even board young persons, were to be sent to England for prosecution. Children of Catholics were encouraged to forsake their parents' religion. A

[25] *Ibid.*, Maryland, Land of Sanc., 417-18.
[26] *Ibid.*, Maryland, Land of Sanc., 378.

duty of twenty shillings per poll was laid on all Irish Papists brought into the Province." [27]

Charles, the third Lord Baltimore, died in 1715. His son, Benedict Leonard, who had conformed to the Established Church, succeeded him, but enjoyed his new honors only a few weeks, the title descending to his son, Charles. "Representation being made to King George, that Charles was also a Protestant, the Palatinate was restored to him under the terms of the original charter. The Assembly of Maryland adopted an address—that the administration of the Province had been finally put upon a wholly Protestant establishment and expressing the hope that further toleration might not be granted to Catholics." [28] Charles was weak and vain, a creature of the court, unscrupulous in aiding and abetting the King, in his intrigues and dishonest alliances and under him Catholics could hope for no relief, as the laws were strengthened and rigidly enforced by the Assembly and the Governors. His son and successor, Frederick, was "a degenerate scion of a noble stock, a selfish and grasping voluptuary, who cared only for his province, which he never visited, as a source of revenue for his pleasures.—He came near adding his name also to the list of noble criminals by figuring as a traverser in a discreditable trial for felony, of which he was acquitted." [29] In 1752, Catholics, discouraged by persecu-

[27] Browne, Maryland, 199.
[28] Russell, Maryland, Land of Sanc., 396.
[29] Browne, Maryland, 217.

tions, through their spokesman, Charles Carroll, the father of Charles Carroll of Carrollton, petitioned for a tract of land in Louisiana, near the Arkansas River where they might enjoy civil and religious freedom. The French minister objected, and the plan was abandoned.[30] Frederick died in 1771 without legitimate heirs, and bequeathed the Province to his natural son, Henry Harford. The outbreak of the Revolution put an end to English rule and in 1780, the landed domains of the illegitimate Henry were sequestered to the State of Maryland.[31]

The Jesuit fathers, Andrew White and John Gravener or Altham, accompanied the first expedition, Mass was said on St. Clement's Island, a cross erected and the river, capes and islands given the names of Catholic saints. A little Indian hut in St. Mary's was assigned to the Fathers as a chapel, until the projected church, adjoining the fort should be erected. Other sites were established at Port Tobacco and St. Inigoes, and additional priests and brothers came to minister to the settlers and evangelize the natives. The strange conduct of the Lord Proprietor and his Secretary, John Lewger, a fellow student at Oxford, and a recent convert from the Anglican ministry, retarded the labors of the missionaries and left a blot on the escutcheon of Cecilius Calvert. He made no provisions for the support of the

[30] Russell, Maryland, Land of Sanc., 414.
[31] Browne, Maryland, 285.

clergy, through state donations and popular contributions, but compelled them to take up lands like the other settlers. Their servants were forced to perform military services, the fathers were obliged to till the fields and neglect their spiritual obligations. He neither built nor endowed chapels for whites or Indians, and confiscated the lands given by the grateful tribesmen.[33] "This difficulty between Baltimore and the Jesuits is still wrapped in considerable mystery. It appears to be one of those lamentable instances of which we too have often experienced, when sincere, honest and devoted men through misunderstandings become involved in an inextricable labyrinth of suspicion, mutual recrimination and bitterness."[34] The zealous fathers, although discouraged by the troubles, labored assiduously to safeguard the faith of the colonists, to win converts among the non-Catholic settlers and the natives. "Father White devoting himself to the study of the languages, soon compiled a grammar, dictionary and catechism in the Piscataway language, while Rigbie at a later period compiled a catechism for the Patuxents."[35] Chilemacon, King of the Piscataways, with his wife and daughter were baptized, and many warriors and squaws were received into the church. Four other chieftains were subsequently converted. Father Altham succumbed

[33] Hughes, So. of Jesus in N. Am., I-410-446.
[34] Russell, Maryland, Land of Sanc., 171.
[35] Shea, Hist. of Cath. Ch. Among Indians, 487.

to the rigors of the climate, others were incapacitated but additional workers came. Owing to the disputes with Lord Baltimore, several secular priests were assigned to labor in the virgin field, but their names and the result of their labors are unknown. During Claiborne's rebellion, Fathers White and Copley were carried to England in chains, Fathers Rigbie, Hartwell and Cooper, were either carried or escaped to Virginia, where all three died in 1646. When peace was restored, Father Copley and his devoted confreres returned and revived the missions. The civil war in England, the execution of Charles I, the triumph of the Parliamentary Party, the accession of Cromwell as Lord Protector, assured Puritan ascendancy in Maryland. The Indian missions were broken up, and the settlers left without spiritual guides. Sixteen priests had shared the missionary labors, "all but two were Jesuits, all true soldiers of the Cross. Eight of them died in the performance of their heroic duties." [37]

When the Calvert rights were restored, the Jesuits resumed their stations. In 1673, two or three Franciscans came to Maryland and during the next century and a half, seven or nine others labored in the colony. As Catholics were hopelessly in a minority, only the tact and wisdom of the clergy prevented heated controversies. Charges were continually preferred in London against the Papists and their Popish proprietor, and

[37] Russell, Maryland, Land of Sanc., 182.

Calvert and his sons were ever on the defensive.[38] It was a common rumor, that the colony was infested with fanatics and Jesuits who led the inhabitants to "Popery, Quakerism, or fanaticism," although all religions were tolerated, all provided with ministers, all supported by voluntary contributions, or the produce of the plantations. It was merely the echo of the No-Popery cry which brought such dire consequences to the English Catholics during the Stuart dynasty. Rumors of alliance with the Indians, to massacre the Protestants, or a coalition with the French or Spanish to deprive England of her American colonies was another charge, frequently laid before the King and his council. Even James II gave heed to these charges, and determined to forfeit the Proprietor's Charter.

The accession of William and Mary brought additional woes to the clergy of the colony. A royal governor was named, and Anglicanism proclaimed as the state religion. All the inhabitants were taxed for the support of its ministers. New laws were enacted bearing heavily on the Catholics and especially on the priests, who on several occasions were brought to trial, and although acquitted, were grossly insulted by the trial judges.[39] The chapel at St. Mary's was closed by the sheriff, and only the clemency of Queen Ann enabled priests to say Mass in private houses. Yet the clergy

[38] *Ibid.*, Maryland, Land of Sanc., 325.
[39] Shea, Hist. of Cath. Ch., I-354-56.

labored incessantly, the Catholic population actually increased, and many converts joined the church,—a circumstance which aroused all the fury of the established church. "They were fined, disfranchised, and their possessions taken from them, they were socially ostracized, yet they held to their faith in spite of all, and what was the greatest crime of all,—they increased." [41] From 1700 to 1771, seventy Jesuits came to the province. [42] When freedom came, they were the only clerical body in the new republic. "The field of missionary labor during colonial times comprised Maryland, Virginia, New Jersey, Delaware, Pennsylvania and New York." [43] From the landing of the pilgrims in 1634, the devoted Jesuits planned educational facilities for the colonists, although the disputes with Lord Baltimore and the rebellions of Ingle and Claiborne crippled and retarded their activities, and the triumph of the Parliamentary Party and the accession of Oliver Cromwell were almost fatal to the project. Yet in 1640, Ralph Crouch, a former novice of the Society and later a priest, opened a school and taught for twenty years probably at Newtown. [44] In the ancient registry of wills, various bequests for the support of schools are preserved. In later years, Jesuit priests and brothers especially Gregory Turbeville assisted in the teaching,—"as the Jesuit priests in

[41] Russell, Maryland, Land of Sanc., 614.
[42] *Ibid.*, Maryland, Land of Sanc., 432.
[43] Hughes, So. of Jesus in N. Am., II-V.
[44] Burns, Cath. Sch. Sys. in U. S., 392.

Maryland were as a rule, remarkably learned men, there was a chance for them to lay the foundation for college work by the gradual introduction of such classes as would form the curriculum of a classical preparatory school." [45] In 1677, it was officially announced that a college or school for the Humanities was opened with two Jesuit fathers as teachers. [46] One of the first pupils was Robert Brooke,—later a Jesuit and a laborer for many years in the Maryland missions. A scholastic, Thomas Hathersall, taught the classics for fifteen years. For many years this college at Newtown was the only institution for higher learning in Maryland and ranks as the second college within the present limits of the republic, being antedated only by Harvard. At the beginning of the eighteenth century, another Jesuit school was opened at Bohemia. Its history is obscure, owing to the persecutions, but several illustrious scholars matriculated within its walls, Archbishop John Carroll, his successor, Leonard Neale, and Charles Carroll of Carrollton. Complaints were continually registered with the authorities praying for its closing, and it was suspended on several occasions, but survived until 1765. Other Catholic schools flourished from the earlier years, as is evident from the many references found in the letters and records of the period. When the republic was

[45] *Ibid.*, Cath. Sch. Sys. in U. S., 100.
[46] *Ibid.*, Cath. Sch. Sys. in U. S., 101.

founded, historic Georgetown became the heir and successor to these primitive seats of learning.

The revolution sounded the death knell of religious intolerance in Maryland. Charles Carroll of Carrollton was chosen a member of "the Committee to propose a Declaration of Rights and a Form of Government for this state." The committee incorporated in the Declaration, that principle of religious liberty which had been proclaimed in Maryland, one hundred and forty-two years before,—a principle always in operation while the Catholic Proprietors were in power, always in abeyance when the government was in the hands of Puritans or Prelatists." [47] "We may now place side by side, the three tolerations of Maryland. The tolerations of the Proprietors lasted fifty years and under it all believers in Christ were equal before the law and all support to churches and ministers was voluntary. The Puritan toleration lasted six years and included all but Papists, Prelatists, and those who held objectionable doctrines. The Anglican toleration lasted eighty years and had glebes, and churches, for the Establishment, connivance for Dissenters, the penal laws for Catholics, and for all the forty per poll." [48]

[47] Russell, Maryland, Land of Sanc., 488.
[48] Browne, Maryland, 185-6.

CHAPTER FIVE

New York

IN April, 1524, Giovanni da Verrazano, a Catholic Venetian, in the service of Francis I of France, entered the harbor of New York in the little caravel *Dauphin*, of less than one hundred tons, explored its waters and ascended the river for several leagues. The next year, Estevan Gomez, a Catholic Spaniard, sailed past Cape St. Mary,—as the Florentine called the present Sandy Hook, and entered the bay. He named the harbor, St. Christobel, and the river, San Antonio.[1] In 1542, Allefonce, pilot and captain under Robertval, is said to have explored the shores of Long Island. These voyages were barren of permanent results, although French hunters and trappers came to trade in furs and peltries and explored the river as far north as the present city of Albany.[2] In July, 1609, Samuel de Champlain, and his Algonquin allies entered the lake which bears his name and fought a sanguinary battle with the warriors of the Mohawks. Two months later, Henry Hudson, an Englishman, in the service of the Dutch, came to "The Great River of New Netherland," in the yacht,

[1] Bennett, Cath. Footp. in Old N. Y., 10.
[2] *Ibid.*, Cath. Footp. in Old N. Y., 10.

62

the *Half Moon,* and thinking he had found the North-west Passage, explored its waters as far as the head of navigation. His glowing accounts of the natural resources of the country and especially the abundance of fur-bearing animals, brought about the formation of the Dutch West India Company, and in 1623, Adrian Tienpoint, as Director of the "Prince Maritius" or North River, took possession of Manhattan Island and erected a fort, near the present site of Albany, which he called Fort Orange. Three years later, his successor, Peter Minuit, bought the entire island from the Indians for merchandise valued at twenty-four dollars. Under the new company, New Amsterdam was a trading post and the outlying settlements, depots for collecting beaver skins and peltries, the staple wealth of the colony. The Governor was a salaried official, anxious only to increase the revenues of the colony and insure his retention. Emigrants from New England settled on Long Island and in the present county of Westchester. The people clamored for popular government but their appeals were unheeded. Minuit, Van Twiller and Kieft were unpopular and the unjust and selfish policy of their agents in dealing with the river Indians provoked bloody reprisals which several times brought the colony to the brink of ruin. Even brave, old Peter Stuyvesant was unable to calm the popular discontent. In August 1664, four English frigates mounting one hundred twenty guns, carrying a little army of five hundred soldiers, regulars and New England volunteers appeared before New Amsterdam and demanded its surrender. The gallant but irascible Stuyvesant prepared to resist and called on the citizens for aid, but the weakness of the defences, the lack of powder, the scarcity of food, and the meagreness of the garrison precluded all hope of a successful resistance. The remonstrances of the people, and the prayers of Dominie Megapolensis finally prevailed over the headlong bravery of the old warrior, the white flag was hoisted, the invading army marched in and Dutch rule was at an end. The fort and city were renamed Fort James and New York, in honor of the Duke of York, the king's brother on whom the province had been conferred. Nine years later, during the war between England and Holland, a Dutch fleet recaptured the city but the Treaty of Westminster restored it to the Royal Proprietor.

The change of government was welcome to the majority of the settlers, mostly immigrants from England and Holland, the two European countries most strongly impregnated with the democratic principles derived from the two celebrated documents of Catholic origin,—"The Magna Charta," and "The Great Privilege." Nicholls and his successors, Lovelace and Andros, although more polished and polite than Kieft and Stuyvesant were equally autocratic in their conduct, popular government was again sought and refused, taxes were increased, and restrictions placed on trade. Connecticut claimed a portion of the Hudson Valley, New Jersey was encroaching on the Duke's dominions and trade, Penn was intriguing for the Susquehanna country, the native tribes were restive and eager for hostilities, the French threatened the frontier towns. Charges of peculation and favoritism were lodged against Governor Andros who was summoned to London to explain his conduct. After his departure, the merchants refused to pay the custom duties, claiming that the three years' agreement with the Duke had expired, and could not be renewed during the absence of the Governor. Captain Anthony Brockholles, a Yorkshire Catholic, and Deputy Governor, endeavored to enforce the payments, but was unsuccessful. The whole Province was seething with rebellion when the news arrived that Andros had been exonerated of the charges, and relieved from office, and Thomas Dongan, an Irishman and a Catholic, had been appointed Governor.

Dongan came of a distinguished Irish family, his father, Sir John Dongan a member of the Irish Parliament, his elder brother, William, Baron Dongan and Viscount Claire, later Earl of Limerick. After the fall of Charles I, Thomas, a youth of fifteen, accompanied his family to France, serving as Colonel under Marshall Turenne and winning many laurels in Flanders. He was conversant with the Dutch and French languages and diplomacy,—ideal qualifications for the ruler of a colony, where English and Dutch settlers predominated, and useful accomplishments in the controversies with the Canadian Governors, striving for the possession of Central New York and the friendship of the Five Nations. On October seventeenth 1683, shortly after his arrival, he called the first popular General Assembly to meet at Fort James. Although the records are lost, we know it remained in session for three weeks and passed fourteen enactments. The most important of these was, "The Charter of Libertyes And Privileges, granted by His Royal Highness to the inhabitants of New York and its dependencies." [3] "That the supreme legislative authority under His Majesty and Royal Highness, James, Duke of York—shall forever be and reside in a governor, Councill, and the people met in General Assembly. The Assembly shall meet at least once in three years; Every freeman shall have a voice and a vote in the election of representatives without restraint; The Assembly shall be the judge of the qualifications of its members; No one shall be punished unless found guilty by a jury of his peers; No tax shall be levied without the consent of the Assembly; No soldiers shall be quartered on the people except in actual warfare; No martial law shall be proclaimed; No Man's property shall be sold without his consent unless by due process of the law; a widow shall be entitled to the third part of her husband's estate as her dower. Finally; no person or persons which profess faith in God through Jesus

[3] New York, Eccl. Rec. of, II-864.

Christ, shall at any time be any ways molested, punished or disquieted or called in question, for any difference in opinion or matter of religious concernment, who do not actually disturb the civil peace of the Province but that all and every such person or persons may from time to time and at all times freely have and fully enjoy his or their judgments or consciences in matters of religion throughout all the province, they behaving themselves peacefully, and quietly and not using this liberty to licentiousness nor to the civil injury or outward disturbance of others." [4]

In this document, built on the broad foundations of Magna Charta, Dongan showed himself a ruler of broad mind and rare executive ability, and a constructive statesman with a deep appreciation of popular rights and individual liberty and an intelligent concept of the theory of government. In religious toleration, he shares the honors with Calvert and Penn. In addition, acts were passed to naturalize foreigners, creating twelve counties, and providing a complete judiciary. The charter was signed by the Governor, and sent to England for ratification but was never returned. In the boundary disputes, he protected the rights of the Proprietor. By a treaty with the Cayugas, approved by the Mohawks, the Susquehanna Valley was ceded to New York to the chagrin of Penn who coveted that fertile region. The claims of Connecticut,

[4] *Ibid.*, Eccl. Rec. of, II-864.

Massachusetts and New Jersey were adjusted with credit to Dongan and to the advantage of his patron.

The master stroke of his administration was the alliance with the Iroquois, by which the whole of the present state of New York became an integral part of the Duke's dominions. Dongan realized that the friendship of these tribes would insure the safety of the colony and New England and divert the fur trade from Montreal to Albany. In the disputes with de la Barre and De Denonville he was sagacious and diplomatic defending the rights of the allies and preparing them for the coming conflict. He strengthened Fort James, and erected new fortifications at Albany and Schenectady against the expected attacks of the French and Indians. In these enterprises he received neither aid nor encouragement from the Royal Patron and as the revenues were insufficient for such large outlays, he spent his private fortune and pledged his personal credit.[5] A century later, when the titanic struggle between the two great nations began, the alliance with the Indians brought victory to the English standard. He renewed the ancient privileges enjoyed under former Dutch and English Governors, and confirmed the flour bolting industry to the city. In April 1686, he gave a charter to New York City which remained in force for one hundred and thirty-five years and is the basis of the present

[5] Roberts, New York, I-195.

document, and in July, conferred a charter on Albany, which continued until 1870.[6]

On the death of Charles II, the Duke of York ascended the English throne as James II. He united New England, New York and New Jersey in one province and commissioned Sir Edmund Andros as Governor. Dongan was recalled to London, and offered a Major-General's commission but he refused all honors and re-tired to his country estate on Long Island to recoup his shattered fortunes. His exertions against the French had borne fruit, as his policy proved successful, and was approved and adopted by the home government. The triumph of William of Orange and the flight of James II to France "led in New York to rebellion, open, armed and for a while successful." [7] "The religious fears and prejudices which had precipitated the revolution in Britain were grotesquely paraphrased in New York." [8] Jacob Leissler, a merchant, seized the fort and assumed the authority of the government. "The man was unquestionably honest in his dealings and purposes, his mind was vigorous, his temper ungovernable and vindictive, his vanity inordinate, and his whole nature and character were poisoned by his fanaticism." [9] Stories of a Popish plot "to seize the fort and massacre the inhabitants were circulated although the Catholic popu-

[6] McCarthy, Hist. of U. S., 94.
[7] Roberts, New York, I-200.
[8] *Ibid.*, New York, I-202.
[9] Bennett, Cath. Footp. in Old N. Y., 116.

lation was insignificant. The Catholics were few in numbers, had never been aggressive, and could have exercised no control if they had tried to do so." [10] Warrants were issued for Colonel Dongan, Major Brockholles, Matthew Plowman, the Collector, Major Jervis Baxter, the Councilor, and other well-known Catholics, and Lieutenant Governor Nicholson and many liberal Protestants were stigmatized as "Papists." After many vicissitudes of fortune, Dongan escaped to Boston and took ship for England. He succeeded to his brother's title, Earl of Limerick, but his possessions in New York were forfeited and his family estates confiscated. He died in London in 1718 loyal and true to his country and his religion. "These were evil times which chose such a man for a victim and heaped false charges upon him and drove him even temporarily from the rural home where he was illustrating the modest virtues of a private person." [11] In 1691, Colonel Sloughter, the new governor arrived in New York. Leissler and his son-in-law, Jacob Milborne and his chief supporters were tried for treason and murder, and condemned to death. Leissler and Milborne were executed, the others discharged.

Until the close of the revolutionary period, thirty-three governors ruled the colony.[12] Domestic problems, affecting trade, revenues, and religion agitated the citi-

[10] Roberts, New York, I-212.
[11] *Ibid.*, New York, I-197.
[12] *Ibid.*, New York, I-216.

zens and the officials. The trial and acquittal of John
Peter Zenger on the charge of libel, and the atrocities
committed during the so-called "Negro Plot," illustrated
the feelings of the period. Irish, Scotch, Palatinates settled in the Hudson and Mohawk Valleys bringing a
much needed addition to the population. During the
conflicts with France, Canadians and Indians raided the
border settlements, killing and capturing the settlers
Lake Champlain was the natural waterway from Canada
to the Hudson and the fortified posts at Crown Point
and Ticonderoga were the key to the situation. In the
final struggle, these posts and Fort Niagara were captured after several bloody forays and much loss of life.
In the pre-revolutionary agitation, New York vigor-
ously opposed the enforcement of the Stamp Act and the
other measures inimical to the colonies. In 1765, delegates
from seven colonies assembled at New York and framed
"A Declaration of Rights and Grievances of the Colonies of America." A conflict between the people and
the soldiers at Golden Hill "was the beginning of the
shedding of blood for the independence of America." [13]
Although the Tories were numerous and influential,
New York joined the other colonies in the struggle for
freedom. Crown Point and Ticonderoga were captured
by the Green Mountain Boys and New York City was
garrisoned and fortified. The disasters on Long Island
and the retreat of Washington's army left the entire

[13] *Ibid.*, New York, II-378.

island in the hands of the British until the signing of the treaty of peace. In November 1783, the enemy evacuated the city, Washington and his army marched in, and the stars and stripes were unfurled over the emancipated people.

"Although the States-General frequently intervened in the civil administration of the Province of New Netherlands, there is hardly any trace of its intervention in ecclesiastical matters." [14] In 1640, the Dutch West India Company enacted: "and no other religion shall be publicly admitted in New Netherland except the Reformed, as it is at present preached and practiced by public authority in the United Netherlands." [15] English Presbyterians were welcomed as members of a kindred religion and English Congregationalists as agreeing in fundamentals.[16] "They were not granted, as some historians seem to think, freedom of religion, but freedom of *their* religion." [17] During the administration of Stuyvesant, the Lutherans were forbidden to meet in public or private conventicles but were permitted to hold family prayers and worship in their homes.[18] Quakers were persecuted and expelled from the colony, Jews were unwelcome settlers, from religious and economic causes.[19] The Directors in Holland

[14] Zwierlein, Rel. in New Neth., 144-46.
[15] New York, Eccl. Rec. of, I-130.
[16] Zwierlein, Rel. in New Neth., 145-6.
[17] *Ibid.*, Rel. in New Neth., 144.
[18] *Ibid.*, Rel. in New Neth., 197.
[19] Cobb, Rise Rel. Tol. in Am., 318-320.

granted them rights to land and property but refused them full religious liberty.[20] Later they were admitted to citizenship.[21] Catholics were settlers in the province as is evident from the letter of Dominie Megapolensis of the Classics of Amsterdam, protesting against admission of Jews; "For as we have here, Papists, Mennonites, and Lutherans among the Dutch; also many Puritans or Independents, and many Quakers, and various servants of Baal among the English, under this government who conceal themselves under the name of Christians." [22] Privateering was popular and lucrative in those days and many French and Spanish prizes, with Catholic officers and crews were brought to New Amsterdam.[23] In 1643, St. Isaac Jogues was captured by the Mohawks, tortured and mangled, and carried to Ossernenon, the principal village. Commandant van Corlear rescued him, appeased the savages by a generous ransom and sent him to New Amsterdam where he was honorably received and humanely treated by Governor Kieft and Dominie Megapolensis.[24] He found two Catholics on the island, the Portuguese wife of the ensign and a young Irishman lately arrived from Maryland, who made his confession to the saintly missionary.[25] During the following year, another Jesuit, Father

[20] *Ibid.*, Rise Rel. Tol. in Am., 316.
[21] Zwierlein, Rel. in New Neth., 262.
[22] New York, Eccl. Rec. of, I-335.
[23] Bennett, Cath. Foots. in Old N. Y., 16.
[24] Campbell, Pio. Priests of N. Am., I-15-28.
[25] *Ibid.*, Pio. Priests of N. Am., I-28.

Bressani, was also rescued from the Mohawks by the kindly burghers of Fort Orange, brought to New Amsterdam and sent to France by the warm-hearted Governor Kieft. Father Poncet, S.J., after imprisonment and torture in the Indian country, was brought to Fort Orange where he met the famous Radisson, who had been adopted by the Mohawks but escaped and sought the protection of the Dutch. Father Poncet returned to Canada by the overland route, Radisson journeyed to New Amsterdam and sailed for France.[26] During the administration of Stuyvesant, the celebrated missionary, Father Simon Le Moyne came to New Amsterdam to minister to the few Catholics and the French and Spanish prisoners of war. He was well received by the Governor and secured for the Dutch trading vessels the right to trade with Canadian ports. "Although the Dutch were very generous in their treatment of Father Jogues and later of the other Jesuit missionaries, they were evidently bent on impressing him with the idea that dissenters from the established religion were only present in the colony on the suffrance of the local authorities as he had been informed in all likelihood by the Director himself that the colony had orders to admit none but Calvinists." [27] However the only known instance of intolerance was the case of Nicholas the Frenchman, who with several other settlers of Brooklyn

[26] Bennett, Cath. Foots. in Old N. Y., 42-3.
[27] Zwierlein, Rel. in New Neth., 141.

refused to contribute six guilders for the support of
Dominie Polhemus according to the levy of the village
court, "making none but frivolous excuses one for
instance that he was a Catholic, the other that he did
not understand Dutch." The Director General adjudged
them guilty and fined each twelve guilders.[28]

The Instructions of the Duke of York to Governor
Andros breathe the spirit of Christian toleration. "You
shall permit all persons of what religion whatsoever,
quietly to inhabit within the precincts of your jurisdiction, without giving them any disturbance or dis-
quiet whatsoever, for or by reason of their differing
opinions in the matter of religion; Provided they give
no disturbance to the public peace nor do molest or dis-
quiet others in the free exercise of their religion." [29]
Lieutenant-Governor Brockholles, an English Catholic
was second in command to the Governor. There were
few Catholics in the colony, as Dominie Selyn avers:
"As to Papists there are none; or if there are any, they
attend our service or that of the Lutherans." [30] In 1683,
Thomas Dongan called the Popular Assembly which
passed the famous "Charter of Libertys and Privileges,"
"granting freedom to all persons which profess faith
in God through Jesus Christ." [31] The Jesuit Father,
Thomas Harvey, accompanied him as chaplain and said

[28] New York, Eccl. Rec. of, I-420.
[29] *Ibid.*, Eccl. Rec. of, I-649.
[30] New York, Eccl. Rec. of, I-830.
[31] *Ibid.*, Eccl. Rec. of, I-864.

Mass at Fort James.[32] Later Fathers Henry Harrison and
Charles Gage joined him in New York.[33] Among the
Catholics in the Province were Major Brockholles, formerly Deputy Governor, Matthew Plowman, the Collector, Jarvis Baxter, Councilman, Captain Webb and
Mark Talbot.[34] During the Leissler regime, fears were
expressed lest the Catholics on Staten Island and the
Catholic soldiers of the garrison might massacre the
loyal Protestants of the city.[35] On the accession of William and Mary, Jacob Leissler assumed the title of
Lieutenant Governor and solemnly proclaimed the new
sovereigns. A warrant was issued for Dongan, but he
escaped, and was joined by Baxter and Plowman. Brockholles was imprisoned in the Fort, a guard sent to
Staten Island to disarm and subjugate the Catholics and
the soldiers of the garrison were denounced as papists
and malcontents. Mayor Van Cortland, Major Bayard
and many prominent citizens and loyal Protestants were
denounced as "Popishly affected dogs and rogues." [36]
Dominie Delius, the Reformed minister fled to Boston,
and Dominie Varick was imprisoned. Dominie Selyns
wrote the Classis of Amsterdam: "Dominie Varick and
myself have suffered more than can be believed and are
forced to cultivate patience." [37] Father Gage had left

[32] Hughes, So. of Jesus in N. Am., II-147.
[33] Ibid., So. of Jesus in N. Am., II-148.
[34] Bennett, Cath. Foots. in Old N. Y., 88.
[35] Hughes, So. of Jesus in N. Am., II-148.
[36] Bennett, Cath. Foots. in Old N. Y., 155.
[37] Ibid., Cath. Foots. in Old N. Y., 169.

the colony, Father Harrison had sailed for France,
Father Harvey betook himself to Maryland. Later he
returned, but was forced to leave during the administration of Governor Fletcher.[38] Governor Henry
Sloughter arrived in 1691, and after taking the infamous Test Oath, hanged Leissler and Milborne. His
first assembly passed an act granting freedom of conscience to all,—"Provided always that nothing herein
mentioned or contained shall extend to give liberty for
any persons of the Romish religion to exercise their
manner of worship contrary to the laws and statutes
of their Majesties kingdom of England." [39] Governor
Fletcher established the Church of England and endeavored to bribe the Onondagas to surrender the Jesuit,
Father Milet, but the savages refused the offer. Governor Bellamont placed on the Statute Books the infamous laws against the Jesuits and Popish Priests. Any
priest found in the colony should be "deemed and
accounted an incendiary and disturber of the public
peace and an enemy to the true Christian religion and
shall be adjudged to suffer perpetual imprisonment. If
he escapes, and be recaptured, he is liable to the death
penalty. All who harbor priests are subject to a fine of
Two Hundred and Fifty Pounds and three days in the
pillory." [40] In 1701, another law was passed, depriving
Catholics of the right to vote or hold office unless they

[38] Hughes, So. Jesus in N. Am., II-149-50.
[39] New York, Eccl. Rec. of, II-1016.
[40] *Ibid.*, Eccl. Rec. of, II-1368.

abjured the doctrines of Transubstantiation, the invocation of the Saints, and the Sacrifice of the Mass.[41] The Penal Laws were now in effect,—"and for seventy-five years, Catholics had no place to worship, and lived in constant fear of penal punishments." [42] The Negro Plot of 1741 aroused another no-Popery agitation, many Catholic negroes, kidnapped from the Spanish settlements died on the scaffold or at the stake, and John Ury, a non-juring Minister of the Established Church was hanged as a Popish priest. The Recorder, the infamous Horsmanden, who presided at the trials reviled the Catholic church and denounced its dogmas. During the French and Spanish wars, many prisoners were brought to the port, and some poor Palatines, "poor, persecuted, Protestant Palatines,"—as they were styled, were found to be Catholics.[43] In 1756, several shiploads of Acadians were sent to the colony and distributed in the various towns and villages. Even in this dark and bitter period, there were a few Catholics in the city, who journeyed to Philadelphia for Mass and the Sacraments.[44] Just previous to the Revolution there was a little congregation worshipping in the house of a devout German in Wall Street, and the Jesuit Father, Ferdinand Steinmayer, visited and ministered to them on his trips from Maryland. To avoid arrest, he assumed

[41] Hughes, So. of Jesus in N. Am., II-184.
[42] New York, Eccl. Rec. of, III-1449.
[43] Ibid., Eccl. Rec. of, III-1872.
[44] Bennett, Cath. Foots. in Old N. Y., 249.

the name Farmer, and entered the city in disguise. The little church was burned in the great conflagration following Washington's retreat, and the congregation was broken up.[45] "Before the commencement of the Revolutionary war, Father Farmer had visited the city and according to the French dispatches Catholics actually had a church which was burned during the war in the great conflagration that followed the retreat of Washington's army." [46] The existence of the chapel is denied by many historians, although Barbe Marbois mentions it in his letter to Vergennes, but the visits of Father Farmer—as he called himself—at all times, are authentic. After the war, he exercised his ministry at Warwick and Fishkill, and organized the church in New York City.[47]

Although the Iroquois braves were sworn enemies of the French since the days of Champlain, had ruined the Huron missions, and killed the missionaries, the Jesuit Fathers planned to win them to the faith. Tradition asserts that a priest accompanied Verrazano and offered up the Holy Sacrifice on the banks of the Great River.[48] Yet, Saint Isaac Jogues was undoubtedly the first priest to enter the present limits of the state of New York. [49] He had labored among the Hurons with

[45] New York, Eccl. Rec. of, III-1450.
[46] Shea, Cath. Church in U. S., II-264.
[47] *Ibid.*, Cath. Church in U. S., II-278.
[48] Bennett, Cath. Foots. in Old N. Y., 8.
[49] Campbell, Pio. Priests of N. Am., I-1-10.

Fathers Brebeuf, Daniel, Garnier, Lalemant and the other Jesuit heroes and martyrs, and while returning from his post of duty, was captured by the Mohawks, with his two companions, William Couture and Rene Goupil,—"two donnes or laymen who for religious motives had devoted themselves to the help of the missionaries." [50] His journey to the Mohawk country was a succession of revolting tortures, his fingers mangled, his thumb cut off, his body cut and bruised. Couture was adopted into the tribe, but the gentle Goupil was tomahawked for making the sign of the cross on the head of a child.[51] The kindly Dutch at Fort Orange ransomed him from the savages, and sent him to New Amsterdam where he was warmly received by Governor Kieft and Dominie Megapolensis and provided with passage to France. During his captivity he had baptized seventy persons at the point of death.[52] The Queen Regent, Anne of Austria, kissed his mutilated hands and Pope Urban VII dispensed him from all impediments; "it would be wrong to prevent the martyr of Christ from drinking the blood of Christ." [53] The next year he returned to Canada and was sent to Ossernenon to negotiate peace with the Indians. His mission was successful, and he again set out for the Mohawk country with some Huron guides and his faithful donnee, Lalande. The

[50] *Ibid.*, Pio. Priests of N. Am., I-14.
[51] *Ibid.*, Pio. Priests of N. Am., I-19.
[52] *Ibid.*, Pio. Priests of N. Am., I-21-22.
[53] *Ibid.*, Pio. Priests of N. Am., I-31.

fickle natives were again hostile, a pestilence had broken out, the crops had failed, and all these evils were ascribed to the priest's box, containing the vestments and the sacred vessels. On the nineteenth of October, an infuriated brave struck him down with an ax, his head was impaled on a stake, his body thrown into the river. His faithful Lalande was killed on the following morning.[54] A shrine has been erected at Auriesville, the scene of his martyrdom. As he was sacrificed, "out of hate of the cross, of dislike of his doctrinal teachings, and detestation of the Christian morality which he inculcated," [55] the Plenary Council of Baltimore petitioned for his canonization. In 1925, Pope Pius XI solemnly declared as blessed: Isaac Jogues, John de Brebeuf, Anthony Daniel, Gabriel Lalemant, Charles Garnier, Noel Chabanal, John de la Lande and Réné Goupil and five years later they were raised to the altar as saints.

In 1644, another Jesuit Father, Francis Bressani, was captured, brought to the banks of the Mohawk, tortured, his hands mangled. The kindly Dutch ransomed him for two or three hundred francs and sent him to New Amsterdam, where he was kindly received by the Governor, Kieft, and Dominie Megapolensis and given passage to Europe. Father Poncet, another son of Saint Ignatius, was captured near Quebec, hurried to the Mohawk country, and exposed to the usual tortures.

[54] *Ibid.*, Pio. Priests of N. Am., I-32-39.
[55] *Ibid.*, Pio. Priests of N. Am., I-46-49.

Defeated by the French near Three Rivers, the tribesmen offered to surrender the captive priest. He was sent
to Fort Orange and later, made his way to Canada.[56]
In 1654, the famous Jesuit, Simon Le Moyne, colleague
of Brebeuf, Daniel, and the other martyrs of the Huron
mission, visited the Onondagas. A born orator, a master
of the Huron tongue, his eloquence captivated the as-
semblage and disposed them to ask for a "Black
Gown," [57] and to propose the establishment of a French
settlement on Lake Ganentaa.[57] During his sojourn, he
discovered the salt springs of Syracuse. Father Chaumont, linguist, musician, orator, established the mission
and a French fort was erected at Oswego.[58] The Mohawks declared war and carried the conflict to the gates
of Quebec, the missionaries and settlers escaped by
a stratagem and returned to Canada. "The mission had
lasted only two years, but it was not altogether a failure, as during that time the missionaries had baptized
five hundred children who died shortly after; they had
converted four hundred victims who were burned at
the stake; had ministered to a great number of Huron
captives, and had sown the seeds of the faith in the
minds of many of the far western Indians who had come
down to Onondaga." [59] Father Le Moyne came to the
Cayugas and Onondagas but the outbreak of the hos-

[56] Ibid., Pio. Priests of N. Am., I-64-71.
[57] Ibid., Pio. Priests of N. Am., I-86-87.
[58] Bennett, Cath. Foots. in Old N. Y., 52.
[59] Hughes, Soc. of Jesus in N. Am., II-282.

tilities caused him to abandon the project. When peace
was restored, the Iroquois besought the Jesuits to re-
establish the missions. Fathers Bruyas, De Carheil,
Fremin, Garnier, Milet and Pierron were assigned to the
center, and five fields of labor, extending from Lake
Erie to Lake George, were founded.[60] "The missionaries
were thus at their labors in all the cantons, reviving the
faith of the captured Hurons and winning the better
disposed to the faith." [61] During nineteen years,
Fathers John and James de Lamberville and their companions labored with their brethren in Central New
York but the rivalries of England and France, the traffic
in rum and brandy, badly hampered their efforts, by
debauching and enraging the natives. To protect the
converts, the Jesuits founded a mission, which after-
ward became the Indian village of Caughawaga, of
which St. Regis is an offshoot, the Sulpicians opened the
mission of the Mountain, subsequently transferred to
the Lake of the Two Mountains, and another on the Bay
of Quinte. Here, far from the annoyance and persecution of their pagan relatives, many led lives of Christian
perfection. The Indian sachems and the English officials
protested against this depopulation of the cantons, and
Dongan, eager to exclude the French from Central New
York, proposed to found a reduction near Saratoga
under the guidance of the English Jesuits.[62] Although

[60] *Ibid.*, Soc. of Jesus in N. Am., II-282.
[61] Winsor, Hist. of Am., IV-283.
[62] New York, Eccl. Rec. of, II-679.

Fathers Gage, Harrison and Harvey were in New York, the attempt ended in failure. The invasion of the Iroquois country by De la Barre and Denonville, the fall of James II, the accession of William and Mary sounded the death knell of the missions. Yet during these years, many illustrious converts were won to the faith; Garakonthie, the celebrated Oneida chieftain and friend of Father Le Moyne; Catherine Ganneaktena, an Erie captive who afterwards founded a mission on the St. Lawrence; Catherine Tegakwitha, the Lily of the Mohawks; Chief Assendase, and Kryn, the great Mohawk; Soenrese, the Oneida sachem. In addition, thousands of humbler souls, dying infants, tortured enemies, captive Hurons, were converted or restored to the faith.[63] Many native superstitions and immoral customs had been modified or totally eradicated. Father Milet, captured at Fort Frontenac, remained among the Oneidas for five years, having been adopted by the tribe.[64] Father Bruyas endeavored to revive the missions but war and treachery frustrated his efforts. Forty years later, the Sulpician, Father Piquet, opened the Mission of the Presentation near Ogdensburgh, but the English invasion destroyed the foundation.

These missionaries, "men of intelligence and education, were the first to reveal the character of the interior of the country, its soil and products, the life and

---

[63] Winsor, Hist. of Am., IV-283-4.
[64] Campbell, Pio. Priests of N. Am., I-254.

ideas of the natives and the system of American languages." [65] In the annual letters to the Superior, exact descriptions of Central New York were given, with maps of the region, its rivers, lakes and mountains. Like their brethren in the Spanish dominions they noted the manners and customs of the natives, the climate and the productions of the soil, the variety and habits of the animals and birds. They learned the languages and dialects and reduced them to writing. Fathers Le Moyne and Fremin were famous orators at the tribal councils, Father de Corbeil, an adept in the Iroquois dialects. All the Fathers understood the languages and preached to the people. Father Bruyas is the oldest and foremost authority in Mohawk philology, and his Catechism, Grammar and Mohawk Dictionary are monuments to his learning and perseverance.[66] Father Le Moyne discovered the salt springs of Syracuse and Father Chaumont in the Relations tells of three others, one of salt, one of sulphur, one of oil.[67] On his visit to New Amsterdam, Father Le Moyne informed Dominie Megapolensis of these findings: "Whether all this is true or a mere Jesuit lie, I will not decide. I mention the whole on the responsibility of the Jesuit." [68] Of these mentioned in the Relations, "the first of these springs has never been identified; the burning spring near the

[65] Winsor, Hist. of Am., IV-289.
[66] Campbell, Pio. Priests of N. Am., I-190.
[67] Ibid., Pio. Priests of N. Am., I-133.
[68] New York, Eccl. Rec. of, I-438.

Senecas is near the town of Bristol. The spring towards the country of the Cats was probably the noted oil spring in the town of Cuba, Alleghany County." [69]

Although the conversion of the natives was the primary object of the missions, education was not neglected. A hundred years before the establishment of the much heralded English and Dutch schools, Father John Pierron tried to teach reading and writing to the Indian boys. "Unhappily, his pupils preferred the chase to the class room and their fathers frowned on his efforts to make the boys use a pen instead of an arrow, or to learn the alphabet instead of tracking the deer, so Pierron after a while, like so many other school masters gave up his work in despair." [70] Higher education was also planned. Writing to the Governor at Boston Leissler relates: "I have formerly urged to inform your honor, that Coll. Dongan in his time did erect a Jesuit college upon colour to learne latin to the Judges west,—Mr. Graham, Judge Palmer, and John Tudor did contribute their sons for some time, but no boddy initiating them, the collidge vanished." [71] "A Latin school was set up and the teacher strongly suspected for a Jesuit." [72] The building was situated near the site of the present Trinity Church and was formerly an Episcopal school. [73] Father

---

[69] Campbell, Pio. Priests of N. Am., I-133.
[70] *Ibid.*, Pio. Priests of N. Am., I-210.
[71] New York, Doc. Hist. of, II-23.
[72] Smith, Hist. of N. Y., I-90.
[73] Burns, Cath. Sch. Sys. U. S., 104.

Harvey or Father Harrison reopened the institution under the patronage of the Governor. It was probably a classical as well as a primary school, as there were several prominent Catholics in the city, and the Governor gave ample support and encouragement. Dongan petitioned the King to endow it with a tract of land, known as the King's farm, but James denied the request and during Queen Ann's reign it was granted to Trinity Church.[74] Dongan was superseded, Leissler's insurrection broke out, and the iniquitous acts of Sloughter, Fletcher and Bellamont drove the few Catholics into exile.

The people of the colony bitterly opposed the taxes levied by the English Parliament. The passage of the Quebec Act, granting the Catholics of Canada the rights assured them by the terms of the capitulation and extending the boundaries of the Province of Quebec westward, aroused a storm of unrest throughout the colonies and especially in New York. Appeals to the citizens to resist tyranny were issued, demanding: "No Pensioners, Placemen, Ministerial Hirelings, Popery and Arbitrary Power." The banner of the Sons of Liberty bore the offensive inscription: "George III, Rex, The Liberties of America, No Popery. The Union of the Colonies, the Measures of Congress." [75] The Convention to adopt a new state constitution, convened at King-

[74] *Ibid.*, Cath. Sch. Sys. U. S., 104.
[75] Bennett, Cath. Foots. in Old N. Y., 337.

ston in 1777, and decreed: "That the full exercise and enjoyment of Religious profession and worship without discrimination or preference shall forever be allowed within the state to all mankind." [76] The intolerant John Jay proposed an amendment excluding: "the professors of the religion of the Church of Rome, unless they took an oath, that no Pope, priest or foreign authority on earth hath power to absolve the subjects of the state from their allegiance to the Same"; and furthermore, "that they renounce and believe to be false and wicked the dangerous and damnable doctrines that the Pope or any other earthly authority hath power to absolve men from their sins described in and prohibited by the Gospel of Christ"; and in addition, "that no Pope, Priest or foreign authority hath power to absolve them from the obligations of this oath." [77] However, the fair-minded delegates rejected these amendments. The Convention of 1784 repealed the iniquitous "Anti-Jesuit Law," of 1701, "although practically cancelled by the adoption of the Constitution." [78] Another clause was added by Jay that all foreigners "shall take an oath of allegiance to this state and abjure all allegiance and subjection to all and every foreign king, prince, potentate and state, in matters ecclesiastical as well as civil." [79] This act would have disfranchised Catholic immigrants, but the convention of 1821 abrogated the clause.

[76] New York, Eccl. Rec. of, VI-4301.
[77] Shea, Cath. Church in U. S., II-156-7.
[78] Roberts, New York, II-572.
[79] Shea, Cath. Church in U. S., II-156.

CHAPTER SIX

Pennsylvania and Delaware

IN 1681, Charles II, "granted to William Penn and his successors all the territory between the fortieth and forty-second degrees of latitude extending through five degrees of longitude west from the Delaware River, with the exception of that part which would fall within a circle drawn around New Castle, the northern segments of which was to form the boundary between Penn's Province and the Duke of York's colonies of Delaware." [1] It was not difficult to obtain from the Duke a release of his claims on Pennsylvania, and after much negotiation, the lower province was granted by two deeds of feoffment. [2] The territory included in the grant was originally claimed by four European nations; Spain, by the discovery of Columbus and the explorations of de Allyon and Gomez; France, by the voyages of Verrazano and Cartier; England, by the explorations of John Cabot, the Venetian; Netherlands, by the visit of Henry Hudson. The Dutch and the Swedes attempted to form colonies, and several forts were erected

[1] Winsor, Hist. of Am., III-477.
[2] Bancroft, Hist. of U. S., II-367.

along the South River. In 1632, Sir Edmund Plowden, a Catholic peer, received from Charles I a large tract, comprising the present states of Delaware, Maryland, New Jersey and Pennsylvania, which he called New Albion, and proposed to found a second Utopia, where full religious liberty might be enjoyed by every sect.[3] The Dutch and the Swedes refused to recognize his claims and the downfall of Charles I and the triumph of the Parliamentary Party frustrated his designs. The Dutch also regarded the Swedes as intruders, and during Stuyvesant's administration the settlements were invaded, reduced, and annexed to New Netherland. In 1664, Charles II granted all the lands from Maine to Maryland—Massachusetts, Connecticut, and Rhode Island excepted—to his brother, James, Duke of York. New Amsterdam was captured and the settlements along the Delaware subjugated.

William Penn was the son of Sir John Penn, a distinguished English naval officer, who had captured Jamaica and won laurels during the Dutch war. His son William had embraced the religion of George Fox and had suffered fines and imprisonment for his faith. His interest in colonization began in 1674, by the purchase of West Jersey with his associates, but he proposed to found a province as sole proprietor, "that would be an asylum for those who suffered for conscience sake, and that absolute liberty of worship should

[3] Kirlin, Cath. in Phil., 5.

be granted to all." [4] His father had always been a staunch supporter of the Stuart cause and had left claims amounting to sixteen thousand pounds against the King. To liquidate this indebtedness and as a mark of respect for the memory of the gallant Admiral, the new province was granted to his son. Penn desired to call it either New Wales or Sylvania, but the king added the family name to the latter suggestion, naming it Pennsylvania, to the embarrassment of the modest Quaker. [5] Penn arrived in the fall of 1682, and found a few hamlets established, with five hundred white inhabitants, Finns and Dutch, with a few Quakers from West Jersey. [6] The Great Law, prepared in England, and promulgated on his arrival, insured civil and religious freedom to all, although the Privy Council rejected this provision, and inserted a new clause, restricting this freedom to Trinitarian Christians. [7] A Provincial Council and a General Assembly, both chosen by the people, were created to originate and pass just and equitable laws for the welfare of the colony. Lands were purchased from the natives, and their interests were always safeguarded by the humane proprietor. "The English and the Indian should respect the same moral law, should be alike secure in their pursuits and their possessions, and adjust every difference by a peace-

[4] *Ibid.*, Cath. in Phil., 8.
[5] Smith, Commonweal. of Pa., 24.
[6] Winsor, Hist. of Am., III-480.
[7] Smith, Commonweal. of Pa., 27.

ful tribunal, composed of an equal number of men from each race." [8] In consequence, Indian troubles were unknown until later years, when the cupidity of the officials and the cruelty of the settlers aroused the tribes to retaliation. Such charity and tolerance brought peace and prosperity to the province. "From England and Wales, from Scotland and Ireland, and the Low Countries, emigrants crowded to the land of promise." [9] The Irish immigration was so large that in 1728 an attempt was made to restrict "the importation of Irish Papists and convicts," and a law was passed, "laying a duty on foreigners, Irish servants and persons of redemption," [10] but it proved inoperative and was repealed the next year.

Various contentions interrupted the peace of the colony. In 1692, Penn's enemies, using his friendship for the Stuarts as a charge of disloyalty, had him suspended from his charter rights, and his Province was placed under the jurisdiction of Governor Fletcher of New York. In the following year his property was restored, and although the opposition continued, he and his heirs remained in possession until the outbreak of the revolution. Although factions disturbed the province, incompetent officials annoyed the citizens, the Indians were aroused by unjust treatment, and the Dela-

[8] Bancroft, Hist. of U. S., II-381.
[9] *Ibid.*, Hist. of U. S., II-391.
[10] O'Brien, Hid. Phase of Am. Hist., 254-55.

ware Assembly refused to unite with the Pennsylvania delegates, yet under the benign rule of Penn and his successors, the colony prospered and the population increased. "The census of 1720 showed the number of inhabitants"—in Philadelphia—"to be twenty thousand, so greatly had the place increased from the eighty houses and five hundred inhabitants of 1683. Planted in 1682, nearly fifty years later than her neighbors, Pennsylvania could boast in 1735, that her chief city, Philadelphia, was the second in size in the colonies, and her whole population larger than that of Maryland, Virginia and the Carolinas. During the later years—1765 to 1773— Pennsylvania could be justly called the most flourishing of the English colonies. A fleet of four hundred sail left Philadelphia yearly with the season's produce. The colony's free population numbered two hundred and twenty thousand souls. "The spirit and tenets of the first framers of its government as the Quakers had been, were calculated to attract the attention of oppressed sectaries everywhere, and bodies of many diversified beliefs from different parts of Europe flocked to the land, took up their abodes and are recognized in their descendants today." [11]

During the struggle for supremacy between England and France, Pennsylvania witnessed stirring scenes. Fort Du Quesne, the key to the Ohio Valley, was held by the French and menaced her western frontier.

[11] Winsor, His. of Am., V-189-245.

Washington began his military and diplomatic career by his visit to the fortress, by his success over Jumonville and his surrender at Fort Necessity. Braddock's veteran army was routed a few miles from the fort and the survivors retreated to Philadelphia. During the Revolutionary struggle, Pennsylvania played an honorable role although loyalists were numerous in the state. The First Continental Congress met in Philadelphia and the succeeding sessions were held there, until Howe captured the city, the legislators retiring to York. On the retreat of the British forces, Congress returned to the City of Brotherly Love. The Declaration of Independence was drafted, signed and read to the people in Independence Hall, Philadelphia, the birthplace of American freedom. At Brandywine and Germantown, Washington's army was defeated; at Valley Forge and White Marsh, he passed two cheerless winters. The massacre at Wyoming is a sad page in the history of the state, the murder of sleeping troops at Paoli, an undying blemish on the escutcheon of England. Many of her sons won fame in the sanguinary struggle. Franklin, Wilson, Wayne, Barry and Moylan are only a few who have inscribed their names in the Hall of Fame while the bravery and loyalty of the Pennsylvania Line has been celebrated in song and story. The Constitutional Convention which drafted the immortal document, assembled in Philadelphia in 1787 and Pennsylvania was the second state to ratify the Constitution.[12]

[12] Smith, Commonwealth of Pa., 47-50.

The benign laws of Penn brought Catholics to the colony even in the early days. There is a record of "a Romanist" who came to Germantown in 1683, one John Gray, alias John Tatham, afterwards a leading figure in New Jersey, and George W. Nixon, grandfather of John Nixon who read the Declaration of Independence to the people after its adoption. Irish, French and German Catholics settled in the colony and were visited by a priest, probably Father Thomas Harvey, who accompanied Governor Thomas Dongan to New York.[13] Although few in numbers, their influence was considerable, as converts were made to the faith. The Rev. John Talbot, Episcopalian minister, writing to a colleague in New Jersey reports: "He"—Mr. Bradford—"tells me that Mass is set up and read publicly in Philadelphia and several people are turned to it, amongst whom is Lionel Brittin, the church warden is one, and his son is another." [14] These reports were sent to London by Penn's enemies, and were used to prejudice the ministry against him. Writing to James Logan, the Governor, he complains: "Here is a complaint against your government that you suffer public Mass in a scandalous manner. Pray send the matter of fact, for ill use is maid against us here." [15] The protest evidently was of no avail, as Mass was said publicly by

[13] Kirlin, Cath. in Phil., 17.
[14] Ibid., Cath. in Phil., 24.
[15] Ibid., Cath. in Phil., 25.

the Jesuit missionaries although their names are unknown.

In 1720, Father Joseph Greaton was assigned to the
missions of Maryland and placed in charge of the
Catholics of Philadelphia. In 1729, he took up his residence in the city, probably officiating in private houses.
For some years, the Maryland Proprietor claimed all the
region as far north as the fortieth degree of latitude
which included the site of Philadelphia. As the laws
of Calvert's colony forbade Catholic churches, the
faithful feared to erect a public chapel, but in 1732
the heirs of Calvert and Penn came to an agreement
and the boundary line was fixed some fifteen miles be-
low the city. In the following year, Father Greaton
through his friend, John Dixon, purchased a site for
the new church and built old St. Joseph's, the first public
Catholic chapel in the English colonies.[16] It was an
unpretentious edifice, eighteen by twenty-eight feet,
with a two-story rectory. In this modest abode, the
small Catholic population, composed of English, Irish
and Germans, worshipped until 1763, when St. Mary's
was built and became the parish church. Both edifices
still exist, the pride and glory of the Catholics of
Philadelphia.

Under the early laws of the colony, Catholics enjoyed full civil and religious liberty, voting and holding
office. Under William and Mary, these benign ordi-

[16] *Ibid.*, Cath. in Phil., 35.

nances were revoked, and the offensive Oaths prescribed in England were enforced. Penn endeavored to restore the old conditions and the legislature passed a series of laws reëstablishing religious freedom, but the Ministry of Queen Ann repealed these statutes and extended the religious discriminations to judicial and all other offices. "The oath was designed in England as a test discriminating against Romanists, Jews and Unitarians. It especially abjured the Roman doctrines of Transubstantiation, the adoration of Mary and the sacrifice of the Mass." [17] The colonial officers and the assembly yielded, and these religious tests remained in force until 1776. Catholics however, were not molested in the practise of religion although occasionally threatened by bigoted outbreaks. At the opening of St. Joseph's chapel, representation was made to the council that the laws of Queen Ann had been violated and the difficulty referred to the Governor, but no decision was rendered. During the wars with France and Spain, both Catholics and Quakers were under suspicion, the former as co-religionists of the enemies, the latter as opposed to arms and bloodshed. Malicious reports of Catholic disloyalty in the other colonies, especially in New York during the quasi-Negro Plot, were published in the newspapers and aroused the hatred of the fanatics. George Whitefield, the famous English evangelist, denounced "The Mischiefs of Popery," adding to the popular unrest, and

[17] Cobb, Rise of Rel. Tol. in Am., 445.

Braddock's defeat revived the agitation against the
Catholics and a mob set out to burn the Catholic chapel,
but the Quakers persuaded the rioters to disperse.[18] In
1757, the assembly passed a law depriving all Papists
and suspected Papists of arms and ammunition, and
levying a tax of twenty shillings on all men between the
ages of seventeen and forty-five.[19] "This fear was the
result of an unjust suspicion and the law, due to a
moment of panic, was never put in force." [20] The historian of the church in Philadelphia gives a different
explanation: "The bill, however, the only anti-Catholic
act passed in Pennsylvania, was rejected by the King,
George III, and did not become a law. Its rejection was
not due to its anti-Catholic tenor, but because it gave
to the regiments the right to elect their own officers." [21]
The spiritual growth of the church was not impeded
by these attacks; it kept pace with the commercial and
numerical increase of the city and its population. Cobb
aptly sums up these anti-Catholic crusades: "In the
Maryland of the eighteenth century, it was the voice
of a monstrous ingratitude. In the other colonies, it
was so needless as to be ridiculous." [22]

The founders of the faith in Pennsylvania did not
neglect the education of their flocks. "There is no docu-

[18] Kirlin, Cath. in Phil., 77.
[19] Hughes, So. of Jesus in N. Am., II-192.
[20] Cobb, Rise of Rel. Tol. in Am., 450.
[21] Kirlin, Cath. in Phil., 84.
[22] Cobb, Rise of Rel. Tol. in Am., 451.

mentary proof to show the time of the establishment of the first Catholic schools in Pennsylvania, but there is a strong, traditional evidence for the belief that they date back to the time of the first organization of the church in the various centers of Catholic life." [23] The Jesuits were men of exceptional talents and training and deeply interested in education. Father Schneider had been "Rector Magnificus" of Heidelberg University and many of his colleagues had taught in European institutions.[24] It is certain that these zealous scholars and teachers established schools for rudimentary education. From several wills made before the revolutionary era, it would seem that Catholic schools had been in existence since the coming of the priests to the colony. Even before churches were erected, children were assembled in private houses for instruction in catechism and the elementary branches. Outside the city of Philadelphia, and especially at Gossenhoppen, Catholic and Protestant children attended Father Schneider's school. In the earlier years, the priest taught the classes, but in later years, teachers were employed whose names are honorably inscribed in the early church records. These able and energetic Jesuits laid the broad and firm foundations of Catholic education on which have been erected the magnificent system of today.

The history of Delaware is closely connected with

[23] Burns, Cath. Sch. Sys. in U. S., 122.
[24] *Ibid.*, Cath. Sch. Sys. in U. S., 126.

that of Pennsylvania. Henry Hudson, in 1609, was undoubtedly the first European to enter Delaware Bay. By virtue of his discoveries, the Dutch claimed all the territory, and sent out settlers who purchased lands from the natives. Troubles with the tribesmen brought on war, the fort was destroyed, the inhabitants slain. In 1638, the Swedes dispatched an expedition under Peter Minuit, former Governor of New Netherland, and formed a settlement near the present site of Wilmington. The colony was feeble and in 1655, a Dutch fleet conquered and annexed the region. After the surrender of New Amsterdam the Delaware colony was annexed to the dominions of the Duke of York but in 1681 he relinquished his claims to William Penn. Ten years later, Penn permitted the "three lower counties" to become a separate government. In 1693, they were again joined to Penn's colony although after 1702 each colony had its own assembly under the authority of the Governor of Pennsylvania. Delaware sent representatives to the Continental Congress and voted to adopt the Declaration of Independence. During the revolutionary struggle, her continentals were famous for discipline and valor. Delaware was the first state to ratify the Federal Constitution.

Catholics settled in Delaware at an early date, although definite records are lacking. Owing to the proximity of the Jesuit residence at Bohemia, priests visited the scattered worshipers at intervals. The priests of St. Xavier's mission laid the foundation of Catholicity in Delaware by establishing a mission at Apoquinimick where Mass was said at stated times. The first Mass in New Castle County, perhaps in Delaware, was offered at Cornelius Holohan's house at Mt. Cuba.[25] In 1772, Father Manners, S.J. purchased a farm at Mill Hill Hundred and erected a log refectory and chapel dedicated to the Blessed Virgin. This became the center of Catholic activity until after the revolution. Religious intolerance was almost unknown in Delaware and Catholics enjoyed the same freedom as their brethren in Pennsylvania. One act of discrimination is mentioned. "Act seventeen of George II empowered Protestant churches and societies to secure and hold real estate."[26]

[25] Shea, Cath. Church in U. S., I-369.
[26] Cobb, Rise of Rel. Tol. in Am., 452.

CHAPTER SEVEN

New Jersey

THE first settlement in New Jersey was probably established by the Danes or Norwegians who came to America under the auspices of the Dutch West India Company in 1624,[1] although England claimed the entire territory by reason of the discoveries of John Cabot. In 1584, Queen Elizabeth granted patents to Sir Humphrey Gilbert and his half-brother, Sir Walter Raleigh, including all the lands from the Hudson to the St. Lawrence, but no permanent colony was established. In 1606, James I chartered two companies, the London and the Plymouth, and bestowed on them in equal proportions the vast territory known as Virginia, lying between the thirty-fourth and forty-fifth degree of north latitude together with the islands within one hundred miles of the coast, stretching from Cape Fear to Halifax.[2] Three years before, "a French Calvinist, Seigneur De Monte, received from his King, Henry IV, a concession to colonize Le Cadie, Canada, and other places in New France from the fortieth to the forty-

[1] Cath. Ency., Vol. X.
[2] Winsor, Hist. of Am., III-127.

sixth degrees of latitude, that is from the latitude of New Jersey and Pennsylvania to that of Nova Scotia and the River Ottawa." [3] The voyage of Verrazano, the exploration of the harbor of New York and the Great River, strengthened the claims of France to the entire region. Spain also claimed this territory by reason of the discovery of Columbus and the voyages of D'Ayllon and Gomez. In 1609, Henry Hudson, an Englishman in the service of the Dutch West India Company, entered New York Bay, and sailed up the river which bears his name. In consequence, the Dutch assumed title to all that section and founded New Amsterdam and Fort Orange. Settlements were likewise begun at Weehawken, Hoboken, Ahasimus, Pavonia, Constable's Hook, and Bergen, on the west side of the Hudson, although little is known of their population or growth. [4] In 1632, Cornelius May explored the Delaware River to Gloucester, where he founded Fort Nassau, the first permanent settlement in New Jersey. [5] But to the Swedes must be accorded the credit of making the first successful settlements, although few in numbers and insignificant in extent." [6] The Dutch regarded them as intruders and in 1655, Stuyvesant with an army and fleet seized their forts and annexed their lands to New Amsterdam.

[3] Hughes, So. of Jesus in N. Am., II-231.
[4] Winsor, Hist. of Am., III-422.
[5] Cath. Ency., Vol. X.
[6] Winsor, Hist. of Am., III-422.

Meanwhile, England had not abandoned her claims. In 1632, Sir Edmund Plowden, "the second son of Thomas Plowden Esq., and grandson of Serjeant Edmund Plowden, the celebrated lawyer and editor of 'The Commentaries,' a Catholic who declined the Lord Chancellorship of England offered him by Queen Elizabeth, lest he be forced to countenance her Majesty's persecution of his church, who like his ancestors and other relatives was a Catholic, and at that time resided in Ireland, petitioned Charles I for Manitie or Long Isle and thirty miles square of the coast next adjoining." [7] In a later petition, the island was called "Isle Plowden," and the country "New Albion" or as they are called today, the State of New Jersey, Long Island, and all other islands within ten leagues of that region." [8] The favor was granted, although it embraced almost all the territory of New Netherland. Grants were made to private individuals to settle families in the new concession and a small group of whalers from New Haven came to the present site of Salem. Plowden came to New Albion in 1642, but the opposition of the Dutch and the Swedes, the scarcity of colonists, and the outbreak of the Civil War in England thwarted his plans. In later years his heirs laid claim to the grant, but their efforts were unsuccessful.

In March, 1554, Charles II conveyed to his brother,

[7] *Ibid.*, Hist. of Am., III-457.
[8] Bennett, Cath. Foots. in Old N. Y., 37.

James, Duke of York, a patent, "granting him the Maine territory of Pemaquid, all the islands between Cape Cod and the Narrows, the Hudson River and all the lands from the west side of Connecticut to the east side of Delaware Bay together with the islands of Martha's Vineyard and Nantucket." [9] This unjust spoliation of the Dutch was not due entirely to the perfidy of Charles, but to the policy of successive administrations. "It had been that of Cromwell, the most sagacious of English rulers and was only abandoned by him because of the more immediate advantage secured by his treaty with the Great Pensionary, a statesman only second to Oliver himself. The expedition which Cromwell ordered was countermanded and the Dutch title to New Netherland was formally recognized by the Treaty of 1654. It seemed rational to suppose that the English Protector foresaw the inevitable future fall of the Dutch-American settlements, and that he was willing to wait until the fruit was ripe, and of easy grasp for England." [10] In August, 1664, an expedition captured New Amsterdam and Fort Orange, the settlements on the Delaware were annexed and Dutch rule ceased, except for a few months nine years later.

While the fleet was under way to subdue the Dutch possessions, James granted to Lord Berkeley and Sir George Carteret the territory between the Delaware

[9] Winsor, Hist. of Am., III-388.
[10] *Ibid.*, Hist. of Am., III-386.

River and the lower Hudson, and called it Nova Caesaria or New Jersey. Ten years later, Berkeley sold West Jersey to a company of Quakers and in 1681, William Penn and other members of his society purchased East Jersey.[11] When James ascended the English throne he determined to unite New York and New Jersey to New England under the rule of Edmund Andros. On the accession of William and Mary the proprietors of East and West Jersey surrendered their patents, "that their territory might be combined with New York under one provisional government."[12] After William's death, Queen Ann accepted the offer and vested the joint government in her cousin, Edward Hyde, Lord Cornbury. In 1738, the people petitioned for a separate administration and Lewis Morris was made sole governor of the Province of New Jersey. Until the outbreak of the revolution, a series of royal appointees ruled the colony.

At the beginning of the struggle for freedom, "New Jersey, held back by a strong, loyalist party, led by Governor William Franklin, at first commanded her delegates to vote against independence. But the revolutionary party denounced his act, stopped his salary and sent him under arrest to a Connecticut prison."[13] After the defeat on Long Island, Washington crossed to New Jersey, and retreated southward, pursued by Howe's

[11] *Ibid.*, Hist. of Am., III-435.
[12] Cobb, Rise of Rel. Lib. in Am., 404.
[13] Van Tyne, Am. Rev., 74.

victorious forces. The historic battles of Trenton and Princeton revived the spirit of the patriots and dampened the ardor of the loyalists. At Monmouth, with victory within his grasp, the cowardice and treachery of Charles Lee deprived the Americans of a well-deserved triumph. Washington spent the winter at Morristown where Don Juan de Miralles, the Spanish Agent, died and was interred with the rites of the Catholic Church. In 1781, the united forces of Washington and Rochambeau passed through New Jersey on their way to the glorious triumph of Yorktown. Five delegates from New Jersey signed the Declaration of Independence, four signed the Constitution. "Although her representatives proposed, to add few new powers to the existing system,—the Articles of Confederation, —rather than substitute a national government, yet the state convention unanimously ratified the New Constitution on December 12th, 1787, on the same day as Pennsylvania, and only five days after Delaware, the first state to adopt it." [14]

Catholic explorers were the first to sail along the coast of New Jersey. Cabot, the Genoese, Verrazano, the Florentine, Gomez the Spaniard, and Allefonsce, the Norman, strengthened the claims of England, France and Spain to these shores. Sir Edmund Plowden, scion of an old Catholic family, born and reared in the faith was the first English proprietor. Whether Catholic set-

[14] Winsor, Hist. of Am., VII-238-47.

tlers accompanied him and whether he remained true
to his religion are disputed points. Among the owners
to whom James, Duke of York, ceded New Jersey was
James, Earl of Perth, a distinguished Catholic noble
from Scotland. Whether Catholic settlers came at this
time is unknown but tradition strongly asserts that at
an early date there were Catholics at Woodbridge and
Elizabethtown, who were visited by Jesuits from Maryland or Pennsylvania.[15] In 1683, Father Forster or
Gulick, Superior to the Maryland Missions, came to New
York to meet the English Fathers destined for the New
York Mission. "A baptism at Woodbridge in June 1683,
seems to have been performed by him." [16] During the
administration of Governor Dongan in New York, the
Jesuit Fathers, Harrison, Harvey and Gage, probably
visited the scattered faithful in the neighboring province. The Labbadists, Dankers and Sluyters relate that
during their journeys, the Catholics believed them to be
priests importuning them to say Mass, to hear their confessions and to baptize their children. They speak of a
family of French Catholics who kept a tavern at Elizabethtown, who treated them with every courtesy, convinced to the last that their guests were priests, afraid
to avow their real character.[17] Father Theodore
Schneider frequently visited the colony, and the "bap-

[15] Cath. Ency., Vol. X.
[16] Shea, Cath. Ch. in U. S., I-90.
[17] *Ibid.*, Cath. Ch. in U. S., I-89.

tismal registers of the Jesuit Fathers in Philadelphia show that their missionary excursions extended over the colony (New Jersey), as far as the line of New York." [18] Father Ferdinand Farmer seems to have entered at once on part of the labors borne by Father Schneider as the next year we find him at Concord and at Geiger's in Salem County, N. J. To the close of the period we are considering, his visits to Geiger's and the Glass House in Salem County were constant." [19] Among the prominent Catholics mentioned in the history of the Province was John Tatham, alias John Gray, who purchased land in Philadelphia in 1681, and came to New Jersey in 1685. "He was a person of importance described by William Penn, 'as Rom. Cath. Gent. Be sure to please him in his land.' " [20] He purchased an estate in New Jersey in 1685 and settled in Burlington, where his residence is described as "a great and stately mansion, the best in the province." [21] His home was the refuge of the visiting priests and within its walls the Holy Sacrifice was offered up. "Outside of Maryland, the residence of John Tatham was probably the only stopping place for the priests who said Mass and conducted other ministrations." [22] He was prominent in the political affairs of the colony. "Gov. Robert Bar-

[18] Hughes, So. of Jesus in N. Am., II-508.
[19] Shea, Cath. Ch. in U. S., I-448.
[20] Kirlin, Cath. in Phil., 14.
[21] *Ibid.*, Cath. in Phil., 15.
[22] *Ibid.*, Cath. in Phil., 14-15.

clay died in Oct. 1690, so taking advantage of the confusion at home and the anarchy abroad, the proprietors of Jersey determined to reassert the jurisdiction wrested from them and yielded by nominal cession in Apr. 1688, and therefore proceeded to elect a Governor in Barclay's place. They choose a West Jerseyman, John Tatham, who about the same time was appointed by Gov. Coxe of West Jersey his deputy. 'But being a Jacobite and as such by principles, disqualified him, the assembly rejected him.' For the same reason, the people of East Jersey 'scrupled to obey him.' " [23] Another well known Catholic was William Douglas. He was elected to the General Assembly from Bergen, but the delegates took action and excluded him on religious grounds. "The deputies finding occasion to purge themselves of such a member as cannot be allowed by law, namely William Douglas, the aforesaid member, upon examination owning himself to be a Roman Catholic, we proceed and desire your Honor to issue out yr. Warrant— for a new choice or one to supply his place." [24] It has been urged in palliation of such intolerance, that it was forced by the English law as such discrimination was foreign to the laws of the province. It is difficult to estimate the Catholic population of New Jersey during colonial days although Marbois the French minister, writing to Vergennes in 1785, enumerates seventeen

[23] Griffin, Am. Cath. Hist. Res., 1910-254.
[24] *Ibid.*, Am. Cath. Hist. Res., 1911-213.

hundred Catholics in New York and New Jersey at the close of the Revolutionary War.[25] These figures are probably a rough estimate on his part. "We know of no evidence giving the number of Catholics in New Jersey at the close of the Revolution. If this estimate be near correct, we are of the opinion that the greater part were in New Jersey." [26]

During the Dutch occupation, "there was in all New Netherland except the South River territory, an absolute prohibition of non-conforming religions outside the family," [27] but there is no record of any intolerance against the few Catholics in New Jersey. In the instructions given to Sir Thomas Danby by Sir Edmund Plowden, he was warned not to permit "anyone to live therein who did not believe in or profess the three Christian Creeds—the Apostles, the Athanasian and the Nicene. All Christians were to be welcomed to New Albion, and those who railed and condemned because of their religious belief were to be severely punished.[28] Berkeley and Carteret guaranteed complete religious freedom. The seventh article of "The Concession" decreed: "No person . . . shall be in any way molested, persecuted, disquieted, or called into question in matters of religious concernments; . . . But all . . . may freely and fully have and enjoy his and their judgments and

[25] Bancroft, Form. of Con., I-421.
[26] Griffin, Am. Cath. His. Res., 1888.
[27] Zweirlein, Rel. in New. Neth., 5.
[28] Bennett, Cath. Foots. in Old N. Y., 39.

conscience in matters of religion through the province." [29] When the Quaker proprietors acquired West Jersey they conceded religious liberty to all. The first Assembly (1681) enacted: "Liberty of conscience in matters of faith and worship shall be granted to all people, . . . and none . . . shall be rendered incapable of office in respect to their faith and worship." [30] East Jersey limited toleration to persons "acknowledging One Almighty and Eternal God, and professing faith in Christ Jesus." [31] Yet in 1680, William Douglas, legally elected to the Assembly from Bergen, was excluded; "Owning himself to be a roman Catholick." This has been explained by saying that he was expelled under an English statute as the proceedings were contrary to the laws of the Province. The fall of James II and the rebellion in New York under Leissler aroused religious animosity in New Jersey. In 1698, a law was passed, granting religious liberty to all, "provided that this shall not extend to any of the Romish religion the right to exercise their manner of worship, contrary to the laws and statutes of England." [32] When New Jersey was united to New York, Lord Cornbury's instructions directed him to permit liberty of conscience to all persons "except papists." "Matters remained thus with the

[29] Cobb, Rise of Rel. Lib. in Am., 400.
[30] Cobb, Rise of Rel. Lib. in Am., 402.
[31] *Ibid.*, Rise of Rel. Lib. in Am., 402.
[32] Winsor, Hist. of Am., V-192.

Romish church in New Jersey until the end of British rule." [33]

The provincial Congress assembled at Burlington, July second, 1776, framed the first Constitution for the State of New Jersey. Although it granted liberty of conscience to all, and forbade the establishment of a state religion, yet in Article XVIII it enacted: "That no protestant of this colony, shall be denied the enjoyment of any civil right merely on account of his religious principle; but that all persons professing a belief in the faith of any protestant sect . . . shall be capable of being elected into any office of profit or trust or being a member of either branch of the legislature, and shall fully enjoy every privilege and immunity enjoyed by others, their fellow subjects." [34] This clause which discriminated against Catholics at least by implication, remained in force until 1844, when a new Constitution was adopted, guaranteeing absolute freedom of worship and providing that no religious test should be required as a qualification for office, and that no person shall be deprived of his rights on account of his religious principles.

[33] *Ibid.*, Hist. of Am., V-192.
[34] Shea, Cath. Ch. in U. S., II-158.

CHAPTER EIGHT

New England

NEW ENGLAND received its name from Captain John Smith of Virginia fame, who visited and explored its coasts in 1614.[1] The voyage of John Cabot had given England a claim to all the territory along the Atlantic sea-board, and the expeditions of Frobisher, Gilbert and Hawkins had strengthened these claims. Verrazano had explored this region in the interests of France, and Gomez the Spaniard had entered many of its ports during the first quarter of the sixteenth century. Tradition associates New England with the Vinland of Northmen discovered by Biarne and visited by Leif, son of Eric, in the tenth century.[2] In 1527, John Rut landed on the coast of Maine, the first Englishman to set foot on its shores. Bartholomew Gosnold and Martin Pring also visited the northern section in the vicinity of the Penobscot River and Casco Bay. In 1605, James I created a company with two branches, the London and the Plymouth, the latter extending from the thirty-eighth to the forty-fifth degree of north latitude.

[1] Fiske, Beg. of New Eng., 93.
[2] De Costa, Pre-Col. Dis., 11.

The first attempt to found a colony was made in 1604 by Pierre du Gast who had received from the French ministry authority to colonize all the territory from the fortieth to the fifty-sixth degree of latitude. With him came the famous Samuel de Champlain and a settlement was founded on St. Croix Island, transferred the following year to Port Royal. In 1613, a station was located on Mount Desert Island, called St. Sauveur which the notorious sea-robber and pirate, Samuel Argall of Virginia, destroyed and carried the settlers into captivity. In 1607 an unsuccessful colony was founded at Fort Popham under the auspices of the Plymouth Company, and later Sir Fernando Gorges received a patent for all the lands between the Merrimac and the Kennebec Rivers where, with the aid of his son and his nephew, he endeavored to assert his sovereignty against the encroachments of the French.

In 1620, the Pilgrims, who had separated from the Established Church and fled to Holland, landed at Plymouth Rock. Eight years later, the Puritans who wished to reform the Church of England, formed the Massachusetts Bay Colony and sent settlers to Massachusetts who founded Salem, Boston, Charlestown and other villages. In 1633, emigrants from Plymouth settled Windsor in the present state of Connecticut. Puritans, dissatisfied with religious and civil affairs in Massachusetts established themselves at Wethersfield and Hartford. In 1638, other groups colonized the shores of Long Island Sound and formed the New Haven Colony. The Dutch claimed the Connecticut Valley and had erected trading posts near the present site of Hartford, but soon withdrew although maintaining their title to the territory. In 1662, Charles II united all these towns into the Commonwealth of Massachusetts. In 1636, Roger Williams, banished from the Massachusetts and Plymouth colonies for his religious views, founded Providence, other towns sprang up, and in 1643 he secured a patent from Parliament. In 1663, Charles II granted to Rhode Island and the Providence Plantations the most liberal charter granted to the colonies. During the years from 1621 to 1629, Sir Fernando Gorges and John Mason obtained from the crown various tracts of land embracing not only the present state of New Hampshire but portions of Maine. Settlements were formed near the modern towns of Dover and Portsmouth, but as settlers came slowly, Mason, in 1629, petitioned and obtained a separate grant from the Merrimac to the Piscataqua River which he called New Hampshire from his native county in England. Massachusetts claimed this territory and in 1541, the two colonies were united, but in 1679 New Hampshire became a royal province. In 1684, Charles II annulled the Massachusetts charter as a punishment for not allowing the Episcopal worship and restricted the rights of suffrage to the Congregational Church.[3] Two years later,

[3] McCarthy, Hist. of U. S., 83.

James II united New Jersey and New York to the Eastern colonies as the Dominion of New England under Sir Edmund Andros. The downfall of James and the accession of William of Orange, dissolved that confederacy, Connecticut and Rhode Island retaining their former charters, Massachusetts and Plymouth with portions of Maine, united under a new charter; New Hampshire remained a separate province.[4]

The New England colonies played a prominent role in the events leading up to the revolutionary struggle. Although Virginia, through Patrick Henry, was the first to oppose the Stamp Act, it was at the call of Massachusetts that delegates from nine colonies met in New York in 1765, and framed "A Declaration of Rights and Grievances of the Colonies of America." The opposition to the Townshend Acts was widespread throughout New England, and "The Boston Tea Party" and "The Boston Massacre" are evidences of popular discontent. At Lexington and Concord, the first patriotic blood was shed. At Bunker Hill and the siege of Boston the colonial troops proved their valor and determination. The capture of Crown Point and Ticonderoga, the defeat of Baum at Bennington, harbinger of Burgoyne's surrender, the bravery of John Stark, John Sullivan, Ethan Allen and Nathanael Greene, the naval exploits of the O'Briens of Maine and the legislative services of John Hancock, John and Samuel Adams,

[4] *Ibid.*, Hist. of U. S., 64.

and Matthew Lyon are a few of the many triumphs won by the sons of New England during the struggle for freedom. Massachusetts was usually the leader in these patriotic movements, although the other colonies sent men and supplies to the continental army. All were represented in the Continental Congress, thirteen delegates signed the Declaration of Independence, all but Rhode Island sent representatives to the Constitutional Convention of 1787.

Although the establishment of Congregationalism as the state church in most of the New England colonies, the framing of obnoxious laws and the rigid enforcement of the Test Oaths restricted Catholic immigration to New England, Catholicism has left an indelible mark on many former strongholds of Puritanism. In the story of the Norwegian missions it is claimed that Catholic missionaries came to Vinland to convert the pagan Northmen, who had settled in the vicinity of Narragansett Bay and that Bishop Eric visited the settlement. "After his consecration (1121), Eric returned to America but still attached to his mission, led a body of clergy and colonists to Vinland. Here he found so ample a field for his labor, that he resigned his bishopric and never returned to Greenland." [5] Cabot, Cartier, Champlain, Gomez and Verrazano, the discoverers and explorers of the coast, were members of the ancient faith. Shea speaks of a settlement at St. Croix Island

[5] Shea, Ind. Mis. in U. S., 34.

now known as De Mont's or Neutral Island in 1604.[6]
Two young priests, Nicholas Aubry and a companion,
said Mass in a rude chapel, the first in New England.
The Jesuit Fathers, Baird and Masse, accompanied Bien-
court to Port Royal in 1613, and two years later the
feeble mission of St. Sauveur was founded. Samuel
Argall destroyed the colony, Father Masse was set adrift
in a shallop with fourteen Frenchmen, Brother du Thet
died of wounds, and Fathers Baird and Quentin were
carried to Virginia, where they narrowly escaped death
as pirates.[7] The first Abnaki missions were destroyed
but the Recollects and Capuchins kept the faith alive in
Acadia and along the Kennebec and Penobscot Rivers.[8]
In 1646, Father Gabriel Druillettes, S.J. was sent to the
Kennebec at the request of two chiefs who journeyed to
Quebec to ask for a "Blackrobe." He labored among
them for ten years and converted the entire tribe. Although the frequent bloody wars interrupted the mission, the Jesuits, the Seminary Priests from Quebec, and
the Foreign Mission Fathers ministered to their spiritual
wants.[9] In 1693, Father Sebastian Rale, S.J. came to the
mission and for thirty years, with a single omission,
shared the triumphs and sufferings of his devoted flock.
An accomplished linguist, he composed a dictionary of
the Abnaki tongue which is still preserved in the library

[6] *Ibid.*, Cath. Ch. in U. S., I-217.
[7] Campbell, Pio. Prs. of N. Am., III-270 ff.
[8] Shea, Ind. Mis. in U. S., 135.
[9] *Ibid.*, Ind. Mis. in U. S., 141.

of Harvard University, and wrote many spiritual works for the consolation and edification of the neophytes. European rivalry extended to the Western Continent, and Canadians and New Englanders engaged in bloody conflicts. The English coveted and claimed all the region on both sides of the Kennebec River, and the Abnaki, staunch allies of the French, fought for the freedom of their forests. The devoted missionary was assailed as the instigator of the Indian attacks, and all the atrocities of the campaigns were laid at his door. In consequence, the zealous Rale was singled out for capture or death, and in 1705, an expedition from New England burned and pillaged the chapel, and destroyed the crops and wigwams. In 1722, the village was again attacked, the strong box and library with the famous dictionary carried away as plunder. Finally in 1724, a body of New England troops surrounded the village, Father Rale fell riddled with bullets at the foot of the cross, his skull was cleft with a hatchet, his scalp torn off and sold in Boston as a trophy of victory. The sacred vessels were desecrated, the Blessed Sacrament defiled, the church burned to the ground.[10] Yet the seed of faith, planted by the martyred priest, fructified and grew, and the descendants of his faithful flock still profess the true religion.

Catholics were few in Massachusetts during the early days. "Of course, under the general law, Roman Cath-

[10] Campbell, Pio. Prs. of N. Am., III-270 ff.

olics were not suffered to live in the colony. In 1647,
Jesuits were forbidden to enter. If any should come,
they were at once to be banished; if they returned, to
be put to death." [11] Even in pre-revolutionary days,
their number was small. In 1765 John Adams wrote:
"Roman Catholics are as scarce as a comet or an earthquake." [12] Ten years later, writing to James Warren
from Braintree, he says: "We have a few Jacobites and
Roman Catholics in this town, but they dare not show
themselves." [13] In the earlier days of the colony, Catholics are occasionally mentioned. Miles Standish, the military leader, was evidently a member of the ancient
faith, as he came from an ancient Catholic family,
never attended the state service, and made annual visits
to the Kennebec settlements where the Catholic missionaries were located, presumably to perform his
Easter duty. Sir Christopher Gardiner, who resided at
Quincy for some years, was banished for not attending
the Congregational worship, a circumstance which has
given rise to the tradition that he was a Catholic. Le
Baron, a young French surgeon, shipwrecked on the
coast, acknowledged his Catholicity, and refused to
assist at the Puritan rites, but his medical and surgical
skill made him valuable in the settlements and he was
unmolested. Both Le Baron and Standish married Prot-

[11] Cobb, Ris. of Rel. Lib. in Am., 177.
[12] Griffith, Cath. Hist. Res., 1905-386.
[13] *Ibid.*, Cath. Hist. Res., 1906-32.

estant wives, and their descendants were lost to the church.[14] In 1643, two French priests appeared in Boston harbor but remained on board the vessel, and three years later, two others came, and were permitted to land. The celebrated Jesuit missionary, Gabriel Druillettes, Apostle of the Abnakis, came to New England as the representative of the Canadian government, to arrange a treaty of alliance against the Iroquois, in exchange for trading privileges with Canada, visited the principal towns and conferred with Elliott, Winthrop and the other leading men.[15] Another Jesuit, John Pierron, traveled in disguise through the New England colonies on his way to Maryland. He engaged in a religious controversy with the ministers at Boston; "then it began to be bruited that he was a Jesuit, and he was cited before the Grand Assembly. That he could not afford to do, and probably in another disguise, he disappeared from public view." [16] Undoubtedly there were many Catholics in the colony, although their names are unknown, as French prisoners of war were brought to Boston, among them several priests, while Portuguese names are occasionally found and Irish names in abundance. The town records, the vital statistics, the church rolls, the land and probate accounts of the towns, contain thousands of names, unmistakably Irish.[17] Con-

[14] Leahey, Hist. Dioc. of Boston, 5-6.
[15] Campbell, Pio. Prs. of N. Am., III-89 ff.
[16] Ibid., Pio. Prs. of N. Am., I-218.
[17] O'Brien, Hid. Ph. of Am. Hist., 222.

trary to the usual assertion of some non-Catholic authors, these immigrants were not alone from the province of Ulster, but from every part of Ireland, as we find in the shipping records, not only vessels from Belfast, Derry and Newry, but also from Cork, Dublin, Galway, Waterford and other harbors, where Catholics formed the bulk of the population.[18] In addition to those who voluntarily came to the New World to escape the misery in Ireland, Cromwell caused about nine thousand (some say many more) women and children to be sent to the colonies and the West Indies as slaves."[19] A large number of them came to New England, some at least Catholics,[20] but as there were neither priests nor churches, and the local laws compelled them to have their children baptized by the Protestant clergy under pain of illegitimacy, and to send them to schools where the faith and nationality of their parents were ridiculed, many intermarried with the Protestants and their descendants were lost to the faith.[21] In 1756, two thousand exiled Acadians were landed at Boston and other ports. Lieutenant-Governor Hutchinson showed them much sympathy but denied them the services of the clergy, as they would not consent to the public exercise of religious worship by Roman Catholic priests.[22]

[18] *Ibid.*, Hid. Ph. of Am. Hist., 250.
[19] Maginnis, Ir. Con. to Am. Indep., 25.
[20] *Ibid.*, Ir. Con. to Am. Indep., 44-45.
[21] O'Brien, Hid. Ph. of Am. Hist., 266-7.
[22] Leahey, Hist. Dioc. of Bos., 3.

From its foundation in 1623, "Catholics were effectually shut out of New Hampshire, not only by the exclusive spirit of Puritanism, but by the early charters and penal laws that prevailed in England for the total suppression of Catholic worship." [23] In 1694, during a French and Indian raid Father Thury and another priest said Mass near the present town of Durham. The many laws framed to prevent the growth of Popery, and the penalties prescribed under the infamous Test Oaths during the reign of William and Mary, is evidence that there were some Catholics in New Hampshire. Irish settlers came in large numbers, and the distinctively Catholic names mentioned in the early civil and religious records, show that at least a few members of the proscribed religion had settled there. "But as exiles in the wilds of New England far removed from environments and scenes that were rich with the holiest memories of faith and fatherland, and instinct with the generations of Catholic life, they forgot the priceless heritage and were lost to the church of their birth." [24] During the many colonial wars, French Canadian captives were frequently brought to New Hampshire. The religious fanaticism of the settlers is plainly shown in the expedition against the Abnaki Indians led by Colonel Westbrook who carried off the famous Dictionary and the shocking murder and mutilation of Father Rale by

[23] Finen, Hist. Dioc. of Manchester, 570.
[24] *Ibid.*, Hist. Dioc. of Manchester, 579.

Lieutenant Jacques. When the Acadian exiles were landed in Massachusetts, the Governor and Council appealed to the government of New Hampshire to relieve them of a part of the captives, in the interests of humanity, "the province declined on the pretext that she was on the borders of Canada." [25]

Tradition links Rhode Island with the Vinland of the Sagas, the voyage of Leif, son of Eric, and the visit of Bishop Eric of Gardar in the twelfth century. Its founder was a victim of intolerance and his views on religious freedom were unusually broad for the century, in which he lived. The Charter, granted by Charles II in 1663, was most tolerant, allowing all men to follow their consciences and judgments in matters of religious contentment. Catholics were few in numbers. "Rhode Island," says Cotton Mather, "has everything in the world but Roman Catholics and true Christians." [26] "But the question arises, were there any Catholics in the colony then? There is very little likelihood that there were any." [27] In 1680, the Governor and the Council, replying to the Board of Trade of London writes: "As for Papists, we know of none amongst us." [28] It is said that in 1680, there was not one Catholic in the colony, and for a long period their number

[25] Shea, Cath. Ch. in U. S., I-430.
[26] Dowling, Hist. Dioc. of Prov., 352.
[27] *Ibid.*, Hist. Dioc. of Prov., 373.
[28] *Ibid.*, Hist. Dioc. of Prov., 353.

must have been small." [29] From the very beginnings of
the colony, Irish names are found in the birth, marriage and death records, in wills and land transfers of
every section. "But it is one thing to discover the traces
of Irish infusion in the colony, and another to connect
them in any way with the Catholic religion." [30] As there
were neither priests nor churches, association and inter-
marriage with non-Catholics weaned their descendants
from the ancient faith. Even when the Acadians were
distributed amongst the colonies, few were sent to
Rhode Island. Yet the colony never excluded Catholics
from her shores and her statute books were never
stained by the unjust and intolerant enactments framed
by the neighboring colonies.

"It is not improbable that the first European to sail
along the shores of Connecticut and perhaps to land
upon its soil, was the great Catholic navigator, Verrazano." [31] As French and Spanish expeditions were
usually accompanied by a priest, it may be that Mass
was said in Connecticut as early as 1524. The first settlers were Puritans and Pilgrims, unfriendly to the
Catholic religion, yet Irish names are found in the history of the colony as early as 1639. During the Pequod
war, and at the Great Swamp Fight, in King Philip's
War, Irishmen won distinction for their valor and re-

[29] Cath. Ency., Vol. XIII.
[30] Dowling, Hist. Dioc. of Prov., 353.
[31] O'Donnell, Hist. Dioc. of Hart., 32.

ceived generous grants of land. During the Protectorate of Cromwell, Connecticut received her share of the Irish women and children sent to New England. Almost on the eve of the struggle for independence Irish were publicly sold as slaves.[32] The most noted victim was Matthew Lyon, soldier and statesman of the Revolution, Representative in Congress from Vermont, Kentucky and Arkansas. In the vital statistics, in the town and county records, in the muster rolls, Irish names are common, some of whom were undoubtedly Catholics. "The absence of Priests, the dearth of Catholic neighbors, the total want of Catholic influence, and the spirit of hostility to Catholics then prevalent, as exemplified in vicious legislation, were no doubt among the causes that led many at least into material apostacy." [33] In 1710, a French embassy from the Governor of Canada to the Governor of Massachusetts came to New London, one of the envoys probably a priest, as were many of the attendants. During the colonial wars with Canada many French and Spanish prisoners were brought to the colony, and either bound out to service or confined in the local jails. French and Spanish vessels frequently came to New London, remaining for long periods. Their crews were mainly Catholics, and priests usually accompanied the warships as chaplains. Four hundred Acadians were assigned to Connecticut and although re-

[32] *Ibid.*, Hist. Dioc. of Hart., 40.
[33] *Ibid.*, Hist. Dioc. of Hart., 53.

ceived with more kindness than in the neighboring settlements, were unwelcome guests. They were distributed among the villages, some bound out to the most menial service, others treated as paupers.[34] The adults clung tenaciously to the faith, and although tradition asserts that several priests were among the exiles, the proof is lacking. Perhaps the notion arose from the custom of appointing and authorizing laymen to marry their fellow Catholics rather than appear before the ministers of the established church.[35] Some of these unfortunates returned to Canada or the West Indies, others made their way to Louisiana, the children who remained were sent to Protestant families and became absorbed in the prevailing sects.

The scarcity of Catholics in New England is clearly understood when the nature of the laws and the sentiments of the dominant rulers are realized. The Pilgrims had sought refuge in Holland from the persecution of the English church and came to Plymouth to preserve their religion and their nationality. In the first years all were of the same faith, with few exceptions, and no qualifications were necessary for the estate of a freeman until 1636, when it was merely enacted that a candidate must have been approved by the freemen of his own town. "Two years later, when the colony was overrun with Quaker propagandists, persons of that

[34] *Ibid.*, Hist. Dioc. of Hart., 70.
[35] *Ibid.*, Hist. Dioc. of Hart., 73.

faith, as well as all others who similarly opposed the laws and the established worship, were distinctly excluded from the privileges of freedom—and in the new revision of the laws in 1671, were obliged . . . to be orthodox in the fundamentals of religion." [36] As Catholics were not "orthodox in the fundamentals" from the Puritan standard, they were denied these privileges. In the Massachusetts Bay colony the Puritans were intolerant of all other sects. "It has been a favorite saying with eulogists of Massachusetts that the pious founders came over to the wilderness to establish here the principles of civil and religious liberty and to transmit the same inviolable to their remotest posterity. Probably nothing was farther from their purpose which was simply to find a place where they themselves and all who agreed with them could enjoy such liberty." [37] The Catholic Church and her teachings were especially abhorrent to the Puritans. "The French garrisons on the North, the Spanish fleets which swept the seas, constantly fed their fear of the monster, and they took care by their enactments that no authentic teachers of its doctrines should enter their midst and enlighten them." [38] "Of course, under the general law Roman Catholics were not suffered to live in the colony." By formal statute, Congregationalism became a law and

[36] Winsor, Hist. of Am., III-280.
[37] Ibid., Hist. of Am., III-312.
[38] Leahey, Hist. Dioc. of Boston, 3.

any attempt to institute another form of worship became a punishable offense.[39] Although the Puritans had left England to escape the tyranny of the State Church, yet the union of church and state in their new home was absolute and church membership was an indispensable requisite for the franchise or for holding office. All must pay tithes for the support of the established religion and all arrears of taxes must be collected by the civil authority.[40] The entire system was founded on the Old rather than the New Dispensation and the government was a pure theocracy. Catholics were unwelcome and their customs and symbols despised. Endicott cut the cross out of the English flag "on the grounds that it smacked of popery," [41] and in 1659, the observance of Christmas was made a punishable offense.[42] The activities of the Catholic missionaries on the frontiers excited apprehension among the Protestant settlers and a law specifically forbidding priests to enter the colony, under penalty of death for a second offence was placed on the statute books.[43] Racial prejudice was aroused by the advent of French and Irish immigrants, many presumably Catholics, and William of Orange in the new Charter (1691) gave liberty of conscience to all Christians except Papists.[44] As late as 1772, the offi-

[39] Cobb, Rise of Rel. Lib. in Am., 177.
[40] Ibid., Rise of Rel. Lib. in Am., 169.
[41] Ibid., Rise of Rel. Lib. in Am., 186.
[42] Ibid., Rise of Rel. Lib. in Am., 209.
[43] Ibid., Rise of Rel. Lib. in Am., 177.
[44] Ibid., Rise of Rel. Lib. in Am., 233.

cials of Boston excluded Catholics from toleration on the ground that their doctrines were "subversive of society." [45] Even when the Continental army was beseiging Boston, Washington was forced to issue an order to the troops forbidding the celebration of Pope's Day and burning the Pope in effigy. Catholics were not the only sufferers, all non-conformists were banned, Roger Williams banished for expressing and teaching opinions contrary to the established order, Anne Hutchinson expelled for her theological errors. "The whole proceedings were due to religious intolerance and the rancor of the ministers, whose spiritual character had been aspersed." [46] Quakers, both men and women, were whipped, fined, imprisoned and executed. [47] The witchcraft delusion, with its gruesome scenes, was another painful chapter in the history of the colony. In the various expeditions against Canada, French settlements were burned and pillaged, churches desecrated, priests carried away into captivity, and the murder of Father Rale with its shocking barbarities, was a fitting climax to the intolerant spirit of the seventeenth and eighteenth centuries in New England.

New Hampshire equalled Massachusetts in hatred of Catholics. In 1679, it was enacted: "that liberty of Conscience shall be allowed unto all Protestants." [48] The

[45] Leahey, Hist. Dioc. Boston, 3.
[46] Cobb, Rise Rel. Lib. in Am., 194.
[47] Ibid., Rise Rel. Lib. in Am., 217.
[48] Ibid., Rise Rel. Lib. in Am., 294.

first Provincial Assembly ordained: "All Englishmen being Protestants, should be admitted freemen of the commonwealth." It is well to note that the restrictive word "Protestant" wrought no individual wrong and acted simply as a deterrent of any Romanist immigration.[49] These stringent laws apparently were not sufficient to exclude Catholics, and in 1696, the oath of allegiance and supremacy was strengthened by a "Declaration" against the Pope and the doctrine and practises of the Catholic religion.[50] In this appendix, the Mass, Transubstantiation, devotion to the Blessed Virgin, prayers for the Saints were condemned as superstitious and idolatrous.[51] All persons refusing to subscribe to this oath were sent to the common jail for three months or fined forty shillings unless they could give adequate security for their appearance in court. Catholics were debarred from holding the offices of Governor, Senator, Councilor or representative, a restriction not removed until the last quarter of the nineteenth century.[52] Towns and parishes were to provide "Protestant teachers of religion and morality and all taxpayers were assessed for the support of the ministers under pain of imprisonment.[53] Quakers were fined for refusing to attend services, those harboring them were

[49] *Ibid.*, Rise Rel. Lib. in Am. 294.
[50] *Ibid.*, Rise Rel. Lib. in Am., 299.
[51] Finen, Hist. Dioc. Man., 573.
[52] Cath. Ency., Vol. X.
[53] Cobb, Rise of Rel. Lib. in Am., 295.

liable to a similar punishment, and during the union with Massachusetts three Quaker women were beaten through the various towns until they reached the borders of the colony.[54] During the Witchcraft Delusion much excitement prevailed, but none suffered the death penalty.

Rhode Island was founded by a fugitive from intolerance and under "the broadest charter of human liberties ever issued under a royal seal." [55] "Certainly it seems that by this charter, an asylum was opened to Catholics who were persecuted in England." [56] In the first collection of laws, issued in 1719, a statute is found granting to all men professing Christianity, the rights of freemen, "Roman Catholics alone excepted." Evidently this law was passed in 1663, during the lifetime of Williams, when he was serving in the Assembly, on the committee appointed to codify the laws.[57] Although these clauses appear in the different digests and are reaffirmed five times, Bancroft argues that neither the people nor the Assembly passed such laws, that they are clearly an interpolation.[58] Justin Winsor suggests that the words may have been inserted in the manuscript copy sent to England in 1689, but never enforced by the colony.[59] John Fiske explains that the anti-Catholic cru-

[54] Finen, Hist. Dioc. Man., 571.
[55] Cobb, Rise Rel. Lib. in Am., 435.
[56] Dowling, Hist. Dioc. Prov., 353.
[57] *Ibid.*, Hist. Dioc. Prov., 354.
[58] Bancroft, Hist. U. S., II-65.
[59] Winsor, Hist. of Am., III-379.

sade which arose in the last days of James II and the beginning of William of Orange's reign, caused the insertion of the intolerant paragraph.[60] "The law, all agree, was never acted upon. No Test Oath was ever administered in this colony and no question ever asked as to the religion of the candidate for freeman. Rhode Island never excluded Catholics from her shores."[61] The founders of Connecticut were of Puritan extraction and Congregationalism became the established religion of the colony. "While taking care that churches of their own order should be founded and maintained, they never decreed the expulsion of other forms of faith and worship. Her worst sins against religious liberty were in the exercise of authority over the churches and the assessment against the entire community for the support of the Establishment."[62] "There never existed a persecuting spirit in Connecticut," says Bancroft.[63] However the amount of religious liberty allowed to dissenters depended on the will of the General Court. Quakers, Ranters and other like sects were regarded as "loathesome heretics" and the same hostile spirit was displayed towards Catholics. They were referred to as "idolators, grossly superstitious, held in subjection by their clergy, and enveloped in spiritual and intellectual

[60] Fiske, Dut. and Quak. Col., II-115.
[61] Dowling, Hist. Dio. of Prov., 354.
[62] Cobb, Rise of Rel. Lib. in Am., 244.
[63] Bancroft, Hist. U. S., II-56.

darkness." [64] Even Catholic practices, such as kneeling at prayers, instrumental music, and fasting on Good Friday were avoided. The Sayville confession of faith pronounced the Pope "Anti-Christ, the Mass, Abominably injurious to Christ's own sacrifice, Transubstantiation the cause of 'manifold superstitions, yea, of gross idolatry,' and vows of poverty, chastity and obedience 'superstitious and sinful snares.' " [65] As early as 1669, renunciation of the Pope was a necessary qualification for holding office, and by the enactment 1724, all officials must make this declaration against the Pope before taking office. In 1744, the ministers of Windham voted "that baptism by a Popish priest is not to be held valid." [66] In 1743, two acts were framed by the legislature; the first restricting toleration to "Protestants," the second, "to prevent the designs of foreigners and suspected persons." [67] These obnoxious laws remained in force until the era of independence, disbarring all Catholics from civil duties and rendering them socially inferior to their Protestant neighbors. There was one mitigating circumstance. "Unlike Massachusetts, New York and Virginia, the statute books of Connecticut were never stained with enactments against the Jesuits or other Catholic priests." [68]

[64] O'Donnell, Hist. Dio. Hart., 15.
[65] *Ibid.*, Hist. Dio. Hart., 19.
[66] *Ibid.*, Hist. Dio. Hart., 21.
[67] Cobb, Rise of Rel. Lib. in Am., 276-77.
[68] O'Donnell, Hist. Dio. of Hart., 15.

The outbreak of the revolution and the birth of the new Republic abolished or modified most of those intolerant laws. Yet in some colonies the leaven of tolerance only permeated the mass of bigotry after the lapse of years. In 1780, Massachusetts framed its first constitution and "retained the old colonial principle which gave to the church a civil status. Every ratepayer was, as in the last fifty years, allowed to indicate his preference as to the church which should be benefited by his tax. Those who had no choice were required to pay taxes for the support of the State Congregational Church." [69] Equal protection was guaranteed to every Christian sect, although "taxes were levied in the different towns" for the support and maintenance of public Protestant teachers of piety, religion and morality.[70] The beginning of the revolution and the alliance with France slowly tempered the old, intolerant spirit. In 1775, the St. John's River Indians sent a delegation to confer with the Council, pledging their allegiance to the patriotic cause, and asking for a "Black gown." The General Court praised their love of religion and promised to find a priest. "Fifty years had wrought its changes and the same body that offered a reward for the scalp of a Jesuit missionary on the Kennebec and finally compassed his death, was now anxious to give the Indians of these parts a Catholic priest." [71]

[69] Cobb, Rise of Rel. Lib. in Am., 500.
[70] Shea, Cath. Ch. in U. S., II-156.
[71] Ibid., Cath. Ch. in U. S., II-154.

It was not until 1833, however, that the State Church was disestablished, tithes abolished and the towns discharged from all concern and power for church affairs.[72]

The New Hampshire Convention of 1776 adopted a meagre Constitution in which no illiberality appears.[73] The Constitutions of 1781 and 1784 left intact the old colonial law which made the church a town institution and its support a matter of public tax and discriminated also in favor of the Protestant religion.[74] In 1792 provisions were made for the "support and maintenance of the public Protestant teachers" and that the Governor, Councilors, Senators and members of the house of representatives "shall be of the Protestant religion." [75] Various dissenting sects received exemption from time to time, but toleration for all religious bodies was not extended until 1819. It was not until 1877, after a century of agitation, that this law was expunged from the constitution. New Hampshire was the last of the original colonies to abandon religious restrictions.

Although Rhode Island had never excluded Catholics, in 1778 it repealed the clause denying them religious toleration. In 1783, it was decreed: "All rights and privileges of the Protestant citizens of this state . . .

[72] Cobb, Rise of Rel. Lib. in Am., 515.
[73] Shea, Cath. Ch. in U. S., II-155.
[74] Cobb, Rise of Rel. Lib. in Am., 500.
[75] Shea, Cath. Ch. in U. S., I-155.

are fully extended to Roman Catholic citizens." [77] In the Constitutional Convention of 1787 she joined with Virginia and North Carolina in proposing a clause "declaring the rights of conscience and the right to a free exercise of religion and enacting that no religious sect or society ought to be favored or established by law in preference to others." [78] It was based on the provision proposed by Jefferson and adopted by the Virginia convention of 1776.

In Connecticut, the Act of 1776 exempted "separates" from taxes for the support of the Established Church. In 1784, a new law was framed, "that no persons professing the Christian religion . . . should incur a penalty by not attending the established worship, . . . and that all Protestant dissenters . . . shall have liberty . . . for maintaining their respective societies as belonged to societies established by law." [79] It was not until the Convention of 1818 that the state church was abolished and full liberty granted to all Christians. "The exercise and enjoyment of religious profession and worship . . . shall forever be free to all persons in this state. No preference shall be given by law to any Christian sect or worship." [80] "These provisions were intended to establish full liberty, but as the clause touching preference mentioned the Christian religion and might rise

[77] Dowling, Hist. Dioc. of Prov., 354.
[78] Shea, Cath. Ch. in U. S., II-347.
[79] Cobb, Rise of Rel. Lib. in Am., 501.
[80] O'Donnell, Hist. Dioc. Hart., 23.

to the construction that the freedom intended was designed only for Christian churches, an after legislature expressly construed the benefits of this freedom as including Jews." [81]

[81] Cobb, Rise Rel. Lib. in Am., 513.

CHAPTER NINE

Virginia and the Southern Colonies

VIRGINIA, originally comprising a vague and unknown region stretching from Florida to New France, received its name from Queen Elizabeth, in commemoration of her maiden life.[1] Its ownership was bitterly disputed, Spain claiming it by its discovery of Columbus, and its exploration by d'Ayllon, England by the voyage of John Cabot. In 1578, Elizabeth granted a patent to Sir Humphrey Gilbert but the first attempts were failures. Five years later, Gilbert was lost at sea, and his half-brother, Sir Walter Raleigh, obtained a new grant and formed a settlement at Roanoke Island. The threatened invasion of the Spanish Armada prevented the founder from sending aid to the colonists, and when assistance arrived after three years, the settlement was in ruins and the inhabitants had disappeared.

In 1606, James I created two companies, the London and the Plymouth, granting to each an equal share of the vast region called Virginia. The London branch received the southern section from the thirty-fourth to

[1] Winsor, Hist. of Am., III-110.

the forty-first degree of latitude. In December the first expedition sailed, and in 1607, the first permanent English settlement was founded at Jamestown. For some years the colony was feeble, disease, famine, and the hostility of the natives decimating its ranks. The coming of Lord De La Ware with additional settlers and much needed supplies, the establishment of homes, and the cultivation and exportation of tobacco brought increased prosperity and social comforts. In 1619, the first popular Assembly convened, but four years later James I demanded the surrender of the Charter, and in the following year Virginia became a royal province. When Charles I was executed, the burgesses condemned the Parliamentary action as treason and acknowledged Charles II as the lawful monarch.[2] The Long Parliament prohibited trade with Virginia and declared that her people had been guilty of rebellion against the English Commonwealth.[3] Cromwell sent a fleet to reduce the guilty province and after a show of resistance, the Virginians surrendered. The restoration of Charles II freed the colony from the tyranny of the Commissioners; Lord Berkeley was chosen Governor by the Assembly and the King granted him a new commission. This loyalty, it is said, merited for Virginia the honorable title "The Old Dominion," although many other varied and fanciful explanations have been given for

[2] Cooke, Virginia, 193.
[3] *Ibid.*, Virginia, 195.

its origin.[4] The occasional Indian outbreaks, Bacon's rebellion, and the French and Indian wars distracted the colony, but immigration increased and the lucrative trade with the West Indies brought prosperity to the settlement.

The territory, comprising the Carolinas and Georgia, was claimed by England as part of Virginia, by Spain as part of Florida. French Calvinists had settled near its southern boundary, only to be expelled and their forts destroyed by Pedro Menendez. In 1663, Charles II conferred all the lands from the thirty-first to the thirty-sixth degrees of latitude on the Earl of Clarendon, the Duke of Albemarle and six other members of the nobility for their loyalty to the house of Stuart. "It is stated in the grant that this extensive region is called 'Carolina,' a name used before and now, no doubt, retained in honor of the King."[5] Two years later, the Ruler granted a new charter, comprising all the territory of North and South Carolina, Georgia, Tennessee, Alabama, Mississippi, Louisiana, Arkansas, much of Florida, and Missouri, and a large part of Mexico. As Mexico, Florida, and much of the western territory had been explored or colonized by Spain, the royal grant was worthless.[6] Emigrants from Barbadoes, New England and Virginia had formed settlements before the

[4] Fiske, Old Virg., II-26.
[5] Winsor, Hist. of Am., V-286.
[6] Bancroft, Hist. U. S., II-138.

arrival of the new company, the Albemarle and Clarendon colonies were founded in the northern sector and
a village planted on the Ashley River (1670), which
later developed into the city of Charleston. Shaftesbury,
assisted by the philosopher, John Locke, drew up a form
of government, magnificent in design, but wholly un-
suited for the feeble colonies of Carolina, and after a
long and bitter controversy, "The Grand Model" was
rejected. "Before the province was authoritatively divided it had divided itself, as it were, into North and
South Carolina." [7] The selfishness of the proprietors,
incompetent and impolitic government, the hostility of
the Indian tribes, the rivalry with the Spaniards on the
southern frontiers retarded its growth and aroused discontent and indignation among the settlers. Yet large
bodies of immigrants came and settled in the interior
in the fertile regions to the west. Huguenots, Swiss,
Germans, and Scots came in large numbers and Irish
exiles were found among the new arrivals. Domestic
oppression drove thousands from their homes in Ireland,
and it is noted by the historian of South Carolina that
scarcely a ship sailed for Charleston that was not
crowded with men, women and children." [8] "The number of places in this section of the state (South Carolina) bearing names of a decidedly Catholic flavor are
striking evidences of the settlement of Irish people in

[7] Winsor, Hist. Am., V-294.
[8] O'Brien, Hid. Ph. Am. Hist., 256.

these parts." [9] "The line of their settlements . . . may be traced on the high roads leading from Virginia into North Carolina and through the state as far as Roanoke." [10] In the colonial documents abstracts of wills, the records of land conveyances, the register of property grants, hundreds of distinctively Irish names may be found. [11] Finally, the proprietors sold their possessions to the Crown, and North and South Carolina became royal provinces.

Georgia, the last of the original colonies, was founded by James Oglethorpe, a member of the English House of Commons, as a refuge for the oppressed debtors and the persecuted Protestants of Europe. [12] The Carolinians welcomed the project as a protection from the hostile Indians and the Spaniards of Florida. King George II granted a charter in 1732 and the new colony was named Georgia in honor of the royal patron. In the spring of 1733, the first colonists arrived, selected a spot on the Savannah River as a site for a settlement, and a treaty of amity and peace was negotiated with the Indians by which all the lands between the Savannah and the Altamaha Rivers from the Ocean to tide water were ceded to the trustees. Immigration was encouraged, and Italian silk workers from Piedmont, Austrian farmers from Salzburg and Scotch High-

[9] *Ibid.*, Hid. Ph. Am. Hist., 356.
[10] *Ibid.*, Hid. Ph. Am. Hist., 257.
[11] *Ibid.*, Hid. Ph. Am. Hist., 360.
[12] Winsor, Hist. of Am., V-363.

landers came in considerable numbers. Irish settlers were
found in the province as early as 1733, the records and
public documents containing many Irish names. "An
O'Brien founded Augusta, a Mitchell, Atlanta, a Mc-
Cormack, Dublin. Twenty counties are named in honor
of Irishmen or Americans of Irish descent who distinguished themselves in one capacity or another in the
civil or political life of the state." [13] The Spanish claims
were a constant menace to the officials and in 1740,
Oglethorpe with his army, and a British fleet, invested
St. Augustine but the attempt was a failure. In retaliation, a Spanish force attacked Savannah by land and
sea but the invaders were repulsed. In 1752, the trustees
surrendered the Charter and Georgia became a royal
province. Many of the projected industries had failed,
trade was inconsiderable, the population small. Georgia
throughout the colonial period was the weakest member
of the thirteen colonies.

The Southern States played a prominent and honorable role in the struggle for freedom. Patrick Henry
sounded the first note of defiance, in his seven resolutions against the Stamp Act.[14] North Carolina framed
the famous, "Mecklenburg Resolution," harbinger of
the coming "Declaration of Independence." [15] Washington was chosen to lead the Continental Army, Richard Henry Lee moved the resolutions for indepen-

[13] O'Brien, Hid. Ph. Am. Hist., 364-5.
[14] Howard, Beg. of Am. Rev., 142-3.
[15] Winsor, Hist. of Am., VI-256.

dence, Jefferson penned the immortal document, Peyton Randolph presided over the deliberations of the First Congress.

Madison, Monroe, Marshall, Edward and John Rutledge were towers of strength in every patriotic movement. Andrew Lewis, "Light Horse" Harry Lee, Daniel Morgan were Washington's most devoted officers, Francis Marion, Andrew Pickens and Thomas Sumter kept the fires of patriotism burning when the three lower colonies were overrun by British and Tories. The surrender of Charleston, the unsuccessful siege of Savannah, the disastrous rout at Camden, almost broke the spirit of the patriots, but the bravery of Moultrie and Sergeant Jasper at the first investment of Charleston, Morgan's phenomenal success at Cowpens, Greene's stubborn resistance at Eutaw Springs, Guilford Courthouse and Hobkirk's Hill, and the annihilation of the Tories at King's Mountain, redeemed the reputation of the Southern colonies. The last and decisive contest was fought at Yorktown, on Virginian soil, the emblems of America and France entwined in victory.

Many years before the foundation of the English colonies, Catholics had visited this region from Georgia to Virginia. In 1526, D'Ayllon, accompanied by the Dominican priests, Montesinos and Cervantes and the lay brother, de Estrada, landed near the mouth of the Wateree River and sailed north as far as Chesapeake Bay, where a colony was established at Guandape, called

St. Michael, and houses and a temporary chapel erected. The death of D'Ayllon, the outbreak of a pestilence, and the insubordination of the settlers caused the abandonment of the scheme. The site of this colony has been identified by some historians with the peninsula where Jamestown was founded.[16] In 1570, Menendez with the Jesuit fathers, Segura and de Quiros, and six lay brothers sailed up the Potomac to establish a mission. Shortly after the departure of the fleet, the treacherous Indians massacred the entire company.[17] "In 1568, Father Sedeno, S. J. took up his abode on Amelia Island; he is the pioneer priest of Georgia. With him was the lay brother, Baez, who wrote a grammar of the aboriginal language and prepared a catechism. Father Rogel, S. J. —set up a mission on Santa Elena Island, Port Royal Sound; he is the pioneer priest of South Carolina."[18] Although the English colonists were opposed to Catholics, some found their way to the new colonies. A memorial to Pope Innocent XI, from the secretary of the Congregation of the Propaganda mentions that Capuchins and Carmelites had labored in Virginia. As the name, "Virginia," included New England, the reference in all probability was to Avalon, Canada or Maine.[19] Franciscans had been invited to Maryland by Lord Baltimore and during the revolution of 1689,

[16] Shea, Cath. Ch. in U. S., I-106-7.
[17] O'Gorman, Cath. Ch. in U. S., 34.
[18] Ibid., Cath. Ch. in U. S., 34.
[19] Hughes, So. of Jesus in N. Am., I-202.

Coode, the Protestant pursuivant of Maryland, informed the Virginian authorities, that one of their number, Hubbard, was sheltered, "at his Popish patron's, Mr. Brent in Stafford County." [20] The Jesuits came to Maryland with the first expedition and opened missions in the colony. During the Cromwellian agitation, Fathers Roger Rigbie, and John Cooper were carried off to Virginia, and died in the hands of their enemies. Father Bernard Hartwell passed away in the same year. "The coincidence of the three young men dying in the same year, while they lay in the hands of enemies, needs no comment, whether the violence which did away with them was that of hardship or something still more summary." [21] The troubles with the Lord Proprietor were so acute, that in 1647 the General concluded; "that something might be done for the comfort of the Catholics of Virginia." [22] Accordingly Fathers Copley and Starkey came to Virginia, "attracting as little attention as possible," ministering also to the faithful of Maryland. During the troubles of 1689, a mission was destroyed through Protestant opposition, although the colony still was, "a place of refuge for the priests." [23] "One Gulick, a Jesuit," is mentioned by Coode in his complaint to the President of the Council. [24] The anti-

[20] *Ibid.*, So. of Jesus in N. Am., II-158.
[21] *Ibid.*, So. of Jesus in N. Am., I-563.
[22] *Ibid.*, So. of Jesus in N. Am., II-23.
[23] *Ibid.*, So. of Jesus in N. Am., II-156.
[24] *Ibid.*, So. of Jesus in N. Am., II-158.

Popery Act of 1700, provided for such outrageous penalties that the priests were obliged to use the utmost caution in their travels and ministrations. In spite of these sanguinary enactments, Catholics were found in the Provinces as late as 1746, but Virginia joined with Maryland in a proclamation against, "Popery, Jesuits and Popish Priests." [25]

The Catholic population of Virginia was small on account of the intolerant laws, yet the presence of the Jesuits and Franciscans and the various enactments against priests and people show that some members of the detested religion were in the colony. Lord Culpepper reported that in a population of seventy or eighty thousand souls there was only one Papist. This was probably a political fiction on the part of the Executive to show his vigilance in religious matters. George Brent, a Catholic lawyer, had purchased thirty thousand acres of land, receiving from James II, the privilege that "he and all who settled on his lands was exempted from the Penal Laws of England." [26] After the flight and deposition of James, an attempt was made to enforce the Popish Recusant Act on the Proprietor and his tenants. [27] That these Catholics persevered in the faith is evident as in 1746, some Catholic families had settled on the southern shore of the Potomac at Aquia Creek

[25] Shea, Cath. Ch. in U. S., I-406-9.
[26] Griffin, Am. Cath. His. Res., 1905-303.
[27] Hughes, So. Jesus in N. Am., II-160.

and above it, and priests ministered to this remote portion of their flock, entering Virginia from time to time.[28] Immigration brought many Catholics to the Old Dominion; "there were many Irish, Polish, Italian and French Catholics in the colony as servants."[29] The Irish influx was especially large. "The fact that Virginia received a large infusion of Irish blood from a very early period is indisputable and according to the most dependable records, approximately three hundred years have elapsed since the first Irishman appeared in Virginia, which was before the arrival of the Pilgrims of the Mayflower."[30] Many of these settled in the neighborhood of the Blue Ridge Mountains and the Shenandoah Valley and protected the sea-board from Indian incursions. These men are usually styled "Scotch-Irish" as if all came from the province of Ulster, when in truth, every section of Ireland furnished settlers who called themselves Irish. Some at least were Catholics, although the absence of priests and churches weaned many of their descendants from the ancient faith.[31] In 1769, John Fitzgerald, the future secretary and aide-de-camp of Washington, came from County Wicklow and settled in Alexandria. At the beginning of the hostilities he, with eight others, the entire Catholic population of the town, joined the Continental Army. When the

[28] Shea, Cath. Ch. in U. S., II-409.
[29] Griffin, Am. Cath. Hist. Res., 1911-158.
[30] O'Brien, Hid. Ph. of Am. Hist., 323.
[31] Ibid., Hid. Ph. of Am. Hist., 366 ff.

Acadian exiles reached Virginia, the Governor refused to admit them, calling them, "bigoted papists," and sending them to England where they were kept prisoners of war for seven years and then transferred to France.[32]

In the Carolinas and Georgia, Catholics were few, as the local enactments and the use of the Test Oaths deprived them of civil rights unless they apostatized. North Carolina disqualified all who denied the truth of the Protestant religion.[33] "South Carolina established the Anglican Church and like Georgia, gave liberty of conscience to all, except Papists." [34] "Georgia by its charter, positively excluded Catholics not one of whom was allowed to settle within its borders." [35] "As late as the period of the American Revolution, there was scarcely a Catholic to be found in the colony or state of Georgia, nor was there a priest in the state for many years thereafter." [36] Yet the Irish are found in large numbers in the three colonies. The names of these exiles indicate that many came from Connaught and Munster, where the population is almost entirely Catholic.[37] No priests were allowed in the colonies and there is no evidence that the Maryland Fathers visited the region. That some at least, preserved the faith is evident, when

[32] Shea, Cath. Ch. in U. S., I-437.
[33] Hughes, So. Jesus in N. Am., II-192.
[34] Ibid., So. Jesus in N. Am., II-192.
[35] Shea, Cath. Ch. in U. S., I-437.
[36] Cath. Ency., Vol. VI.
[37] O'Brien, Hid. Ph. of Am. Hist., 350 ff.

we understand that Thomas Burke, a Catholic, was Governor of North Carolina during the revolutionary period, and his cousin or near relative, Aedanus Burke, who had studied for the priesthood at St. Omer's, was Chief Justice of South Carolina.[38] The mother of William Gaston, the eminent North Carolina jurist, was a Catholic, and reared her son in the faith. The Acadian exiles were unwelcome arrivals. Five hundred were sent to North Carolina, fifteen hundred to South Carolina, and four hundred to Georgia. "Turbulent people," said Governor Lyttleton of South Carolina, as he handcuffed and fettered them.[39] They were allotted to the different villages but public sentiment allowed them to hire or build vessels, on which some made their way to France, others to Louisiana. Those consigned to Georgia, were grudgingly allowed to remain until spring. In wretchedly constructed boats they endeavored to reach their old home, but some were shipwrecked, and the survivors were distributed in the New England and the Long Island towns. Those who remained in the south were soon absorbed by the other sects and their children lost to the Catholic Church.

The letters patent, issued by James I in 1606, granting license to lead out a colony and to found a plantation in Virginia, began by expressing the hope that such a noble work might tend to the glory of God and propa-

---

[38] Griffin, Am. Cath. His. Res., 1905-27.
[39] Hughes, So. Jesus in N. Am., I-276.

gate the Christian religion among those living in darkness, and prescribing that the Church of England must
be the established form of religion in Virginia.[40] The
second charter, 1609, repeats these pious sentiments, and
adds that no person suspected of affecting the superstitions of the Church of Rome must be admitted, until
he had taken the oath of supremacy. A confirmation
of this charter in 1612, decreed that King James' oath
of allegiance must also be taken. No Catholic could
subscribe to these oaths without denying the most
sacred tenets of his religion.[41] On the departure of Lord
De La Ware and others of the Council of Virginia, an
Episcopal divine admonished them: "Suffer no Papists;
let them not nestle there: nay, let the name of Pope, or
Poperie never be heard in Virginia." [42] It is needless to
say, that the laws were enforced and the exhortation
heeded.

From 1642 to 1756, a series of intolerant enactments were placed on the statute books; Popish
priests were subject to deportation within five days;
recusants were fined twenty pounds sterling for every
month's absence from the Established Church service;
No recusant convict was allowed to vote; Popish recusants, convicts, negroes, mulattoes and Indian servants,
not being Christians, were incapable in law to be witnesses; No Papist or reputed Papist could possess any

[40] Cobb, Rise of Rel. Lib. in Am., 74-5.
[41] Hughes, So. Jesus in N. Am., II-152.
[42] Griffin, Am. Cath. His. Res., 1908-355.

firearms, unless he took an oath of loyalty; nor could he own a horse worth more than five pounds.[43] George Calvert, the first Lord Baltimore, was excluded from the colony on his return from Avalon, because he could not and would not subscribe to the oath. In 1614, when the pirate, Argall, brought Father Baird a prisoner to Virginia, Governor Dale contemplated hanging the priest. In 1698, an attempt was made to force the objectionable oaths on George and Robert Brent although by the patent of 1686 they were exempt from the Penal Laws of England. The Puritans of Nasemond, the Baptists of the Blue Ridge section, were oppressed at intervals and the Quakers were persecuted with a severity only exceeded by the Massachusetts' officials.[44]

In 1746, Governor Gooch issued an order calling on all magistrates, sheriffs, and constables to apprehend and bring to justice, "the Romish Priests," who were seducing His Majesty's good subjects from their fidelity and loyalty.[45] Finally, in 1756, all Papists were required to surrender their arms and ammunition under penalty of three months' imprisonment, the loss of the weapons and a fine.[46] France and England were at war, for the possession of the continent, and Canada and the colonies were arrayed in arms. Fear that the Catholics might aid their co-religionists was the reason assumed for the

[43] Henning, Statutes of Va., I-VII.
[44] Cobb, Rise of Rel. Lib. in Am., 84-100.
[45] Shea, Cath. Ch. in U. S., I-408-9.
[46] Cobb, Rise of Rel. Lib. in Am., 108.

outrage. "Not even England herself, sought to crush, humble and despise the Catholics as Virginia did." [47]

If we glance at the Southern colonies, we find the letter of William III's anti-popery legislation often reproduced, the spirit always.[48] "The Charters of Charles II to the Carolinas given in 1663 and 1665, made the Church of England the established religion." For the first twenty years, the great majority of the immigrants was composed of Dissenters.[49] Huguenots, Irish and Scotch Presbyterians, Baptists, Dutch Reformed and Quakers took up lands. To maintain the supremacy of the Establishment, the Acts of 1704 disfranchised all non-conformists but the Queen and Parliament rejected these rigid laws.[50] As all the settlers were obliged to subscribe to the oaths and articles of the Anglican Church, no Catholic could qualify without denying his faith. Georgia was founded not only as a home for oppressed debtors, but also as a refuge for the persecuted Protestants of Europe. The Charter granted liberty of conscience and the free exercise of religion to all persons, "except Papists." The other settlers were left free to choose their own religious preferences with the sole exception of the Roman Catholics.[51] When the colony came under the crown, the Church of England was for-

[47] Shea, Cath. Ch. in U. S., I-410.
[48] Hughes, So. Jesus in N. Am., II-191.
[49] Cobb, Rise Rel. Lib. in Am., 118.
[50] *Ibid.*, Ris. Rel. Lib. in Am., 127-28.
[51] *Ibid.*, Ris. Rel. Lib. in Am., 420.

mally proclaimed the state religion by the legislature of 1758.[52] The people of the Carolinas and Georgia frequently engaged in wars with the Spaniards of Florida, their religious bias clearly shown in the destruction of the native missions and the pillaging and burning of Catholic churches. Their savage allies burned Father Parga at the stake and shot down Father de Mendoza.[53] At the capture of St. Augustine, not only were the monastery and church of the Franciscans given to the flames, but also a library of the Greek and Latin Fathers, valued at six hundred pounds.[54] "The antipathy to the true faith with which the unprincipled rulers in England had imbued the ignorant settlers of Carolina, prompted them to the work of devastation." [55]

The revolution brought changes in the Southern colonies. The Virginia Convention of 1776, adopted "The Bill of Rights" declaring all men entitled to the free exercise of religion.[56] In 1779, the law compelling all to pay tithes for the support of the Established Church was repealed, each person contributing to the religion of his choice. Jefferson was the leader in all these movements, ably seconded by Madison. "Religious slavery" was Jefferson's summary of the privileges of the Church of England. The passage of the Declaratory Act, in

[52] Ibid., Ris. Rel. Lib. in Am., 421.
[53] Shea, Cath. Ch. in U. S., I-461.
[54] Ibid., Cath. Ch. in U. S., I-460.
[55] Ibid., Cath. Ch. in U. S., I-461.
[56] Ibid., Cath. Ch. in U. S., II-159.

October 1785, conferred religious freedom on all. A previous act "annulled all laws favoring the Church of England, dissolved all the vestries, and left to the church itself, the entire regulation of its own affairs. This was the final and complete disestablishment and from the passage of this act, the State-Church of Virginia ceased to exist.[57]

North Carolina, in the Constitution of 1776, provided; "No person who shall deny the being of God or the truths of the Protestant religion shall be capable of holding office or place of trust in the civil government of this state." Yet it likewise provided: "All men have a natural and inalienable right to worship Almighty God according to the dictates of their own consciences." [58] The former clause and the previous sentiments of the people gave rise to a celebrated controversy in after years. The appointment of William Gaston, a fervent Catholic, to the State Supreme Court, led to the charge that he had taken a blasphemous oath or had committed perjury. Judge Gaston argued against these theories, in the Convention of 1835: "The Protestant religion could not be denied because it was indefinite; Catholicism did not deny or disbelieve any truths contained in Protestantism; and in any case, internal disbelief was not a denial on the sense of a statute." [59]

Thomas Burke, a Catholic, was a member of the Con-

[57] Cobb, Rise of Rel. Lib. in Am., 495.
[58] Shea, Cath. Ch. in U. S., II-160.
[59] Hughes, So. Jesus in N. Am., II-192.

vention which formulated this Constitution—a member of the Continental Congress, and also Governor of the state.[60] Judge Gaston pronounced the clause "a dead letter," and the entire electorate, except a little coterie of radicals, agreed with him. The Convention of 1835, expunged the word "Protestant" and substituted, "Christian." "The old establishment died of inanition, and no provision was made to support any church or religious teaching."[61]

In the Convention of 1776, South Carolina made no reference to religion. In 1778, another Convention enacted: "The Christian, Protestant religion shall be the established religion of the state; No person shall be eligible to the senate or the house of representatives unless he be of the Protestant religion; All denominations of Christian Protestants shall enjoy equal civil and religious privileges; No church shall be incorporated unless it subscribe to five articles; justification by faith alone, the scriptures the sole rule of faith, etc."[62] The Convention of 1790 put aside its elaborate provisions as to churches, ministers and a Protestant establishment. By this action it enfranchised Roman Catholics and in set terms provided for religious freedom without distinction or preference.[63]

Georgia, in the Constitution of 1777, provided, "for

[60] Griffin, Am. Cath. Hist. Res., 1911-327.
[61] Cobb, Rise of Rel. Lib. in Am., 505.
[62] Shea, Cath. Ch. in U. S., II-160.
[63] Cobb, Rise of Rel. Lib. in Am., 517.

freedom of conscience but required that all members of the legislature should be of the Protestant religion." [64] A second Convention convened in 1789, which repealed this provision and, "the elective franchise was extended to all male, tax-paying freemen." [65]

[64] *Ibid.*, Rise of Rel. Lib. in Am., 507.
[65] Cath. Ency., Vol. VII.

CHAPTER TEN

The Catholic Population and Influence

A T the beginning of the revolutionary struggle, Catholics were few in numbers and practically devoid of influence. "Yet the thirteen colonies were all Protestant; even in Maryland, the Catholics formed but an eighth or perhaps not more than a twelfth part of the population; their presence in other provinces was hardly perceptible, except in Pennsylvania." [1] By the Declaration of Queen Ann, in 1702, all officials were obliged to take the Test Oath, and local enactments added to the burdens so that Catholics were disfranchised in every colony. [2] Previous to this ruling, Catholics enjoyed civil liberty under the benign rule of Penn, and even after its enforcement, they possessed full religious freedom. Two churches were opened in Philadelphia, St. Joseph's, (1733), and St. Mary's, (1763). [3] By the Act of 1704, in Maryland, "Catholics were not permitted to practise their religion, priests were forbidden to exercise their faculties, Catholic children were not allowed to be educated in the faith, and an open bid

[1] Bancroft, Hist. of U. S., VII-159.
[2] Shea, Cath. Ch. in U. S., I-365.
[3] Kirlin, Cath. in Phil., 34-93.

was made for them to rebel against their parents." [4] Queen Ann refused to sanction this flagrant outrage, and by her directions, Catholic priests were allowed to officiate in private families. Hence arose the custom in colonial days of having a chapel annexed to the house. The Catholic chapels were usually called, "Priests' Mass Houses." [5] Tradition maintains that a Catholic church was established in New York previous to the Revolution, where Father Farmer secretly said Mass and a positive statement of Bishop John Carroll seems to prove that assertion. The edifice perished in the great conflagration of 1776. [6] There were nineteen priests in Maryland and five in Pennsylvania, all formerly members of the suppressed Society of Jesus. From these two centers, missionaries visited Delaware, New Jersey, New York and Virginia. These visits were dangerous, as the Penal Laws and the colonial acts were rigidly enforced. In New England and the Southern colonies priestly visitations were unknown.

Bishop John Carroll in his "Narrative," explains more clearly and fully the condition of Catholics during this period. "As long as the provinces were subject to the British, the Catholic religion had not penetrated into any but Maryland and Pennsylvania. The laws were most vigorous against the exercise of it; a priest was

[4] Russell, Maryland, Land of Sanc., 376.
[5] *Ibid.*, Maryland, Land of Sanc., 378.
[6] Shea, Cath. Ch. in U. S., II-72.

subject to death for only entering their territories. Catholics were subject to vigorous penalties for adhering to the worship which their consciences approved and were not only excluded from every office under the government, but would hardly have been suffered to remain in any of the other provinces if known to profess the faith of Rome. In this situation, few Catholics settled in other states, or if they did, dissembled their religion and either attached themselves to some other, or intermarried with Protestants and suffered their children to be educated in error. Even in Maryland and Pennsylvania, the condition of Catholics was a state of oppression." [7] The Philadelphia historian, Griffin, disagrees with the Bishop's statement in regard to conditions in Penn's colony: "There are no signs of oppression in Pennsylvania as far as historical inquiry can now determine. Catholics had full religious liberty as today; the right to open public chapels distinct from the private residences of the priests and to perform all functions of religion unrestrained by law as today. Any oppression must have been personal such as may yet today be manifested." [8] Perhaps, Bishop Carroll referred to civil rather than religious freedom. Although Penn enfranchised the Catholics, the Test Oaths devised by William and Mary and repeated during the reign of Ann, debarred them from office as they could not sub-

[7] Griffin, Am. Cath. His. Res., 1906-154.
[8] *Ibid.*, Am. Cath. His. Res., 1906-154.

scribe to the blasphemous oaths. Another oppression
was the law passed by the Assembly during the Seven
Years' War disarming Roman Catholics lest their religious sympathies might cause them to aid the French.
"While Romanists were excluded from civil rights, yet
in the private and public exercise of their faith they
possessed in Pennsylvania a larger liberty than in any
other colony.—No law, 'excepted Papists,' from the
category of intending inhabitants, or made the colony
dangerous ground for 'Popish Priest or Jesuit.' " [9]

It is difficult to estimate the Catholic population of
the colonies, although various statistics enable us to
make a fair approximation of their number. "With the
opening of the Revolution, it is estimated that there
were not more than thirteen hundred Romanists between Canada and Florida." [10] These figures are entirely
misleading and are contradicted by contemporary witnesses and writers. In 1756, Bishop Challoner, of the
London district, the spiritual superior of the American
clergy, writing to Rome describes the religious conditions in America: "There are no missions in any of our
colonies upon the continent, excepting Mariland and
Pennsilvania. I have had different accounts as to their
numbers in Mariland, where they are the most numerous. By one account they were about four thousand
communicants; another makes them amount to seven

[9] Cobb, Rise of Rel. Lib. in Am., 444-52.
[10] *Ibid.*, Rise of Rel. Lib. in Am., 451.

thousand; but perhaps the latter might design to include those in Pennsilvania, where I believe there may be two thousand. There are about twelve missionaries in Mariland, and four in Pennsilvania, all of them of the Society. These also assist some few Catholics in Virginia upon the borders of Mariland, and in New Jersey bordering on Pennsilvania. As to the rest, of the provinces on the continent, New England, New York etc. if there be any straggling Catholics, they can have no exercise of their religion, as no priests ever come near them; nor to judge by what appears to be the present disposition of the inhabitants, are ever likely to be admitted amongst them." [11] Writing to the Propaganda the same year, he gives additional information. "There are about twelve missionaries in Mariland and as they say, sixteen thousand Catholics including children; and in Pennsilvania, about six to seven thousand under five missionaries. Some of these also make excursions into the neighboring province of Jersey; and on the other, into that of Virginia and secretly administer the sacraments to the Catholics residing there." [12] Nine years later, Father George Hunter in his report, estimates the Catholic population as ten thousand adult customers or communicants, with as many under age and non-communicants in Maryland, with three thousand adult customers or communicants with as many

[11] Shea, Cath. Ch. in U. S., II-53-54.
[12] Ibid., Cath. Ch. in U. S., II-55.

more under age, and non-communicants in Pennsylvania.[13] In 1785, Rev. John Carroll writing to Cardinal Antonelli gave a relation of the state of religion in the new Republic: "There are in Maryland, about 15,800 Catholics; of these about 9,000 are freemen, adults over twelve years of age; children under that age, about 3,000; and about that number of slaves of all ages, of African origin, called negroes. There are in Pennsylvania, about 7,000, very few of whom are negroes. There are not more than 200 in Virginia, who are visited four or five times a year by a priest.—In the state of New York, I hear, there are at least 1,500.—As to the Catholics who are in the territory bordering on the river called Mississippi,—contains, I hear, many Catholics formerly Canadians, who speak French, and I fear are destitute of priests." [14] Bancroft, speaking of the Revolutionary period states: "America was most thoroughly a Protestant country. The whole number of Catholics within the Thirteen Colonies, as reported by themselves, about the year 1784, was 32,500. The four southern-most states had but 2,500; New England but 600; New York and New Jersey, collectively, about 1,700; Maryland, 12,000, slaves 8,000; Pennsylvania and Delaware, lands of toleration, 7,700. The French Catholics settled between the Western boundary of the states and the Mississippi, were estimated at 12,000 more." [15]

[13] *Ibid.*, Cath. Ch. in U. S., I-449.
[14] *Ibid.*, Cath. Ch. in U. S., II-257-58.
[15] Bancroft, For. of Con., I-224.

These figures are undoubtedly taken from the report of Marbois, the French Minister, in a letter to Vergennes in 1785.[16] The estimate for New England and the Southern states is evidently overestimated although the sum total agrees with the figures of Bishop Carroll. The Catholic population along the Atlantic seaboard did not exceed thirty or thirty five thousand souls and adding the settlers along the Mississippi, and the Catholic Indians was probably less than fifty thousand.

Although fifty thousand people was a negligible quantity in a population of three millions, yet during the colonial period the Catholic Church was regarded "as a constant and threatening foe to colonial institutions. The fact was far otherwise. During the half century in which the Romanists governed Maryland, they were not guilty of a single act of religious oppression."[17] The anti-Catholic spirit never abated but increased from year to year, especially during the struggle between England and France for the possession of the continent. "In the Maryland of the eighteenth century, it was the voice of monstrous ingratitude. In the other colonies, it was so needless as to be ridiculous."[18] On the eve of the Revolution, the same intolerant spirit prevailed. The passage of the Quebec Act, granting the Canadian Catholics the same rights which they had enjoyed under the French regime, and annexing the Illi-

[16] Griffin, Am. Cath. His. Res., 1911-324.
[17] Cobb, Rise of Rel. Lib. in Am., 451.
[18] *Ibid.*, Rise of Rel. Lib. in Am., 451.

nois country to Canada, rekindled all the old flames of
hatred. "The members of Congress had not purged
themselves of Protestant bigotry." [19] The First Continental Congress adopted an address to the people of
Great Britain, condemning Parliament and questioning
its right "to establish a religion fraught with sanguinary
and impious tenets, or to erect an arbitrary form of
government in any part of the world; a Religion that
has deluged your island in blood, and dispersed, Impiety, Bigotry, Persecution, Murder and Rebellion
through every part of the world." [20] These resolutions
were prepared by John Jay of New York and adopted
and distributed by Congress. At the same time, a Memorial to "The inhabitants of the colonies" was issued
condemning the Catholic Canadians as "in favor of
our open and secret enemies, whose intrigues for several
years past, have been wholly exercised in sapping the
foundations of civil and religious liberty." [21] The leading patriots were outspoken against the Quebec Act,
denouncing and ridiculing the Catholic rites. Alexander
Hamilton complained that "their implicit devotion to
their priests and the superstitious reverence they bear
those who countenance or favor their religion will be
ready to second offensive designs against other parts of
the empire." [22] Thomas Paine, in "Crisis No. I," main-

[19] Bancroft, Hist. of U. S., VII-159.
[20] Griffin, Caths. in Am. Rev., I-246.
[21] Ibid., Caths. in Am. Rev., I-250.
[22] Ibid., Caths. in Am. Rev., I-10.

tained "that the aim of Parliament was to subvert the Protestant religion." [23] John Adams feared "if Parliament can do this in Canada, they can do the same in all the other colonies." [24] John Sullivan, the son of an Irish Catholic and grandson of a defender of Limerick, who had deserted his religion, denounced the faith of his ancestors as "a cursed religion so dangerous to the state and favorable to despotism." [25] John Jay's attitude is clearly indicated in the address to the people of Great Britain. The pulpit, the bar, the newspapers, the magazines, inveighed against the King and Parliament for passing and enforcing "this iniquitous Act," although their fellow Catholics had been oppressed in every colony except Pennsylvania by the English Penal Laws. To grant justice to the people of Quebec, overwhelmingly Catholic, was a sacrilege against the Protestant religion, yet, it was "a very judicious measure of religious toleration, which concerned the other colonies but little, however, it might in some cases offend their prejudices." [26]

The Catholic religion and its tenets were likewise publicly exposed to ridicule and sarcasm in many places. "As late as 1774, the Pope in effigy, had been paraded with the Devil through the streets of not only New England towns but even in Charleston and burned in

[23] *Ibid.*, Caths. in Am. Rev., I-10.
[24] *Ibid.*, Caths. in Am. Rev., I-8.
[25] *Ibid.*, Caths. in Am. Rev., I-242.
[26] Fiske, Am. Rev., I-115.

presence of a numerous crowd of people." [27] In some localities, two rival popes were exhibited, the partizans of each engaging in bloody encounters and riotous scenes. In New York, the friends of freedom assembled at the Liberty Pole, bearing a banner with the inscription, "George III, Rex, and the liberties of America. No Popery." On the reverse side, "Union of Colonies, The Measures of Congress." [28] When the American army was besieging Boston, Washington was obliged to issue a special order, forbidding "the observance of that ridiculous and childish notion of burning the effigy of the Pope," and "expressing his surprise that there should be officers and men in his army so void of common sense as not to see the impropriety of such a step." [29] The American forces had invaded Canada, St. John's and Montreal had fallen, and Montgomery was marching on Quebec to unite with Arnold who was traversing the wilderness of Maine. It was indeed most impolitic to insult the religion of those to whom "we are so much indebted for every late, happy success over the common enemy in Canada." [30]

The unjust laws which disgraced the statute books of the colonies were only partially repealed during the war years. "It was virtually only in Pennsylvania, Delaware, Maryland and Virginia that the Penal Laws against

[27] Shea, Cath. Ch. in U. S., II-148.
[28] Griffin, Caths. in Am. Rev., I-26.
[29] Ibid., Caths. in Am. Rev., I-129.
[30] Griffin, Caths. in Am. Rev., I-129.

Catholics were entirely swept away and the professors
of the ancient faith admitted to the rights of citizenship, although Connecticut and Georgia placed no apparent restriction on their freedom. Rhode Island repealed the clause denying toleration to Catholics, and
Connecticut had no express enactment, although a prior
law established Congregationalism." [31] Various re-
straints in regard to civil and religious liberty for all
sects and classes were adopted by different states. New
Hampshire, New Jersey, Connecticut, the two Carolinas and Georgia insisted on Protestantism. New
Hampshire, Massachusetts, Connecticut, Maryland and
South Carolina adhered to an established religion. Pennsylvania, Delaware, and the Carolinas demanded faith
in the divine inspiration of the Bible. Delaware and
Maryland insisted on belief in the Christian religion.
Pennsylvania and South Carolina demanded faith in one
eternal God and the existence of Heaven and Hell.
Delaware in the Holy Trinity, Rhode Island and Virginia imposed no restrictions.[32] Many circumstances
tended to modify or obliterate the traditional opposition
to Catholicity. The embassy to Canada, with Charles
Carroll of Carrollton as a commissioner and his cousin
Rev. John Carroll as assistant, the alliance with France,
bringing thousands of sailors and soldiers to our
shores, at least nominally Catholics, with their chap-

[31] Shea, Cath. Ch. in U. S., II-160-1.
[32] Cobb, Rise of Rel. Lib. in Am., 507.

lains, and the gallant conduct of the colonial Catholics contributed to this happy change. Catholics were guided by the motto of their great leader, Charles Carroll of Carrollton, "We remember and we forgive." [33] Their loyalty and patriotism may be aptly and fittingly summed up in the words of Bishop John Carroll: "Their blood flowed as freely, in proportion to their numbers, to cement the fabric of independence as that of their fellow citizens. They concurred with perhaps greater unanimity than any other body of men in recommending and promoting that government from whose influence America anticipates all the blessings of justice, peace, plenty, good order, and civil and religious liberty." [34]

[33] Russell, Maryland, Land of Sanc., 512.
[34] O'Gorman, Cath. Ch. in U. S., 255.

CHAPTER ELEVEN

Catholic Revolutionary Heroes

MARYLAND was founded under Catholic auspices, with civil and religious toleration for all sects. Catholics and Protestants were among the first settlers, "and regardless of religious belief, all were allowed the franchise as soon as they became freemen." [1] The persecuted of every clime found peace in this modern Utopia. "From France came Huguenots; from Germany, from Holland, from Sweden, from Finland, I believe from Piedmont, the children of misfortune sought protection under the tolerant sceptre of the Roman Catholic. Bohemia itself sent forth its sons who at once were made citizens of Maryland with equal franchises.[2] From the other colonies came Protestants to escape religious persecution. Virginia expelled all non-conformists, and many Puritans accepted the invitation of the Catholic Proprietor. Episcopalians, driven from New England, received shelter in this Catholic haven. "And religious liberty obtained a home, its only home in the wide world at the humble village which bore the name of St.

[1] Russell, Maryland, Land of Sanc., 30.
[2] Bancroft, Hist. of U. S., II-236-37.

Mary's." [3] The Assembly of 1649 had framed the famous Act of Toleration, securing to all men equal freedom. Yet when Cromwell and the Parliament triumphed, these ungrateful exiles, deposed the legitimate officials, disfranchised Catholics and Episcopalians and drove the Catholic priests from the province. The fall of James II and the accession of William and Mary brought additional persecution to the founders of the colony. Episcopalianism was made the established religion, Catholics were disfranchised and doubly taxed, freedom of worship was denied them and Catholic children were debarred from education. [4] For almost a century, Catholics were persecuted and only the dawn of the new era, and the appeal to arms, relieved them of their disabilities.

When the acts of oppression aroused the spirit of the colonists, and the call to arms sounded, "the patriots of Maryland—hastened to bury all private animosities, all local differences, all religious disputes, all memory of past persecution; to equalize all rights, and in the name of God, their country and posterity, to unite in the defence of the common rights and liberties." [5]

Charles Carroll of Carrollton, the popular champion, leader of the Catholics, was chosen delegate to the Convention of 1774 by a Protestant constituency. [6] From

[3] *Ibid.*, Hist. of U. S., I-247.
[4] Russell, Maryland, Land of Sanc., 33.
[5] Ms Sherry, Hist. of Maryland, 180.
[6] *Ibid.*, Hist. of Maryland, 180.

the beginning of the agitation, he favored independence and frowned on compromise. "No argument but bayonets will settle the dispute" was his answer to that sterling patriot, Samuel Adams of Massachusetts.[7] His coreligionists were equally loyal. The discriminations and persecutions of a century were forgiven, all vindictiveness suppressed in the desire for freedom. The achievements of the Carrolls,—Charles, Daniel and John,— overshadowed the deeds of the lesser heroes yet their loyalty is unquestioned. "The Catholics of Maryland, both clergy and laity, warmly espoused the patriotic cause. On the roster of the Maryland Line are found the names of representatives of the Catholic families of Maryland."[8] The Rev. Jonathan Boucher, Episcopalian and Loyalist, furnishes some valuable information on that score: "At length a Catholic gentleman espoused the cause of Congress. Soon after he became a member of that body.—Under so respectable a leader as Mr. Carroll, they all became good whigs and concurred with their fellow revolutionists in declaiming against the mismanagement of Great Britain."[9] A British captain, who had served in the war gives additional testimony; "By far the greatest number of Roman Catholics are on the Western shore, and what is more surprising it was also the most violently rebellious and disaffected."[10]

[7] Murray, Cath. Pio. of Am., 363.
[8] Cath. Ency., Vol. IX.
[9] Russell, Maryland, Land of Sanc., 487.
[10] Griffin, Am. Cath. Hist. Res., 1910-222.

The enlistment rolls make no reference to the religion of the recruits yet it is evident that the old Catholic families of the province were represented in the State Line. "Maryland contributed Neales, Bearmans, Brents, Semmes, Mattinglys, Brookes and Kiltys. The rank and file contained numbers of Catholics." [11] Among the Catholic officers listed are Lieutenant William Clarke, whose ancestors came to Maryland with the Jesuits in 1638 and represented them in the Assembly. He fought at the battles of Long Island, Brandywine and Germantown and his regiment participated in the Southern campaigns, winning renown at Camden. Among the other Catholic officers who fought in the Maryland Line during the struggle for freedom, were Captain Henry Neale, and Lieutenants James and Ignatius Semmes who followed the fortunes of Washington until the triumph at Yorktown. "Among the Catholics of Maryland who served in the war were George Digges, Edward Dyer, John Boone, Walter Dyer, James Winchester, John Lowe, Hezekiah Ford, John Hamilton, Josua Miles, John Lynch, Joseph Ford, Alexander Magruder, John Hawkins Lowe, John Brooke, Edward Mattingly, William Scarff." [12] Irish immigration to Maryland had been steady even in the early days of the colony, and these exiles remained faithful to their religion through the ministrations and zeal of the Jesuit

[11] Shea, Cath. Ch. in U. S., II-153.
[12] Griffin, Am. Cath. Hist. Res., 1908-341.

fathers. "The numerous Irish names that appear in Maryland records justify the conclusion that the Irish were a strong element among Maryland Catholics." [13] "They were especially numerous on the western shore, where the most violently rebellious and disaffected were found." [14] The Catholic population was small, due to Puritan and Anglican persecution. In 1708, they numbered 2974 in a population of over 40,000; at the close of the Revolution, 16,000.[15] Yet in proportion to their numbers, they contributed as generously to the cause of freedom as their more numerous Protestant brethren.

The most prominent figure among the Maryland patriots was the illustrious Charles Carroll of Carrollton, whose grandfather came from Ireland during the reign of James II, (1688), and became agent for the Lord Proprietor. His father was a large landowner, a lawyer, and one of the founders of the city of Baltimore. The third Charles, who added to his name, "of Carrollton" in 1756, was educated at Bohemia, the Jesuit School at St. Omer's, the College of Louis Le Grand at Paris and in the Law Schools of Bruges, and the Inner Temple, London. On his return to his native colony, he found the settlers in revolt against the tyrannical laws framed by the British Parliament. Daniel Dulany, "the Pitt of Maryland," had deserted the popular cause and supported the royal authority and enactments. In a mas-

[13] O'Brien, Hid. Pha. Am. Hist., 262.
[14] Griffin, Am. Cath. His. Res., 1910-222.
[15] Shea, Cath. Ch. in U. S., II-257.

terly series of letters, Carroll completely vanquished his
doughty opponent. "Jesuit," "Nursling of St. Omer's,"
"Unable to offer his puny vote," were some of the in-
sults hurled at him during the controversy. Although
disfranchised on account of his religion, and debarred
from holding office, his loyalty to the cause of independence won him the title, "First Citizen." He was
chosen to serve in the Convention and assigned to the
committee which restored the old Catholic principles
of religious liberty. With Chase and Franklin, he was
appointed to solicit an alliance with Canada or secure
its neutrality. The mission was unsuccessful, owing to
the loyalty of the Canadian clergy, the weakness and
conduct of the invaders, the antipathy of the patriots
to the Quebec Act and the loyalty of Bishop Briand.
On his return he was chosen to the Continental Congress, and by his influence and example induced the
state legislature to favor complete independence and to
instruct its delegates to Congress to support the Declaration. He signed the Declaration of Independence,
cheerfully jeopardizing his life and his fortune for the
patriot cause. During the dark days following the disasters on Long Island, the occupation of Philadelphia, the
gloomy winters at Valley Forge and Whitemarsh, the
intrigues of the "Conway Cabal," the events leading to
the French alliance, the financial troubles, the charter-
ing of the Bank of North America, he was most devoted
to Washington, most assiduous in aiding the struggling

Continentals. "Charles Carroll of Carrollton easily ranks next to Washington in the value of the services rendered the patriotic cause in our revolutionary struggle. He devoted more of his time and more of his money to the cause of the people than any other patriot. He spent more time with Washington at army headquarters than any other civilian and was more closely identified with the purposes, impulses and activities of the great commander than any man, in or out of the army. He served the people in more different positions of responsibility and usefulness than did any other man, and never failed, in a single instance to measure up to the highest standard of statesmanship and patriotism.—He was the richest man that signed the Declaration of Independence, the first man that signed, the only Roman Catholic that signed, and the last man to die of those who signed it." [16] His ideals were God and Country; "to obtain religious as well as civil liberty, I entered zealously into the revolution." [17] His patriotic efforts were crowned with success. Maryland gratefully revived the ancient heritage granted by Lord Baltimore and his worthy successors in the Act of Toleration.

The Rev. John Carroll and his brother Daniel ably seconded the efforts of their illustrious cousin. John Carroll studied at Bohemia, and St. Omer's, entered the Society of Jesus and was ordained to the holy priest-

[16] Leonard, Chas. Carroll of Carr., 17-18.
[17] *Ibid.*, Chas. Carroll of Carr., 253.

hood. After the suppression of the Society, he labored in England; but when the crisis between the colonists and the home government became acute, he realized his country needed his services and returned to Maryland in 1774. He accompanied the Embassy to Canada at the request of Congress; "his religious sentiments, character, and knowledge of the French language, his presence and counsel, might be useful in promoting the object of the mission with the Canadians." [18] The mission was a failure not from want of ability or zeal on the part of the members, but owing to Canadian loyalty and colonial intolerance. Father Carroll returned to his ministry, serving his little flock in Maryland and making excursions into Virginia. During the years of warfare, his voice and pen defended and expounded the purposes and principles of the patriots and inspired the dispirited Continentals to bring the conflict to a successful conclusion. His brother, Daniel, was also an ardent patriot, only excelled by his cousin, Charles. He was foremost in every movement, recruiting troops, furnishing supplies, guarding the extensive sea-board from hostile attack. He served four years in the Continental Congress, an honored member of the various committees of his native state. Church and Country rewarded the devotion and loyalty of this patriotic trio. Rev. John Carroll became the first Bishop and Archbishop of the Church in the new republic, Charles Carroll of Carroll-

[18] Murray, Cath. Pio. of Am., 348.

ton was the first United States Senator from Maryland, Daniel Carroll served as a delegate to the Constitutional Convention of 1787 and represented his native state for four years in the first and second Federal Congress.

Penn, in his "Great Law," ordained: "All persons living in this province shall in no way be molested or prejudiced in their religious persuasion or practise or in matters of faith or worship." [19] Although Penn did not admire or approve certain Catholic doctrines and practises, his true charity would not permit him to exclude Catholics from these privileges, as Catholics and Quakers alike had endured religious persecution in England and her colonies.[20] Catholics enjoyed both civil and religious freedom as "under this early constitution, a Romanist could both vote and hold office." [21] The same toleration had been granted in this region by Sir Edward Plowden to whom Charles I had granted all the lands embracing Delaware, Maryland, New Jersey and Pennsylvania under the name, New Albion.[22] Under William and Mary, the English Test Oaths were required for all officials and the reign of Queen Ann repeated these hardships. All Catholics were debarred from office as these oaths abjured the Mass, Transubstantiation, and devotion to the Blessed Virgin and the

[19] Kirlin, Cath. in Phil., 10.
[20] Ibid., Cath. in Phil., 11.
[21] Cobb, Rise of Rel. Lib. in Am., 444.
[22] Griffin, Am. Cath. Hist. Res., 1888-165-6.

Saints.[23] However, Catholics always enjoyed full religious freedom. Jesuit missionaries from Maryland visited Philadelphia and the outlying districts until 1720, when Father Greaton was placed in permanent charge of the Pennsylvania faithful. When the boundary dispute with Maryland was adjudicated, St. Joseph's Church in Willing's Alley was opened and chapels at Gosshenhoppen, Lancaster and Reading. The congregation of St. Joseph's increased so rapidly that a new church, St. Mary's, was erected in 1763.[24] The pre-revolutionary Catholic population numbered about seven thousand souls with five priests ministering to their wants and making frequent visits to New Jersey, New York and the scattered individuals in other parts of the colony.[25]

As the Pennsylvania Catholics enjoyed full religious freedom, their grievances against Britain were civil rather than religious. Consequently all were not patriots nor were all Tories. "Of the Catholics as a body, it cannot be said that they supported either side. Individuals followed their personal judgment in the matter, for the Catholic Church does not influence the political sentiments of her members." [26] These Catholics were mainly of German or Irish birth or extraction. "In 1750, the German settlers in Pennsylvania were estimated

[23] Cobb, Rise of Rel. Lib. in Am., 445.
[24] Kirlin, Cath. in Phil., 26.
[25] Shea, Cath. Ch. in U. S., II-257 ff.
[26] Kirlin, Cath. in Phil., 100.

at ninety thousand out of a total population of two hundred and seventy thousand and in 1790, at one hundred forty-four thousand." [27] Irish settlers accompanied Penn in 1682, and after the beginning of the eighteenth century, came each year in increasing numbers, settling in the Cumberland Valley and west of the Susquehanna River. Many of these who came from Ulster, were either Episcopalians or Presbyterians, driven from home by economic or religious conditions. Others, who came from the south or the west of Ireland were Catholics, bearing the names of ancient Catholic septs. [28] The little band of devoted Jesuits gathered them into congregations and preserved their faith although some who penetrated to the western wilderness, deprived of church and priest, surrounded by hostile sects, intermarried outside the faith and their children were lost to the church. "Despite all laws, Pennsylvania became of all the colonies, the most favorable and the safest field for the priests and missionaries of the church of Rome.—Before the Revolution, Pennsylvania harbored five Catholic churches with about double the number of priests and several thousand communicants mostly Irish or Germans." [29] The report of Father Farmer to Earl Louden shows that the Germans outnumbered their Irish brethren. [30] A comparison of the baptismal and

[27] Baumgartner, Germans in U. S. Wars, 30.
[28] O'Brien, Hid. Ph. of Am. Hist., 253 ff.
[29] Winsor, Hist. of Am., V-191.
[30] Kirlin, Cath. in Phil., 82-3.

marriage records with the enlistment rolls, and a scrutiny of the names of the officers who served in the Continental army prove that the greater part of these German and Irish Catholics were loyal to the patriotic cause. "When the revolution broke out the comparatively small body of Catholics furnished a number of men who attained distinction, in the military, naval and political service." [31]

Although the military records give no clue to the religious status of the enlisted men, the names of many Catholics are enscribed on the honor roll of the colony. The most illustrious name is that of John Barry, the Wexford Irishman, popularly known to late generations as "Commodore" Barry, although this rank was unknown in the Continental navy. "In Dec. 7th, 1775, he was appointed to command the Lexington, by the marine committee of the Continental Congress. The first Catholic, the first officer appointed to the first vessel purchased, named after the place of the first battle, made the first capture of a British vessel which was brought to Philadelphia as a prize." [32] After the disaster on Long Island, and the retreat through New Jersey, Captain Barry recruited a company of volunteers, aided in transporting the American army across the Delaware, and fought at Trenton and Princeton. When the British occupied Philadelphia and his fleet was useless, he

[31] Cath. Ency., Vol. XI.
[32] Griffin, John Barry, 24-5.

organized a light flotilla, annoying the enemy shipping, and capturing supplies which were sent to the starving troops at Valley Forge. Appointed to command the *Alliance,* the finest vessel of the infant navy, he carried Colonel John Laurens to France as a special commissioner. On the outgoing voyage he captured two British frigates, the *Atlanta* and the *Trepassy,* and on the return trip won another double victory, capturing the *Mars* and the *Minerva.* At various times he commanded the *Effingham,* the *Raleigh,* the *America.* In March 1783, he sailed from Havana in the *Alliance* with the French vessel, *Duc de Luzon,* as consort, carrying seventy-two thousand dollars of public money consigned to Robert Morris, Superintendent of Finance. Three British frigates pursued and attacked him and in a bloody engagement, he captured the *Sybil.* He won the first and last naval battles of the Revolution, sailed the best ships of the navy, and at the close of hostilities, commanded the entire navy of the colonies.[33] He is justly styled, "The Father of the American Navy" not only on account of his revolutionary services, but especially as Washington named him Captain Number One on the organization of the Federal Navy and under him were trained, Stewart, Dale and Jacob Jones naval heroes of the second war with England.[34] He superintended the construction of the frigate, *United*

[33] *Ibid.,* Am. Cath. His. Res., 1907-129.
[34] *Ibid.,* Am. Cath. His. Res., 1907-155.

States, and following the threatened war with France carried the American envoys to France and commanded the American fleet. He died in 1803 and was interred in St. Mary's Catholic cemetery in Philadelphia.

The leading Catholic soldier was Stephen Moylan, a native of Cork, Ireland, educated in France, who came to Philadelphia in 1768. His family was well represented in the clergy of Ireland, his brother Francis being consecrated Bishop of Cork in 1785. He joined Washington's army at Cambridge and was commissioned Muster Master.[35] In coöperation with Colonel John Glover of Marblehead, he fitted out some armed vessels to intercept British supply ships, capturing arms, ammunition, cannon, clothing and food which was sent to the American army. In 1776, he was named Secretary and Aide-de-Camp to Washington and selected by Congress as Quartermaster General. When New York was threatened by the enemy, he was sent to obstruct the harbor and delay the British fleet. During the battles on Long Island, and the subsequent retreat through the Jerseys, his heroic conduct won the praise of his chieftain. In January 1777, he was commissioned to recruit a light horse regiment famed as "Moylan's Dragoons." At Brandywine and Germantown his troops fought bravely and in the following year after the resignation of Count Pulaski, he became Commander-in-chief of the Continental cavalry.[36] At Yorktown, the Fourth

[35] *Ibid.,* Stephen Moylan, 9.
[36] *Ibid.,* Stephen Moylan, 65.

Pennsylvania Regiment under Colonel Moylan was assigned to the right division, an honorable and dangerous position.[37] Ordered south to assist General Greene, he was detained by ill-health and the expedition was disbanded. "On November third 1783, Congress resolved that Colonel Stephen Moylan be promoted to the rank of Brigadier by brevet.[38] After the organization of the Federal government, he was appointed Commissioner of Loans and Major General of the State militia. He was a member of the Society of the Cincinnati, and the first President of the Friendly Sons of St. Patrick.[39] He died in 1811, and was interred in St. Mary's Cemetery.

His brother, James Moylan, resided in Philadelphia, but went to France before the outbreak of hostilities. He was helpful to the American cause as commercial agent at L'Orient and acted as prize agent for the American privateers. He fitted out the *Ranger* for John Paul Jones and the *Alliance* for Captains Barry and Landais, and secured the *Duras* from the French authorities, which he named the *Bonne Homme Richard*, which won undying fame for Jones at the battle off the mouth of the Humber River.[40] Another brother, John Moylan, came from Cadiz and entering the army, was commissioned Clothier-General. The scarcity of supplies, the depreciation of the Continental currency, and the

[37] *Ibid.*, Stephen Moylan, 121.
[38] *Ibid.*, Stephen Moylan, 131.
[39] *Ibid.*, Stephen Moylan, 7.
[40] *Ibid.*, Stephen Moylan, 140-41.

lack of "hard money," made his position most difficult yet he won the praise of Washington for his efficiency.[41] His half-brother, Jasper Moylan, came to Philadelphia from Spain, and immediately took the oath of allegiance to the colony. He became an ensign in the colonial militia, and after the war resided in Philadelphia.[42]

Thomas FitzSimons, another Irish Catholic, was a prominent patriot in Pennsylvania in revolutionary days. Among the delegates at Carpenter's hall urging the Assembly to send representatives to the first Continental Congress he was an inspiring figure. In the same year he was selected as a provincial deputy, the first Catholic chosen to office in the province. He was commissioned Captain of the State Militia, serving three months in New Jersey resisting the Tories and defending the approaches to Staten Island. During the closing months of 1776, when Washington was almost at the end of his resources Captain FitzSimons and his company joined the patriotic forces. Although unable to reach Trenton on account of the swollen river, he participated in the battle of Princeton. During the financial crisis of 1780, the Bank of Pennsylvania was chartered to supply the army with food and clothing, the merchants of Philadelphia subscribing three hundred and fifteen thousand pounds, FitzSimons and his partner, George Meade, contributing two thousand pounds.

[41] *Ibid.*, Cath. Am. Hist. Res., 1888-2-27.
[42] Haltigan, Irish in Am. Rev., 184-5.

In 1782, he was elected to the Congress of the Confederacy, in 1787, a delegate to the Convention which framed the Constitution. He represented his native state in the Federal Congress for three terms, advocating a protective tariff. He was a Trustee of the College of Philadelphia, a Director of the Bank of North America, a member of the Friendly Sons of St. Patrick. He died in 1811 and was buried in St. Mary's Cemetery. George Meade, his business associate, was the son of a Limerick Irishman, active in every patriotic movement, a soldier of the Third Battalion of ASSOCIATORS, and a member of committees to recruit and equip the troops. His firm contributed two thousand pounds to found the Bank of Pennsylvania. He died in 1808 and was interred in St. Mary's Cemetery. General George Meade and Commodore Meade were his grandsons.

Among the lesser heroes, we find men of every nationality. Sergeant Andrew Wallace a Scotch Catholic, hero of Culloden, and a staunch partizan of the Stuart cause, came to Pennsylvania, and served in the French and Indian war. He enlisted in the Continental army, accompanied the expedition to Canada, and participated in the battles of Brandywine, Germantown and Monmouth. He was one of the survivors of the massacre of Paoli, where his brother was killed. Although captured by the British he was released in time to share in Wayne's desperate storming of Stony Point. He joined the southern expedition, fighting at Camden, Cowpens and Eutaw Springs, completing his brave deeds at Yorktown. After the Treaty of 1783, he again enlisted in the army, participating in St. Clair's defeat and Wayne's victory, serving continuously until 1811 when he was mustered out of the service for disability, being eighty years of age.[43]

Anthony Selin, a Swiss enlisted in 1776, served at Brandywine and Germantown and survived the dreadful winter at Valley Forge. He became a member of the Cincinnati, and founded the town of Selin's Grove.[44] Colonel Morgan Connor, enlisted in 1775, serving with gallantry in the southern department until incapacitated by ill-health.[45] Major Michael Ryan served under Colonel Wayne so gallantly that Washington presented him with a testimonial and made him Inspector General of the state militia.[46] Captain Thomas Doyle, of the Sixth Pennsylvania Regiment, fought under Wayne at Brandywine and Germantown, and took part in the siege and capture of Yorktown.[47] Major John Doyle, his brother, organized a military company after the adoption of the Declaration of Independence, joined Wayne's regiment, fought at Brandywine and Germantown and was seriously wounded during the western campaign.[48] Colonel John

[43] Griffin, Caths. in Am. Rev., II-185.
[44] Ibid., Caths. in Am. Rev., II-197.
[45] Ibid., Caths. in Am. Rev., I-132.
[46] Ibid., Caths. in Am. Rev., II-193.
[47] Ibid., Caths. in Am. Rev., II-206.
[48] Ibid., Caths. in Am. Rev., II-208.

Moore, a Dublin Irishman, was active in the patriotic movements around Lancaster in the early days of the struggle, was commissioned Major in Colonel Lewis' regiment, was promoted for gallantry, and given the rank of Colonel. In Federal days he was elected to Congress, and was well known in political circles.[49] Emanuel Holmes, a Portuguese "who loved liberty," was a member of the Rifle Company of Philadelphia. He died in 1776 and was interred in St. Mary's Cemetery with every mark of respect for his sterling patriotism.[50] Dr. Joseph Cauffman, an eminent physician, was assigned to the frigate, *Randolf,* and lost his life during an engagement.[51] Paul and Rudolf Essling served in the German regiment and the Second Artillery.

Nine of the colonies maintained navies which did much damage to British shipping and brought needed supplies to the Continental army. Among the Philadelphia merchants who equipped these vessels were the following Catholics: James Oellers, John and Thomas Flahavan, George Meade and Company, Thomas Fitz-Simons and Company, George Meade and Thomas FitzSimons. Among the Catholic Captains of Volunteers were the following Catholics: Roger Keane, John Walsh, William Keeler, John Baxter, John Rodman and John Kelly. All were pew holders in St. Mary's church

[49] *Ibid.,* Caths. in Am. Rev., II-207.
[50] *Ibid.,* Am. Cath. Hist. Res., 1907-354.
[51] *Ibid.,* Caths. in Am. Rev., II-215.

and most of them were buried in the cemetery.[52] This list gives only the printed records of Catholics who served in the army or navy, but it is a fair indication of Catholic loyalty and a proof that in proportion to their numbers they supplied their quota of enlistments.

In the other colonies, Catholics were few and the intolerant laws led some to conceal their religious belief or to affiliate with the Protestant sects. Yet the names of some are known proving that the members of the Old Religion were loyal to their adopted country. When hostilities began, there were nine Catholics in Alexandria, and all enlisted in the service of the patriots. The names of three are known: John Fitzgerald, Clement Sewall and John Byrne. Colonel Fitzgerald was a native of Wicklow, Ireland, who came to Virginia in 1769 or 1770, joined the army at Cambridge, and was appointed Aide-de-Camp and secretary to Washington. He accompanied his chief in all campaigns until the surrender at Yorktown, discovered the plans of the "Conway Cabal" to place Gates or Lee at the head of the Continental army, and apprised the Commander of the danger. After the war, he was the friend and business associate of the great warrior. Thomas Burke, an Irishman, was one of the framers of the North Carolina Constitution of 1776, and a member of the Continental Congress from 1776 to 1780. He enlisted in the local militia and fought bravely at Brandywine. He was

[52] *Ibid.*, Am. Cath. Hist. Res., 1908-1-16.

chosen first governor of North Carolina in 1781. In the fall of that year, he was surprised and captured by the British but escaped. The cruel treatment of his captors had undermined his health and he died in his thirty-third year.[53] His cousin or near relative, Aedanus Burke, a native of Galway, had studied for the priesthood at St. Omer's but left the school and came to South Carolina shortly before the outbreak of the Revolution. He enlisted as a private, was promoted to be Major for his gallant conduct on the field, and in 1778, was chosen Judge of the Supreme Court. After the disasters at Charlestcn and Savannah, he rejoined the army serving until the surrender at Yorktown. He returned to the bench, "long filling with justice and mercy that highly respectable office." He represented his district in the first Federal Congress, served in the legislature of his state and was elected Chancellor.[54] Patrick Colvin, the patriotic boatman of Trenton, was a member of St. Mary's congregation in Philadelphia. During Washington's retreat through the Jerseys, toward the close of 1776, he ferried the weary Continentals across the Delaware. He was prepared to carry Ewing's men to Trenton but the failure of several detachments to arrive prevented a junction with Washington. A few days later, he brought reinforcements, the enemy was defeated and the victory at Princeton achieved. When

[53] Haltigan, Irish in Am. Rev., 275.
[54] *Ibid.*, Irish in Am. Rev., 81.

Washington was chosen President of the new Republic and was making his triumphal march to the capital, New York, for his inauguration, the old hero once more manned the boats and ferried the party across the Delaware.[55] Timothy Murphy, a New York patriot, although enlisted in the Pennsylvania Riflemen, is another stirring figure in Revolutionary annals. He joined the American army besieging Boston, fought with Daniel Morgan at Stillwater and Saratoga, and is reputed to have shot General Fraser, thus bringing confusion into the British ranks. He accompanied Sullivan in the expedition to punish the Indian tribes for the massacre of Wyoming and Cherry Valley, narrowly escaping death on several occasions. Stories of his courage and coolness as an Indian fighter and his remarkable aptitude with the rifle are told in the literature of the period. He escaped every peril and died an honored and respected resident of Schoharie County in 1818.[56]

[55] Griffin, Caths. in Am. Rev., III-329.
[56] Ibid., Caths. in Am. Rev., III-369.

CHAPTER TWELVE

The Mississippi and the Penobscot

IN the charters granted by Great Britain to the colonies during the seventeenth century, the western boundaries stretched from ocean to ocean, as the mythical South Sea was supposed to be not far distant from the Atlantic sea-board, and the crown officials were ignorant of the vast extent of territory included in the grants. The first colonists settled along the coast, only hunters and trappers penetrating to the western lands. France based its claim to sovereignty over the Mississippi Valley on the discoveries and explorations of Marquette, La Salle, Joliet and other daring voyagers and founded many trading posts and feeble villages along the great waterway. At the close of the French and Indian War, the Treaty of Paris (1763) transferred Canada and all that portion of Louisiana between the Alleghanies and the Mississippi Valley to Great Britain.[1] The acquisition of this great tract brought increased responsibilities and raised issues which contributed to the revolt of the colonies. Its conquest and defense required large expenditures of money, and the colonists were heavily taxed

[1] Winsor, Hist. of Am., VI-685.

to meet the expenses. The passage of the Quebec Act, granting religious freedom to the Canadian Catholics and extending the boundaries of the province north of the Ohio River and westward to the Mississippi, gave great offence to the Protestant colonies.[2] It was a violation of colonial rights, it impeded the expansion of the eastern settlements, it encouraged Papacy. Various colonies claimed these lands; "Massachusetts and Connecticut claimed strips extending through the Northwest and over them like blankets extended New York's claims, based on her protectorate over the Iroquois domain, and Virginia's stronger claim based on her early charter." [3] During the revolutionary struggle, these states continued to assert their claims to this territory on the basis of their old colonial charters.

As the French-Canadian settlers scattered through the feeble villages constituted the bulk of the population, England was anxious to win their allegiance and granted them the same religious privileges they had enjoyed under the old French regime. To further conciliate them, General Gage applied to Father Harding of Philadelphia, requesting him to send a priest to them, as Father Meurin alone remained in the Illinois country after the expulsion of his Jesuit brethren. The Penal Laws were still in force in England and many of the colonies, so this demand seems to have been a political

[2] Van Tyne, Am. Rev., 270.
[3] *Ibid.*, Am. Rev., 287.

move to increase the loyalty of the French settlers.[4] Several years elapsed before the request was granted, but in 1768, Bishop Briand of Quebec assigned Father Pierre Gibault, just ordained, to assist Father Meurin.

Although the colonies failed to occupy these regions granted by their charters, England, recognizing the importance of these positions, garrisoned and fortified the old French forts at Detroit, Cahokia, Kaskaskia and Vincennes. Pioneers from Virginia and the Carolinas had penetrated the wilds of Kentucky and established flourishing villages. At the outset of the revolution these settlers suffered from Indian invasions, encouraged if not planned and abetted by Governor Henry Hamilton of Detroit, who was most successful in making alliances with the savage tribes. Among those who fought against these native hordes was a young Virginian, George Rogers Clark, who conceived the plan of attacking the Illinois country as the best protection from the forays of the Anglo-Indian marauders. He communicated his plans to Patrick Henry, then Governor of Virginia, and to Thomas Jefferson, and through their influence he was commissioned Lieutenant-Colonel, granted permission to enlist soldiers and provided with twelve hundred pounds of Continental money. Sailing down the Ohio to the mouth of the Tennessee with four companies of troops to invest Kaskaskia, he heard the news of the French alliance and realized it would

[4] Griffin, Am. Cath. His. Res., 1909-268.

rally the French settlers to the standard of freedom. Scouts had reported that the inhabitants were not interested in the conflict between England and the colonies but feared the Virginian heroes who had inflicted such defeats on the Indian invaders.[5] Encouraged by these rumors, he marched secretly and speedily surprised the garrison at midnight and took possession of the town.

The inhabitants were momentarily alarmed, but Clark's humane and liberal treatment soon won their hearts. "They were told of the Treaty of Alliance with France and that if he could have surety of their attachment to the American cause, they could enjoy all the privileges of its government and their property would be secured to them." [6] The parish priest, Father Gibault, who understood the disputes between England and the colonies, aided in the transfer of their allegiance. Clark assured him "he had nothing to do with churches more than to defend them from insult. That by the laws of the state, his religion had as great privileges as any other." [7] The enthusiastic people took the oath of allegiance, raised the American flag, recruited a company of volunteers,[8] and took possession of Cahokia, sixty miles distant, where the settlers swore fealty to

[5] Lodge, Am. Rev., 331.
[6] Winsor, Hist. of Am., VI-722.
[7] Shea, Cath. Ch. in U. S., II-187.
[8] Van Tyne, Am. Rev., 282.

the new government.[9] Clark now proposed to attack Vincennes, two hundred miles from Kaskaskia, as his presence was known to the enemy, and surprise was impossible. The friendship of Father Gibault relieved his anxiety, as in company with Dr. La Font the local physician and several influential parishioners he set out on the long and dangerous journey through a wilderness teeming with hostile Indians bearing a proclamation from Clark. His mission was successful, the people of Vincennes took the oath of allegiance and raised the American flag.[10] The effect on the Indian tribes was great. Seeing the French and the missionary accepted the friendship of the Virginians, the Kaskaskias, Peorias, and Michiganeas proposed peace, and when Clark sent a messenger to the Kickapoos and Piankeshaws near Vincennes, they also agreed to lay down their arms.[11]

The news of Clark's success reached General Hamilton at Detroit, so collecting an army of British and Indians he appeared before Vincennes, overwhelmed the feeble garrison and took possession of the village. This catastrophe did not discourage the American commander, who prepared to attack the fort and recover the settlement. Colonel Francis Vigo, a patriotic Italian and a devoted Catholic, who had served in the Spanish army, was sent as a spy to Vincennes. "He was captured by the Indians and taken before Hamilton, who sus-

[9] Winsor, Hist. of Am., VI-722.
[10] Shea, Cath. Ch. in U. S., II-188.
[11] Ibid., Cath. Ch. in U. S., II-188.

pected the character of his mission, but he was released
on the ground of his being a Spanish subject and having influential friends among the French residents." [12]
Vigo was an influential figure in the annals of the
Northwest. He had served in the Spanish army and was
stationed in Louisiana. Leaving the army, he became a
merchant. A friendship sprang up between him and
Clark and he transferred his allegiance to the United
States. He was a financial power throughout all that
country and rendered Clark much pecuniary service.[13] He reported to Clark that Hamilton had sent
away his Indians and most of his troops, intending to
collect them in the spring and reduce Kaskaskia and
the other villages. Clark planned to attack him before
his schemes were matured, but the term of enlistment of
many of his soldiers had expired and they had returned
to their homes in Virginia. Money and supplies were
wanting, but the influence of Father Gibault enabled
him to recruit two companies at Kaskaskia and Cohokia
under Captains McCarthy and Charleville, and a generous loan from Colonel Vigo supplied him with arms
and equipment. Before his little force marched away,
the patriotic Gibault addressed them and gave absolution to his parishioners.[14] They marched over muddy
trails, forded swollen rivers, waded through submerged
lands, covered two hundred miles, stormed and captured

[12] Winsor, Hist. of Am., VI-724.
[13] Schuyler, Trans. in Ill., 69.
[14] *Ibid.*, Trans. in Ill., 71.

the fort, and sent the Governor and his officers prisoners to Virginia. During the remaining years of the struggle the patriots retained this territory, and when the Treaty of Paris was signed, Clark's occupation of the North-west was a contributing factor in securing the entire region for the new Republic.

The success of the campaign was primarily due to the bravery and daring of Clark, partly to the enthusiasm of the inhabitants who admired and trusted him, and to the loyalty and devotion of Father Gibault, Colonel Vigo and Dr. La Font. History has not only preserved the record of his bravery and prudence, but also acknowledges its debt to the Catholic heroes. "Next to Clark and Vigo," says Judge Law in his history of Vincennes, "the United States are indebted more to Father Gibault for the accession of the states comprised in what was the original Northwest Territory than to any other man." The legislature of Virginia adopted a resolution in 1780, acknowledging the brave service he had rendered.[15] Patrick Henry honored him "as the priest to whom this country owes many thanks for his zeal and service." [16] Perhaps the best tribute to his patriotism was the bitter and unjust criticism heaped on him by Colonel Hamilton. The greatest monument to the memory of Clark, Gibault and Vigo are the states of Indiana, Illinois, Michigan and Wisconsin,

[15] Shea, Cath. Ch. in U. S., II-189.
[16] Griffin, Caths. in Am. Rev., III-235.

formed from the territory won and preserved by their valor.

The Catholic Indians of Maine and Nova Scotia, the Micmacs, Penobscots, Passamaquoddy and St. John's tribes were loyal to the patriots during the revolutionary struggle. The Micmacs were probably the first Indians seen by John Cabot, Cortereal and Cartier on their northern voyages. The Abnaki tribes were visited by Champlain and the other French navigators who endeavored to colonize New Brunswick and Nova Scotia. Friendly to the French, they became early converts to Catholicity, as the Jesuits, Fathers Biard, Masse and Quentin, ministered to them until Argall destroyed the settlement and carried the priests away captives. Capuchins, Recollects, and secular priests from Quebec visited them at frequent intervals. The Jesuit missionaries, Druillettes, Bogot and Thury labored among them until the arrival of Sebastian Rale, who spent more than thirty years in their villages. Their loyalty to France aroused the hatred of the New Englanders and led to a series of attacks on their territory, culminating in the martyrdom of the saintly Rale. The permanent mission was destroyed, although priests visited them occasionally, and they made frequent excursions to the missions of Quebec. They remained faithful to the religion and their descendants are today devoted Catholics.

When the colonists revolted against England, the British agents endeavored to enlist the service of the

Indians in harassing the patriots. Sir John Johnson in Central New York had rallied the Iroquois to his stand- ard, Stuart at Pensacola negotiated with the Southern tribes to lay waste the Carolinas and Georgia, and Ham- ilton at Detroit instigated the Northwestern Indians to attack the rebel frontiers. Although Congress had de- nounced their religion to win the favor of the Mohawks and Oneidas, and the New England leaders had scourged their villages and slain their priest, they pledged their fidelity to Washington and were loyal to their former oppressors. In May, 1775, the Provincial Congress of Massachusetts sent a petition to the Eastern Indians advising them "the ministry of Great Britain had deep laid plans to take away our liberty and your liberty." [17]

In the same month, a deputation of Caughnawaga braves living near Montreal visited Washington's camp and assured him of the loyalty of their brethren. The Commander wrote to the St. John's tribes, seeking their neutrality or assistance, and delegates, headed by Am- brose Var, came to Watertown, pledged their allegiance and asked for a priest. "The General Council expressed their gratification at this love of religion and declared their readiness to obtain a priest for them, though they did not know where to find one." [18] Two days after the battle of Bunker Hill a deputation of Penobscots, with their celebrated chieftain Orono, came to Cambridge,

[17] *Ibid.,* Caths. in Am. Rev., II-98.
[18] Shea, Cath. Ch. in U. S., II-154.

tendered their assistance to Washington, and also asked for "a Black Robe." Their request was not granted until 1779, when Father de la Motte, an Augustinian who had been attached to a French vessel, was assigned to their missions.[19] On his departure, application was made to Admiral De Ternay and one of the fleet chaplains was appointed. De Valnais, the French Consul at Boston, informed the messenger: "the King of France sends you a priest to direct your consciences." His name is unknown, although tradition asserts he was a Capuchin.[20] The Continental Congress voted that Washington be permitted to employ these Indians "as he shall judge necessary," and empowering him "to employ in Canada a number not exceeding two thousand."[21]

The most illustrious leader of the Indian tribes was Joseph Orono. His stature, features and complexion were not of the Indian type, and tradition has thrown the glamor of romance around his supposed ancestry. Many stories are related about his early life; he was a native of York, captured in a raid and reared among the savages; he was a descendant of the celebrated Baron de Castine; "he himself told Captain Munsell his father was a Frenchman, and his mother was half French and half Indian, but who they were he did not state."[22] He was patient, intelligent and a man of peace,

[19] *Ibid.*, Cath. Ch. in U. S., II-181.
[20] Griffin, Caths. in Am. Rev., II-121.
[21] *Ibid.*, Caths. in Am. Rev., II-110.
[22] *Ibid.*, Caths. in Am. Rev., II-131.

although ready to defend his people from oppression. He spoke the Indian, French and English languages and understood the Latin church prayers. He was a devoted Catholic and his piety inspired his people to practise their religion. "We know our religion and we love it" was his answer to a Protestant minister urging him to attend the Congregational service.[23] He was honest, chaste, temperate and industrious, and his example influenced his fellow tribesmen. From the beginning of hostilities, he was a devoted patriot and his followers emulated his loyalty. His actions influenced other tribes to support the American cause. He watched the movements of the British and the hostile Indians and communicated valuable information to the government. For his services he was thanked by Congress and Washington and received many pecuniary rewards. He died in 1801 at the advanced age of one hundred thirteen years. His native state has honored his memory by calling the town which sprang up in the section where he lived Orono, a well deserved tribute to his bravery and loyalty.[24]

Many of the Eastern Indians participated in the war, some fought at the battle of Bunker Hill, others accompanied Arnold on his march through the wilderness to Quebec, acting as guides and interpreters, bringing food to the starving soldiers, guiding the frail craft through

[23] Shea, Cath. Ch. in U. S., II-155.
[24] Griffin, Caths. in Am. Rev., II-126.

the angry streams. They were supplied with arms and ammunition and guarded the frontier from surprise or hostile attack. Had they been unfriendly, every American settler east of the Penobscot would have been killed or driven away and their clearings laid waste. Urged by the influence and example of Orono, the Penobscots, Passamaquoddy and St. John's braves entered into a treaty of amity with the Massachusetts Provincial Congress and on July 19th, 1776, acknowledged the independence of the United States and raised the American flag over their villages. The other tribes remained neutral and refused all alliance with the enemy, although the British agents endeavored to win their favor by compliments and presents. The news of the French alliance increased their ardor for the patriotic cause and when the French fleet came to Rhode Island, a deputation of chiefs visited Rochambeau, who entertained them most hospitably. To weaken their devotion to the popular cause, British agents denied that France would send material aid, but the arrival of the army and the fleet strengthened their devotion to the cause of freedom.

Colonel John Allen was appointed by the Continental Congress as Superintendent of the Eastern Indians and Colonel in the army and entrusted with a small force to defend the borders and to protect the maritime towns. The Indians formed the bulk of his forces. An expedition of soldiers and Catholic Indians to capture Nova

Scotia was planned, but the weakness of the army prevented Washington from supplying reinforcements and the depreciation of the Continental money and the scarcity of supplies delayed the movement. Had Colonel Allen been given a regiment or a division well equipped, acting in conjunction with Orono and his faithful Indians, Nova Scotia and New Brunswick might have been added to the future republic.

CHAPTER THIRTEEN

France, Spain, Poland

WHEN the agitation against the Stamp Act became known in France, Choiseul, the Chief Minister, predicted the revolt of the colonies. For centuries England and France had been hereditary enemies, their armies battling in France, Flanders, India and Germany, their navies clashing in the Mediterranean Sea, the Atlantic and Indian Oceans, victory invariably favoring the English. In the new world the rivalry was so tense that a series of wars broke out, devastating the colonies and Canada, culminating in the complete defeat of France and the cession of her possessions to her hated rival. On the accession of Louis XVI, Comte de Vergennes was selected as Secretary for Foreign Affairs. Less brilliant than his predecessor, he was sagacious and prudent, and believed that the loss of America would be a fatal blow to the prestige of Great Britain. "The selection of Vergennes was of much importance to the American colonists. . . . During five years of war, he did his best for his allies. . . . His memory is not green in America like that of Lafayette. . . . He did more than any other Frenchman to secure independence for the

American colonies." [1] Subsequent historians insinuate that his interest in the struggle was mercenary, a desire to humble a rival and avenge past defeats, and even the struggling patriots were suspicious of his motives. John Adams feared he would demand a portion of the conquered territory for France, and even Washington was perplexed by his disinterested zeal. Yet the great statesman never flinched during the years of defeat and failure, maintaining that peace should not be made until the independence of the United States was assured." [2]

The French exchequer, depleted by the Seven Years' War, was ruined by the alliance, taxes increased enormously, and commerce suffered during the struggle, yet France kept her word, no conquest was attempted, and her only recompense was the thanks of a liberated nation. Although the colonists fought to despoil France of her possessions in America they looked to her for assistance. "Meanwhile, France and the Thirteen Colonies were mutually attracted to each other, and it is not easy to decide which of them made the first movement towards an intercourse." [3] Choiseul and Vergennes had been interested spectators for ten years and Washington, after the first disaster, declared: "If we do not have money and soldiers from France our cause is lost." In September, 1775, a resolution to send envoys to France was defeated by Congress, but in March of the

[1] Perkins, France in Am. Rev., 35-36.
[2] *Ibid.*, France in Am. Rev., 36.
[3] Bancroft, Hist. of U. S., VIII-215.

following year Silas Deane was sent to Paris to solicit arms, ammunition, clothing and money, and Arthur Lee, who had been in England, soon joined him. Neither envoy was qualified for such a delicate mission and their rivalry provoked interminable quarrels until the arrival of Benjamin Franklin brought united effort, at least in public, although his fellow commissioners were suspicious of his methods and disliked his diplomacy, but he was hailed with enthusiasm in literary circles and lionized by the middle classes and the peasantry. Vergennes was anxious to assist the patriots but the laws of neutrality precluded public aid, so he employed as his agent Beaumarchais, watchmaker, dramatist, creator of Figaro, petty court official, eccentric in manners, yet the earliest and best friend of the Americans. He formed the fictitious firm of Roderigue Hortalez et Compagnie, engaging to send supplies and munitions of war from the royal arsenals to the colonists. Vergennes advanced one million livres and persuaded Grimaldi, the Spanish Minister, to obtain a like amount. "Three vessels, containing the first consignment of clothing and stores, got off early in 1777, in spite of many obstacles. Five more vessels followed, all but one of which reached America." [4] These supplies and munitions were used principally in the campaign against Burgoyne. Beaumarchais obtained, mostly from French arsenals, over two hundred cannon, twenty-five thousand guns, two

[4] Winsor, Hist. of Am., VII-31.

hundred thousand pounds of powder, twenty or thirty
brass mortars, and clothing and tents for twenty-five
thousand men, and these he loaded on boats which he
himself provided." [b] By September, 1777, he had
shipped munitions of war to the value of five million
livres.[6] When the alliance was signed, larger donations
were given. "February, 1778, it amounted in money
lent to eighteen million livres. The next year a final loan
of six millions was granted. In addition to this, the King
of France made sundry presents to the United States.
. . . In 1781, six millions were directly presented, and
two more in 1782.[7] The present made to Washington in
1781 purchased arms, ammunition and clothing, and
financed the Yorktown campaign. In 1780, the General
Assembly of the French clergy voted six million livres
to the King as a gratuity to aid in the war against England for the independence of America. The money was
raised by the sale of bonds, the church property given
as security." [8]

The equipment of volunteers was early advocated by
the revolting colonies. The hardy New England sailors
captured British merchantmen and sold the cargoes for
the benefit of the crews, and frequently supplied the
army with needed stores. Not satisfied with operating in
American waters they crossed the ocean, terrorizing the

[5] Perkins, France in Am. Rev., 92.
[6] *Ibid.*, France in Am. Rev., 95.
[7] Winsor, Hist. of Am., VII-71-2.
[8] Griffin, Caths. in Am. Rev., II-389.

English channel and the Irish Sea. The captured vessel⸱ and cargoes were carried to French ports and sold, and the ships refitted and provisioned. As England and France were at peace, these visits violated the neutrality laws. International laws were not clearly defined and although England had been a flagrant offender, especially during the reign of Elizabeth, when Drake, Hawkins, and other corsairs ranged the seas, the English minister protested and in some cases secured the arrest of the captain and crew and the seizure of the privateer and its cargo. Usually, however, the crews were pardoned after a short imprisonment and the ship released to begin another raiding career. Among these who sent out these free lances were some Catholic Philadelphians, Meade, FitzSimons, Oellers and Flahaven with Catholic officers and crews. English towns were raided, English commerce destroyed or captured. Without the tacit consent of the French ministry these expeditions would have failed. The American navy owes much to the bravery of these daring mariners and their success was due to the complaisance of the French officials who furnished refuge and protection in their ports to these adventurers.

Many officers were recruited in France to aid the colonists. Some were soldiers of fortune or impecunious noblemen actuated by personal motives or love of adventure. The American cause was popular in Paris and young men attracted through sympathy offered their services. Deane engaged many volunteers to the annoyance of Washington and the embarrassment of Congress. Franklin was overwhelmed by applications for commissions but was more circumspect in his selections than his colleagues. Many of the volunteers had fought in the European wars under many flags, but were ignorant of colonial warfare and demanded high rank in the Continental service. Vergennes made no opposition to these enlistments, although the British Minister objected strenuously. Among the volunteers were some who distinguished themselves by their bravery, especially the Catholics, Kosciusko and Pulaski, the Protestants, de Kalb and von Steuben and the "foreign papist," Arundell, an artillery officer who was killed in Virginia. The most famous recruit was Marquis de Lafayette, the scion of an ancient and illustrious Catholic family, whose ancestors had fought in the Crusades and in all the campaigns against England since Poitiers and whose father fell at Hastenbeck. He offered his services to America and although his family protested and the King forbade him to leave the country, he purchased a ship and after a stormy voyage landed at Philadelphia. Unlike many other foreign recruits, he asked to serve as a volunteer and was wounded at Brandywine. Washington recognized his enthusiasm and devotion, employing him in many difficult and delicate missions. At Brandywine, Monmouth, the Virginian campaign, and Yorktown, during the privations at Valley Forge, amidst the intrigues of the "Conway Cabal," he was the devoted friend and loyal associate of the Commander and a staunch defender of American liberty. His influence with the French ministry brought Rochambeau and his army to coöperate with the patriots and his private fortune was expended to clothe and arm the soldiers of his division. He was the most useful and the most illustrious volunteer who came to America.

Vergennes maintained that if the Continental army withstood the British forces France must openly espouse their cause and secure their independence, and the American envoys constantly urged the necessity of recognizing the confederacy. The Declaration of Independence aroused much enthusiasm in political circles, but the disasters on Long Island, Washington's retreat through Jersey, and the capture of Philadelphia retarded the alliance. When the news of Burgoyne's surrender reached Paris, Vergennes decided to openly espouse the American cause. On February sixth, 1778, treaties of commerce and alliance were signed by the French representatives for France, by Franklin, Deane and Arthur Lee for the Congress. The first granted free access to all the harbors of France, the second guaranteed to the United States her independence and to France her possessions in the West Indies and that no peace should be made until the independence of the colonies was acknowledged.[9] By a secret treaty, Spain might enter into

[9] Perkins, France in Am. Rev., 239-40.

the alliance, but this clause was never fulfilled. Spain united with France but made no alliance with America.

Four French fleets and two French armies participated in the Revolutionary struggle on American soil and in American waters. Five weeks after the signing of the treaty, Count D'Estaing with twelve vessels and four frigates sailed for America and united with the patriots in attacking Rhode Island. The failure of the army to properly coöperate with the fleet delayed operations and a violent storm damaged the French vessels so badly the Admiral was obliged to sail to Boston harbor for repairs. The expedition was not entirely unsuccessfull as five British frigates were taken or destroyed and the garrison evacuated Rhode Island, leaving behind large stores of artillery and munitions of war. In the fall of 1779, D'Estaing joined General Lincoln in attacking Savannah, but the assault was repulsed and the fleet returned to the West Indies to refit. Two battalions of the famous Irish brigade from the Dillon and Walsh regiments participated in the siege.[10] Although defeated, the arrival of the French fleet off the southern coast, delayed for a time the offensive movement against the Southern colonies. In 1780, another French expedition commanded by Admiral De Ternay, bringing five thousand six hundred troops under Rochambeau arrived in Newport. On the death of De Ternay, Destouches succeeded to the command and engaged Hood's fleet off

[10] Griffin, Am. Cath. Hist. Res., 1909-290.

Chesapeake Bay, the rival squadron being badly disabled but saved from capture by a violent storm. De Barras succeeded Destouches and took part in the decisive engagement at Yorktown. Count de Guichen was stationed in the Antilles and coöperated only indirectly in the war, although his operations in southern waters hampered the British and several of his frigates were added to the fleet which blockaded the Bay. In 1781, Count De Grasse with twenty-six ships and several frigates sailed from the West Indies. Washington and Rochambeau marched from the North and united with Lafayette and three thousand four hundred soldiers under Count Saint Simon. The combined fleets of Hood and Graves were defeated by the French squadron under De Grasse and De Barras, while the French and American armies surrounded Cornwallis and forced his surrender, thus insuring the independence of the United States. "The Compte De Grasse performed his part with great exactitude and is entitled to a large share of the credit for the capture of Yorktown. He brought an important reinforcement to the forces on land, he prevented the English from relieving Cornwallis. The capture of Yorktown would have been impossible if his fleet had not arrived promptly and remained until the work was done." [11] Rochambeau shares in the triumphs of the land forces with Washington. His prudence and sagacity prevented rivalries between the allies, and his

[11] Perkins, France in Am. Rev., 376.

promptness in coöperating with Washington and his valor and skill during the siege were important factors in the successful issue of the campaign.

The French soldiers and sailors, with few exceptions, were at least nominally members of the Catholic church. Every vessel had a chaplain listed among its officers and the French naval records give the names of "ninety priests, of whom seventeen were Capuchins, thirteen Recollects, four seculars, three Carmelites, and two Premontarians." [12] The other chaplains were not assigned to either seculars or regulars. The best known of these was Abbé Bandol, chaplain to the French Ministers, Gerard and Luzere, who preached the sermon at the first Catholic celebration at St. Mary's church, July fourth, 1779, and the following year officiated or preached at the burial of Don Juan de Miralles, the Spanish agent. Among these priests were some bearing unmistakably Irish patronymics, Maccabe, Morrison, Omahony, Machunery and Dowd to his name is affixed "of Ireland." [13] Although the French army records omit the names of the chaplains, it is certain that priests accompanied Rochambeau's forces. Twelve chaplains attended the interment of Admiral de Ternay at Newport, Abbé Robin officiated at Baltimore, Father Charles Whelan at New York, and Abbé Berthalet, Father de St. Pierre and Abbé Reynal were well-known

[12] Griffin, Caths. in Am. Rev., III-289.
[13] *Ibid.*, Caths. in Am. Rev., III-289.

figures in the closing years of the struggle. The suspicion of the patriots and the hatred of the loyalists for the "French Papists" are additional proofs of the Catholicity of the French allies. Washington in his reply to the Address of the Catholics on his assumption of the presidency strengthens the theory. "And I presume your fellow citizens will not forget . . . the important assistance which they received from a nation in which the Roman Catholic faith is professed." [14] French aid was certainly an important factor in the outcome of the revolutionary struggle. "Whether or not we should have eventually established our independence without the help of France, it is impossible to say. So judicious a scholar as Mr. Lecky believes that most of the states would have given up the struggle without this help." [15]

Although Spain did not pursue the same consistent policy as France during the Revolution, she gave substantial assistance to the patriotic cause. American historians have impugned and condemned her motives as "greedy, mercenary and selfish," the expansion of her boundaries, the recovery of Gibraltar, revenge for past injuries, and the revival of her former prestige. Yet there were many and excellent reasons for her seeming indifference to the colonies and her distrust and hatred of England. The stern Puritans, the intolerant Episcopalians abhorred "Popery" and associated Spain with the

[14] *Ibid.*, Am. Cath. His. Res., 1911-298.
[15] Muzzey, Life of Jeff., 48-9.

supposed Catholic superstitions and "the atrocities of the Inquisition." In the colonial wars the settlers from the north had invaded Spanish towns, villages and missions, desecrating the churches, destroying their schools and religious houses. The opposition to the Quebec Act, the addresses of Congress to the inhabitants and the English people, the sentiments of the leading patriots convinced the Spanish government that the ancient racial and religious bitterness had not subsided. Her grievances against England were many and of long standing. English pirates had burned her towns, plundered her treasure ships in time of peace with the tacit approbation of the ministry and the rulers. English soldiers had routed her armies, assisted her rebellious subjects and seized the Rock of Gibraltar. These injuries rankled in the bosom of every Spaniard and stimulated him to cripple the ancient foe in her hour of trial. France and Spain were united by family and friendly ties, Charles II being the uncle of Louis XVI. Both had been embroiled in war with Britain, both had suffered grievously on land and sea.

The friendship of Vergennes for the revolting colonists was shared by Grimaldi, the Spanish Premier, and when France advanced a million livres to aid them, Spain loaned a like sum. A political change overthrew the regime of Grimaldi and placed Florida Blanco at the head of the government. The new leader was friendly to America but the weakness of the Spanish

army and navy, and a depleted treasury, warned him to
avoid a conflict with his powerful foe. He refused to
receive the American envoys, although he made profuse
and friendly promises.[16] Yet in the reports of Arthur
Lee to Congress, mention is made of supplies sent to
the patriots and magazines of ammunition and clothing
at New Orleans and Havana which would be loaned to
Congress. Franklin in his dealings with Count Aran-
dano, the Spanish minister, a firm friend of the patriots,
proposed to attack Florida and to reduce Portugal and
Brazil. In addition, privateers and naval vessels were
permitted to refit and provision in Spanish ports and
although the British cabinet protested, no action was
taken. The adoption of the Declaration of Independence evidently lessened Spain's interest in the struggle
lest the example of the rebels might incite her own colonial subjects to throw off her sovereignty.

When the Treaty between France and the United
States was signed, Spain refused to enter the alliance,
although Vergennes importuned her ministry to do so.
Florida Blanco suggested a settlement and the King pro-
posed a truce, offering his services as mediator, but
Congress rejected the proposal. In the following year
France and Spain made a separate treaty, and declared
war on England. To recover Gibraltar, to acquire the
Mississippi country were the reasons assigned for enter-
ing the conflict, yet it helped the colonies by raising up

[16] Van Tyne, Am. Rev., 214-5.

another enemy for England. A joint naval demonstration was planned, a squadron of fifty ships entered the English channel, although without results, another fleet blockaded Gibraltar and captured Minorca. While the Spanish ministry was vacillating and neglected many opportunities of humbling Britain and impairing her power, yet ships and soldiers were detained in Europe which might have overwhelmed the Continentals. These dilatory tactics and the various changes of ministries obscure the material assistance received from Spain.

It was on American soil that Spain was destined to play a prominent role in the revolutionary struggle. The people of Louisiana gave both sympathy and support to their rebellious neighbors. Oliver Pollock, American merchant, devoted Catholic, Congressional Agent, collected military supplies, especially arms and ammunition and shipped them to Pennsylvania by way of the Mississippi and Ohio Rivers.[17] With him were associated other merchants from Baltimore, Boston, New York and Philadelphia. Pollock had rendered valuable assistance to George Rogers Clark, honoring the drafts drawn by him on Virginia, and forwarding recruits and supplies.[18] In this traffic the people of Louisiana cheerfully participated and the Governor sent seventy thousand dollars to the Kentucky defenders. When Spain joined France, England attempted to reduce Louisiana and as Florida

[17] Phelps, Louisiana, 139.
[18] Schuyler, Trans. in Illi., 51.

and the region around Detroit was British territory, General Campbell, the Commandant, planned to subjugate the Spanish possessions and annex the lands conquered by George Rogers Clark. Bernardo de Galvez, the Spanish Governor, a youth of twenty-four, was ambitious, enthusiastic and brilliant, a brave soldier and an excellent administrator, and as the plans of the enemy were revealed to him by an intercepted letter he resolved to strike a sudden blow and cripple the British army. Sinclair from Michilimackinac was to march southward and capture St. Louis, St. Genevieve, and the other villages, thus holding Clark in check, while Campbell with his motley army of British and Indians, Hessians and Tories seized New Orleans. This move would insure the defeat of Clark and secure for England all the territory from the Gulf to the Great Lakes. Galvez at once recruited a volunteer army, in whose ranks Pollock and the other Americans enlisted, stormed and captured Baton Rouge and Natchez. From Havanna he secured additional soldiers and reduced Mobile and Pensacola. When Sinclair learned that Campbell was captured and Clark on the march, he retreated and as his auxiliaries deserted him all hope of conquest was abandoned. The Mississippi Valley and the Illinois country were once more secured by the valor of the Catholic Spaniards and their brave allies. "Galvez's success made it possible for the new country to hold its territory intact from Canada to Florida. Had the English expedition succeeded, Great Britain could have set up a claim to this territory when the western boundary was fixed, several years later at the declaration of peace.[19]

Among the foreign heroes who came to America to fight for freedom were two Polish officers, Thaddeus Kosciusko, "The Father of the American Artillery Service," Casimir Pulaski, "the Father of the American Cavalry." Pulaski was famous in European annals for his heroic bravery in defending his native land from the invading armies of Austria, Prussia and Russia, but after three years of herculean warfare, his troops were overwhelmed and he fled to Turkey. He came to Paris, but as his estates were confiscated, he lived in poverty. He at once offered his services to the American cause and in 1777 arrived at Boston. A few days later he joined Washington at Philadelphia and fought as a private at Brandywine. Congress then commissioned him "Commander of the Horse, with the rank of Brigadier." [20] The four scattered troops of cavalry were united under his command, and during the doleful winter at Valley Forge he drilled them in cavalry tactics, prepared a manual of instruction, long adopted in the Federal army, raided British convoys and brought large stores to the impoverished camp.[20] In 1778, he resigned his commission and recruited an independent corps, "The

[19] Phelps, Louisiana, 148.
[20] Griffin, Caths. in Am. Rev., III-11.

Pulaski Legion." To repress the Indians and Tories who had ravaged Cherry Valley the Legion was sent to northern New Jersey and in the spring of 1779 was ordered to reinforce General Lincoln. He aided in the defense of Charleston and joined the expedition to recapture Savannah. During that memorable siege he performed prodigies of valor and in the unsuccessful assault was mortally wounded leading his men in a desperate charge, his last words: "Jesus, Mary Joseph." [21] "The Colonel's valor and active zeal on all occasions," wrote Washington to Congress, "have done him great honor." The Committee appointed by the Fifty-Seventh Congress (1903) approving the bill for the erection of a monument to his memory in the capital of the nation reported: "His invaluable service to America entitles him to be numbered among the heroes of America and to be perpetuated in the memory of the people for whom he sacrificed his life." He fought to preserve the liberty of his own land and died to secure freedom for his adopted country.

Kosciusko also served in the patriot army of Poland, fighting against the invading triumvirate of nations, and when the movement collapsed came to Paris. He arrived in Boston in 1776 and offered his services to the struggling patriots. In all probability he participated in the Trenton-Princeton campaign with his fellow Catholics, John Barry, John Fitzgerald, Thomas FitzSim-

[21] *Ibid.*, Caths. in Am. Rev., III-108.

ons and Stephen Moylan. In August, 1776, Congress commissioned him "an Engineer in the service of the United States, with the pay of sixty dollars a month and the rank of Colonel." [22] Engineers were scarce in the Continental ranks and four French engineers had been engaged by the American representatives in Paris, so the arrival of Kosciusko was timely. He was assigned to the Northern Army under Schuyler threatened by Burgoyne's invasion from Canada. General St. Clair was ordered to fortify Ticonderoga, and Kosciusko was commissioned to superintendent the operations, but before the neighboring Mount Independence could be secured, the defenders were overwhelmed by the superior forces of the enemy, so the army retreated southward, obstructing the roads and destroying the bridges. Gates superseded Schuyler, and the Polish engineer selected and fortified Bemis Heights, a site which resisted every attack. The British army was surrounded and captured, the turning point of the Revolution, securing the alliance with France and the recognition of independence. After the close of the campaign, Kosciusko was ordered by Congress: "To repair to the army of General Putnam, to be employed as shall be thought proper as an engineer." [23] He altered and strengthened the defenses of West Point and made it the most impregnable fortress in America. Governor

[22] *Ibid.*, Caths. in Am. Rev., III-134.
[23] *Ibid.*, Caths. in Am. Rev., III-150.

Clinton praised his skill, and Washington paid him a well deserved tribute; "to his care and sedulous appreciation the American people are indebted for the defense of West Point." [24] He was assigned to the Southern Department, but before his arrival Gates had been routed at Camden and Sumpter surprised at Fishing Creek. He joined Greene's forces and participated in the engagements which restored the Southern states to the patriotic cause. At the close of the hostilities, Congress at the recommendation of Washington voted: "That the Secretary of War transmit to Col. Kosciusko the brevet commission of Brigadier General and signify to that officer that Congress entertains a high sense of his long, faithful and meritorious service." [25] He returned to Europe and during the Polish struggle for freedom commanded an army of raw recruits, was wounded and taken prisoner by the Russians. On his release, he again visited America, receiving an enthusiastic welcome from Adams, Jefferson, Washington and his other comrades of revolutionary days. Congress adjusted his salary claims and a land grant was given him in token of his loyalty. He returned to Europe and died in Switzerland in 1817. "He was one of our great revolutionary worthies," was the tribute of Jefferson to this Catholic, Polish patriot.

[24] *Ibid.*, Caths. in Am. Rev., III-153.
[25] *Ibid.*, Caths. in Am. Rev., III-183.

CHAPTER FOURTEEN

Catholic Loyalists

DURING the revolutionary struggle, all the colonists were not patriots; some were loyal to the King. While Washington was besieging Boston, several Tory companies were formed to reinforce the regulars and to perform patrol duty.[1] These supporters of England were drawn from various classes, the office holders, the Anglican clergy, and those who were satisfied with the existing conditions.[2] When the city was evacuated, more than nine hundred loyalists accompanied the army to Halifax. In the other colonies they were equally strong and active. John Adams contended that were it not for the proximity of New England and Virginia, New York and Pennsylvania would have remained loyal.[3] Many regiments of Tories were formed to assist the enemy. The Scotch Highlanders of Georgia and North Carolina, under the leadership of Donald McDonald, organized a regiment to coöperate with Clinton and Parker on the first attack on Charleston, but were al-

[1] Van Tyne, Loyalists in Am. Rev., 55.
[2] *Ibid.*, Loyalists in Am. Rev., 25-26.
[3] *Ibid.*, Loyalists in Am. Rev., 101-2.

most annihilated by Caswell.[4] Sir John Johnson, with
"The Royal Greens," and Butler with his "Tory Legion," devastated Wyoming and Cherry Valley in conjunction with Brandt and his Indians. In Burgoyne's
campaign, and in the expeditions to the Illinois country,
Tory regiments fought side by side with the British
regulars. When Charleston and Savannah fell, and Gates
was routed at Camden, the Tories joined the ranks of
Clinton or Cornwallis or attacked or destroyed the
Whig settlements. Tarleton and his "Tory Legion,"
raised in New York, were especially active. Their bravery at Camden turned the tide of battle and their defeat of Sumpter was a crushing blow to the patriots.
Daniel Morgan's victory at Cowpens and the route of
Ferguson's forces at King's Mountain were serious reverses and dampened the ardor of the Tories. Expeditions under Tryon and Arnold invaded Connecticut,
New Jersey and Virginia, and privateers manned by
loyalists preyed on American shipping and ravaged
maritime towns. Many enlisted in the army or navy,
"New York alone furnished about fifteen thousand men
to the British army and navy and over eight thousand
loyalist militia. All of the other colonies furnished
about as many more, so that we may safely state that
fifty thousand soldiers, either regulars or militia were
drawn into the service of Great Britain from her Ameri-

[4] *Ibid.*, Loyalists in Am. Rev., 97.

can sympathizers." [5] After the victory at Yorktown, more than three thousand refugees went to the West Indies, Halifax and New York from Charleston, and seven thousand from Savannah.[6] More than twenty-nine thousand left New York and after the signing of the treaty of independence, sixty thousand exiles arrived in Nova Scotia and other British possessions.[7] Computing those who were banished, those who were killed more than a hundred thousand loyalists resisted independence. Those who took the oath of allegiance although devoted to England, those who escaped the vengeance of the Whigs cannot be estimated.

The various religious sects were divided, some Whigs, some Tories. "Peace-loving Quakers became warriors, and even the Presbyterians, though they were more loyal than any other sect, gave an almost unanimous support to the cause of America. Yet they had Tories among them." [8] "Pennsylvania," wrote Chevalier de Fleury, "is the province most infested with loyalists. The Quakers, Methodists, Anglicans and other sects which have a sort of affinity with Monarchy, are intestine but paralytic enemies." [9] Catholics were likewise divided in their allegiance, although the Historian of the American Church has written: "The Catholics spontaneously, universally

[5] *Ibid.*, Loyalists in Am. Rev., 182-3.
[6] *Ibid.*, Loyalists in Am. Rev., 289.
[7] *Ibid.*, Loyalists in Am. Rev., 289-93.
[8] Griffin, Caths. in Am. Rev., I-325.
[9] *Ibid.*, Caths. In Am. Rev., I-330.

and energetically gave their adherence to the cause of America. . . . There was no faltering, no division. Every Catholic in the land was a Whig. There were no Catholic Tories." [10] The records of the period disprove this statement. Like all other denominations, Catholics disagreed on purely political questions. "All Catholics did not take the part of the Colonies, . . . they were divided as all others were. Speaking in general terms it may be believed that the Maryland Catholics were 'rebels,' the Pennsylvania Catholics 'Loyalists.' The Maryland Catholics wanted religious liberty as well as civil freedom is the testimony of Charles Carroll of Carrollton. In Pennsylvania Catholics had both." [11] This assertion seems too broad and not warranted by the history of the colony. The tolerance of Penn and his successors had welcomed Catholics to the province, and full religious freedom was granted. The list of officers in the Pennsylvania Line and the Continental navy and privateer service furnishes the names of English, French, Irish, German, Portuguese, Scotch and Swiss Catholics, and it seems reasonable to maintain that many of the rank and file were also Catholics. Nor is it surprising that some Catholics were true to England as the colonists had bitterly assailed their religion and persecuted its adherents and Pennsylvania alone had granted them religious freedom. The leading patriots had displayed

[10] Shea, Cath. Hist. Rec., 1885.
[11] Griffin, Am. Cath. Hist. Res., 1907-277.

flagrant bigotry after the passage of the Quebec Act, and in the colonial wars, religious as well as racial antipathy embittered the strife with France and Spain, the representative Catholic nations. "Popery and Papacy" had been terms of reproach and symbols of disloyalty. Under such conditions, it is not surprising that some Catholics refused to support the patriotic cause. The loyalty of the vast majority of the Catholics may be explained in the words of the Fathers of the Third Plenary Council of Baltimore: "We believe that our heroes were the instruments of the God of nations in establishing this home of freedom."

"While it was no longer possible for the Americans to keep up their army by enlistments, the British gained numerous recruits from immigrants. In Philadelphia, Howe had formed a regiment of Roman Catholics." [12] As the people of Philadelphia seemed friendly to the cause, Howe planned to recruit three regiments of Loyalists, under Colonels Allen, Chambers, and Clifton, the latter regiment the Roman Catholic Regiment. "The organization of a distinctively Roman Catholic Regiment in Philadelphia during British occupation was in full accord with the policy of the government. The effort was made, where the only chance of success . . . in Pennsylvania under British control where Catholics were the most numerous." [13] Some Catholic historians

[12] Bancroft, Hist. of U. S., X-175.
[13] Griffin, Caths. in Am. Rev., I-330.

deny that the regiment was ever recruited; "it never existed except on paper. The regiment was already defunct." [14] "The attempt failed most miserably. The recruits were not forthcoming." [15] These conclusions are incorrect, as the regiment, although weak in numbers, was actually organized and fought in the loyal ranks. Its commander was Alfred Clifton, a well-known Catholic and landowner of Philadelphia; "an English gentleman of an Irish mother," who had served in the Prussian and Russian service. Major John Lynch and many of the other officers were well known in Catholic circles, their names appearing in the baptismal and marriage records of St. Mary's Church. Father Ferdinand Farmer, one of the pastors of the Church, was named chaplain, but he did not accept the offer; "which embarrasseth me on account of my age and several other reasons." [16] The regiment, however, was only a battalion, in May, 1778, one hundred ninety-seven names on the rolls, in the following August, one hundred seventy-three.[17]

When the British evacuated Philadelphia, the Catholic Volunteers were attached to General Knyphausen's corps and fought at Monmouth. On its arrival in New York, death and desertion had so thinned its ranks that efforts were made to strengthen it by offering bounties

[14] Shea, Cath. Ch. in U. S., II-170.
[15] O'Gorman, Cath. Ch. in U. S., 256.
[16] Ibid., Cath. Ch. in U. S., 328.
[17] Griffin, Am. Cath. Hist. Res., 1912-83.

of money and clothes to all recruits. The attempt was unsuccessful and the battalion, now reduced to "near eighty men," was absorbed by the Volunteers of Ireland. Sir Henry Clinton assigns a reason for its amalgamation with the other corps: "From the inattention of the officers to the terms of their warrant, and their utter disregard of discipline, I found it necessary to reduce it." [18] Colonel Clifton died in New York in 1780, described in the mortuary records as "a stranger," and Major John Lynch in 1782. Both were interred in Trinity Cemetery, but as the graves were unmarked the site is unknown. Of the other officers, some were dismissed or reduced, others enlisted in other British regiments, others returned to Philadelphia and were either punished or pardoned. The Volunteers of Ireland served in the Southern Department under Lord Rawdon, at Camden, Hobskirk's Hill and Yorktown. The few survivors of the Roman Catholic Regiment were captured at Yorktown and shared the fate of the Irish volunteers.

The attempt to establish episcopacy in Scotland drove many immigrants to America.[19] They settled in New England, the middle colonies and the south. Later-day historians have included in their ranks the Protestant Irish from Ulster, but these early settlers were native Scots and not the hybrid Scotch-Irish. After the defeat of the so-called "Pretender" at Culloden, many High-

[18] *Ibid.*, Caths. in Am. Rev., I-337.
[19] Bancroft, Hist. U. S., II-410.

landers of the Clans Macdonald and Macleod settled in the uplands of Georgia and South Carolina, and in Central New York. Among them was "the celebrated Flora Macdonald, the romantic woman who had saved Charles Edward from capture and death in 1746." [20] The Southern Scots were Protestants, those in New York mainly Catholics, and the Highlanders of the South and the Catholics and Presbyterians of New York were mostly Tories.[21] The activities of Ashe and Caswell kept them under restraint until the British overran the Carolinas, and the rout of Ferguson's detachment at King's Mountain was a crushing blow to these Scotch loyalists. In New York the vigilance and harshness of the patriots caused many to flee to Canada, others enlisted under Butler and Johnson, and with the Indians under Brandt, devastated the Whig settlements. They participated in the massacre of Cherry Valley and Wyoming Valley, the siege of Fort Stanwix, and the battle of Oriskany, and were attached to Burgoyne's invading army. The surrender at Saratoga and Sullivan's expedition were disastrous to their hopes, but until the close of hostilities they scourged the patriotic settlers of Central New York.

The patriots viewed these Scotch settlers with suspicion, and in 1775 presented a petition to the New York Provincial Congress, asking for a regiment "in

[20] Fiske, Am. Rev., I-207.
[21] *Ibid.*, Am. Rev., II-200.

order to keep under proper subjection, Regulars, Roman Catholics and Savages." [23] These Highlanders came to New York under the patronage of Sir William Johnson and his son and successor, Sir John Johnson, and settled near Johnstown, Tryon County. Sir William Johnson, although born in Ireland, traced his ancestry to the Macdonnels of Glencoe.[24] General Schuyler with an army overawed Johnson, an avowed Tory, disarmed his Scotch vassals, and received six hostages to ensure their neutrality. "Though Johnson had signed a parole and his Highlanders and other armed men had been disarmed, they were held in suspicion as endeavoring to instigate the Indians to warfare against the patriots. Finally, it was determined to make him a prisoner and remove the entire body of Highlanders from the county." [25] In May, 1776, Johnson with one hundred thirty Highlanders and one hundred twenty other inhabitants escaped the vigilance of the guards and fled to Canada. The remaining Scotch settlers remained in the province and were neutral during the war, refusing to serve with either Tories or Whigs and suffering persecution from both.

Dr. Shea attributes their flight to religious intolerance: "The outburst of bigotry in New York excited by the Quebec Act, stimulated by narrow-minded

[23] Griffin, Am. Cath. Hist. Res., 1908-45. ·
[24] *Ibid.*, Caths. in Am. Rev., II-135.
[25] *Ibid.*, Caths. in Am. Rev., II-144.

fanatics like John Jay, caused the only serious trouble experienced by Catholics during the period. . . . A number of Scotch Highlanders, chiefly Catholics from Glengarry, had settled near Johnson's Hall in the Mohawk Valley. . . . They were attended by the Rev. John McKenna, an Irish priest educated at Louvain. . . . They knew little of the points on which the colonies based their complaints against the English government. . . . Thus did anti-Catholic bigotry deprive New York of industrious settlers, . . . who longed to avenge the defeat of Culloden and draw their claymores against England." [26] These statements are not in accord with the opinions of contemporary critics or the testimony of the Scotch refugees. After the battle of Culloden, the Highlanders took an oath not to again take up arms against England. The Catholics of New York and the Presbyterians in the South refused to violate this oath, although they were urged to by emissaries sent by Congress. Many joined the royal forces, others remained neutral. The Scotch Catholics who enlisted were few, as only one hundred thirty emigrated to Canada under Johnson. In 1785, a memorial, addressed to Lieutenant-Governor Hamilton, affirmed: "Prior to the last war they were inhabitants of the Back Settlements of the Province of New York, adhering strictly to their Duty and Allegiance, until being unsupported, they were overwhelmed by the numbers of the enemy, then retir-

[26] Shea, Cath. Ch. in U. S., II-142.

ing through the woods to Canada they served in the Eighty-Fourth Royal Yorkers and other regiments . . . until peace as Sir Guy Carleton, General Haldemand, Brigadier General Maclean, Sir John Johnson and other officers can testify." [27] The petitioner was a Catholic priest, the Rev. Roderick or Alexander MacDonnel, who was assigned as their clergyman. The identity of their first pastor, the Rev. John McKenna is shrouded in mystery. Contemporary writers make no reference to him. On the contrary, it is affirmed: "Sir William Johnson or his son and successor, Sir John, took no steps to procure them a religious teacher in the principles of their faith. They were not so provided until after the Revolution and then only when they were settled in the lands that had been allotted to them (in Canada)." [28] The Catholic Scotch were as loyal to their faith as they were to their oath of allegiance, some remaining neutral, others fighting in the British ranks.

To conquer the rebellious colonies King George and his Ministry resolved to employ foreign soldiers. As Catherine II of Russia had concluded a treaty of peace with Turkey, England hoped to secure from her from ten to twenty thousand troops to serve in America. They were to be mercenaries rather than auxiliaries under the command of British officers, but Catherine scornfully rejected the proposal. Holland was petitioned

[27] Griffin, Caths. in Am. Rev., I-131.
[28] Ibid., Caths. in Am. Rev., II-146.

to loan its Foreign Brigade, composed of men of every nation and commanded by Scotch officers, but the States-General refused to allow the soldiers to leave Europe.[29] The Cabinet then applied to the petty princes of Germany, many of them relatives or close associates of George III. Arthur Deane had already been approached by these dealers in human lives, offering to supply officers and men to assist the patriots. "I have been offered troops from Germany on the following general terms: Officers to recruit as for the service of France and embark for San Domingo from Dunkirk and by altering their route land in the American states. The same has been proposed with Switzerland. . . . I submit it for your consideration whether it would not be well to purchase at Leghorn five or six stout frigates which might at once transport some companies of Swiss and a quantity of stores and the whole to be defended by the Swiss soldiers on the passage. Or, if you prefer Germans, which I really do not, the vessel might go from Dunkirk."[30] Franklin relates in a letter to Congress that a German Prince offered to furnish soldiers at the usual stipend.[31] For over a century, German rulers had loaned troops to various countries, to Venice, to Italy, to the Maritime Powers, and to England to conquer the Irish and Scotch.[32] America had neither money

[29] Winsor, Hist. of Am., VII-17-18.
[30] Winsor, Hist. of Am., VII-35-40.
[31] Ibid., Hist. of Am., VII-40.
[32] Lowell, Hessians in Am. Rev., 2.

nor inclination to hire these mercenary bands. France sent armies and fleets, armed and equipped by the government, seeking neither subsidies nor territory from their American allies.

Six German rulers furnished twenty-nine thousand, eight hundred and seventy-five men for service in America. Frederick II, Landgrave of Hesse-Cassel, his son, Count of Hesse-Hanau, Charles I, Duke of Brunswick, Frederick, Prince of Waldeck, Charles Alexander, Margrave of Anspach-Bayreuth, and Frederick Augustus, Prince of Anhalt-Zerbst.[33] As the Landgrave of Hesse-Cassel furnished the largest division, all the auxiliaries were called Hessians. Each ruler made a separate treaty with England stipulating certain amounts for each soldier. England paid in levy money and subsidies to the princes more than one million, seven hundred and seventy thousand pounds sterling.[34] The first division landed at Staten Island in August 1776, and participated in the battle of Long Island and until the close of the struggle served in the Northern and Southern Departments, many being captured at Trenton, Saratoga and Yorktown. "Seventeen thousand three hundred and thirteen Germans or about fifty-eight per cent of those who came over as mercenaries returned to Europe. Of the twelve thousand, five hundred fifty-four that remained, a small portion had been killed in bat-

[33] *Ibid.*, Hessians in Am. Rev., 5.
[34] *Ibid.*, Hessians in Am. Rev., 283.

tle or had died of their wounds, many had died of sickness, many had deserted, some had remained in America
after peace was concluded with the consent of the authorities." [35] Some Hessian officers and privates received
land grants in Nova Scotia and other parts of Canada.

Among the Teutonic soldiers were some Catholics.
In the Washington papers, the testimony of a German
deserter is given: "In February, two thousand Hessians,
three thousand Brunswickers and three thousand West-
phalians, the latter all Roman Catholics embarked,—
and sailed for America." Naturally, some Catholic recruits were enlisted but the deserter's estimate seems exaggerated. "It is noticeable that they" (the recruits)
"all come from Protestant principalities.—The Catholic
princes of the Empire seemed to wish to discourage the
service.—Besides the British government from its constitution preferred the employment of Protestants in
the army as well as in all other departments." [36] Frederick II of Hesse-Cassel provided the largest number of
troops. "This prince was the Catholic ruler of a Protestant country.—He showed some personal dignity and
he was one of the least disreputable of the princes who
sent mercenaries to America.[37] He was a convert to
Catholicity, but despotic and immoral. His court was
notorious for frivolity and his private life was scanda-

[35] *Ibid.*, Hessians in Am. Rev., 291.
[36] Bancroft, Hist. U. S., IX-317-18.
[37] Lowell, Hessians in Am. Rev., 5-6.

lous." The Landgrave of Hesse, although a Catholic convert, can hardly pass for a Catholic prince.[38] In the Bland papers, mention is made of a "Father Theobald," Catholic chaplain to the troops from Westphalia or Hesse-Hanau, but no further information is obtainable.[39] That there were Catholics in certain regiments is evident from the fact that Father Farmer married several Hessians at St. Mary's church, and the records show the regiments in which they served. Many of the prisoners captured at Trenton and Saratoga were confined in Pennsylvania and Virginia, and the Catholic historian of Carlisle, the Rev. H. G. Gans refers to them: "Our cemetery gives evidence that some of them by birth or conversion were Catholics and their bodies lie interred in consecrated ground." [40]

Individual Catholics became Tories, especially in Philadelphia. During the British occupation, some took the oath of allegiance, and served in official capacities. After the evacuation of the city, some were imprisoned, some executed for disloyalty. Even families were divided on the question of independence. Captain John Barry, the Father of the American Navy, was an ardent patriot, Captain Patrick Barry, his near relative, espoused the loyalist cause. Joseph Cauffman, a prominent Catholic was a Tory, his son, Dr. Joseph Cauffman was surgeon on the American frigate, *Randolph*, and perished

[38] Bancroft, Hist. U. S., IX-318.
[39] Griffin, Caths. in Am. Rev., I-174.
[40] *Ibid.*, Caths. in Am. Rev., I-278.

in an engagement with the British ship, *Yarmouth*. In the ranks of the Roman Catholic Volunteers, were a few Catholics, while in the Pennsylvania Line and the Continental Navy, many followed Barry and Moylan, FitzSimons and Meade and were true to the patriotic cause. In Maryland, where the influence of the Carrolls inspired patriotism, almost all were true Whigs. In the other colonies, Catholics were so few, and the records so incomplete, it is impossible to enumerate them. Like all other religious bodies Catholics were divided but the Tories had few Catholics in their ranks.

During the Revolution, the loyalists were treated contumeliously by the Whigs, seized and imprisoned, their property confiscated, many eventually sent into exile. In retaliation, they committed many outrages, enlisted in the regulars or the militia, engaged in marauding expeditions, and committed outrages on defenceless settlers. As a result, they were held in execration by all lovers of liberty. Yet many acted from conscientious motives. The colonists had excluded Catholics from many provinces, and had persecuted them in others, and opposed all propositions to alleviate their sufferings. The Scotch Highlanders refused to break the solemn oath they had taken not to take up arms against England. The Germans were the victims of the avarice and tyranny of their despotic rulers. Had England conquered the revolting colonies these loyalists would have gone down in history as patriots, while Washington and his Continentals would be hailed as rebels. The colonists triumphed, and those who opposed them are stigmatized as enemies and traitors.

CHAPTER FIFTEEN

The Catholic Canadians

BY the Treaty of Paris, (1763), Canada was ceded to England, and after the conquest, the Catholic Canadians were governed by a military regime and "disfranchised in a land where there were few Protestants, except attendants of the army and government officials." [1] The civil officers were mostly English adventurers, "ignorant, greedy, factious," unacquainted with the language or customs of the inhabitants, eager to amass fortunes by exorbitant fees. "All the laws, customs and forms of judicature of a populous and long-established colony were in one hour overturned by the Ordinances of the seventeenth of September; and English laws, even the penal statutes against Catholics, all unknown to the Canadians and unpublished, were introduced in their stead." [2] At this time the Catholics numbered one hundred fifty thousand, the Protestants, three hundred sixty. [3] They had a filial love for France, a devoted loyalty to Catholicism, and a natural detestation for the tyranny of the conquerors. This spirit of

[1] Bancroft, Hist. U. S., VIII-156.
[2] *Ibid.*, Hist. U. S., V-212.
[3] Russell, Maryland, Land of Sanc., 490.

unrest alarmed the British Cabinet and when the Southern colonists resisted the Stamp Act and threatened separation, special concessions were made to ensure the loyalty of the Canadians. The Quebec Act of 1774, passed by the British Parliament and approved by the King, restored to them all the rights and privileges enjoyed under the French regime. The clergy were permitted to collect tithes for the support of the churches, and religious houses, Catholics were eligible for all posts of honor and trust under the government, and the French system of laws were restored. To overawe the rebellious colonists, "it erected into one province the territory of Canada, together with all the country northwest of the Ohio, to the head of Lake Superior and the Mississippi River, and consolidated all authority over this boundless region in the hands of the executive power." [4] The colonists bitterly resented this concession and considered it one of their chief grievances against England, since, "it recognized the Roman Catholic religion, abolished English laws and established a civil and spiritual tyranny in Canada to the danger of the other provinces." [5] Catholicity was abhorred by the people of the Protestant colonies, France was an ancient enemy, and blood had been spilled and treasure expended in expelling her from the continent. The English Penal Laws had been rigidly enforced in most of the colonies

[4] Bancroft, Hist. U. S., VII-156.
[5] Griffin, Caths. in Am. Rev., III-391.

and local enactments were devised to prevent Catholics from settling and to overawe those who had found a foothold in certain places. Pennsylvania alone granted Catholics full religious freedom. The Quebec Act prevented the loyal Protestants from subduing the Canadians and destroying French power, as, "the Roman Catholic worship was as effectually established in Canada as the Presbyterian church in Scotland." [6] The united colonies denounced this outrage to religion and country, mass meetings were held protesting against the ministry and Parliament, for violating their oaths and the leading patriots inveighed against the unchristian measure. In 1774, the Continental Congress pronounced it, an attempt, "to dispose the inhabitants to act with hostility against the free, Protestant colonies wherever a wicked ministry shall choose to direct them. —Nor can we express our astonishment that a British Parliament should ever consent to establish in that country, a Religion that has deluged your island in blood, and dispersed Impiety, Bigotry, Persecution, Murder and Rebellion through every part of the world." [7] It seemed doubly ungrateful since it oppressed the loyal colonists, by the assistance of whose blood and treasure the said country was conquered from France. [8] In these impassioned speeches, addresses and pamphlets, the patriots were urged to unite in resisting these tyran-

[6] Bancroft, Hist. U. S., VII-158.
[7] Griffin, Caths. in Am. Rev., I-15-6.
[8] Ibid., Caths. in Am. Rev., I-15.

nical measures, and the people of Great Britain were apprised of the perfidy of the King and Parliament. "That we think the Legislature of Great Britain is not authorized by the Constitution to establish a religion fraught with sanguinary and impious tenets." [9] In the Declaration of Independence, one of the charges against the King was "for abolishing the free system of English laws in a neighboring province, establishing therein an arbitrary government, and enlarging its boundaries, so as to render it at once an example and fit instrument for introducing the same absolute rule into these colonies."

When the war was inevitable, Congress endeavored to conciliate their Northern neighbors. "The members of Congress had not wholly purged themselves of Protestant bigotry.—But the desire of including Canada in the Confederacy compelled the Protestants of America to adopt and promulgate the principles of religious equality and freedom." [10] In 1774, an Address was sent to the people of Quebec in which "all old, religious jealousies were condemned as low-minded infirmities; and the Swiss Cantons were cited as an example of a union composed of Catholic and Protestant states." [11] An expedition under Schuyler and Montgomery was organized in the summer of 1775, and a committee com-

[9] *Ibid.*, Caths. in Am. Rev., I-15.
[10] Bancroft, Hist. U. S., VII-159.
[11] *Ibid.*, Hist. U. S., VII-159.

posed of Adams, Deane and Jay appointed to draw up an address of conciliation to the Canadians.

"The enjoyment of your very religion, on the present system depends on a legislature in which you have no share and over which you have no control and your priests are exposed to expulsion and ruin whenever their wealth and possessions furnish sufficient temptations. We are your friends and not your enemies." [12] The Canadians were not only friendly to the invaders, many were avowed allies. Arnold paid a tribute to their interest in the patriotic movement: "Great numbers of the Canadians have expected us at Montreal for some time, and are impatient at our delay, being determined to join us in great numbers." [13] "The Canadians are friendly and join us in great numbers," wrote Schuyler to the New York Provincial Congress. Ticonderoga had fallen, Montgomery had captured St. John's, Montreal surrendered without a struggle. Arnold journeyed through the wilderness of Maine and down the Chaudiere River, and united his little force with Montgomery's army besieging Quebec. On December 31st, 1775, the city was assaulted, Montgomery killed, Arnold wounded and Morgan captured. The feeble remnants of the American troops blockaded the town until spring although hunger and cold enfeebled them, and smallpox decimated their ranks. In May, Congress sent three

[12] Griffin, Caths. in Am. Rev., I-18.
[13] *Ibid.*, Caths. in Am. Rev., III-324.

commissioners, Chase, Franklin and Charles Carroll of Carrollton to examine into the condition of the army and to induce the Canadians to unite with the Americans or at least, to remain neutral. "By a special resolution, Mr. Carroll was desired, 'to prevail on "Mr." John Carroll,' "—the Rev. John Carroll, afterwards Bishop and Archbishop of Baltimore,—"to accompany the committee to Canada to assist them in such matters as they thought useful." ' It was expected that Rev. Dr. Carroll would exercise a potent influence upon the Bishop and clergy and through them the laity of Canada." [14] The commissioners found on their arrival, a general apprehension that the Americans would be driven out of the province; and that without a restoration of credit, by the use of hard money and without a large army, they could not ask the people to take part in continuing the war.[15] The arrival of the British fleet with reinforcements obliged the besiegers to abandon Quebec and although Sullivan came with a fresh brigade, the entire force retired across the border and found safety at Crown Point. When Carleton heard the news of the invasion, he "proclaimed the American borderers to be a rebellious band of traitors, established martial law, and summoned the French peasantry to serve under the old colonial nobility, while the converted Indian tribes, and the savages of the Northwest, were

[14] Russell, Maryland, Land of Sanc., 496.
[15] Bancroft, Hist. U. S., VII-423-4.

urged to take up the hatchet against New England and New York. These movements affected the intentions of Congress and made the occupation of Canada an act of self-defence." [16] Congress however refused to abandon the hope of conquering the northern country.

When the French fleet arrived after the signing of the Treaty of Alliance, another invasion was proposed. D'Estaing issued an address to the Canadians "to throw off the British rule." Lafayette was to command the expedition, the patriotic forces should reduce Detroit, Oswego, Niagara, and Montreal, the French army and fleet would invest Halifax and Quebec. "Washington however realized that equipping and manning the contemplated army was far beyond the resources of Congress, so in deference to his advice, the speculative scheme was abandoned." [17]

Failure to win the support of the Canadians, and to make Canada an integral part of the American confederacy, was due to racial, religious and financial conditions. The antipathy of the colonists during the bitter struggle culminating in 1763, and the attitude of Congress and the leading patriots towards the Quebec Act, were potent factors in maintaining the royal power. "The instincts of the Canadian peasantry inclined them to take part with the united colonies; they denied the authority of the French nobility as magistrates and re-

[16] *Ibid.*, Hist. U. S., VIII-176.
[17] *Ibid.*, Hist. U. S., X-176.

sisted their claim of a right as seignors to command their military service." [18] Without the hardihood to rise of themselves, they were willing to welcome an invasion. The strictures of Congress on the Quebec Act and the denunciation of the Catholic religion had awakened their animosity. "O, the perfidious Congress! Let us bless and obey our honored prince, whose humanity is consistent, and extends to all religions." [19] To efface the memory of this bigotry, Congress addressed them in a conciliatory strain and Washington assured them: "The Cause of America is the cause of every Virtuous American Citizen, whatever be his religion or his descent." In his instructions to Arnold, Washington cautions him: "As the contempt of the religion of a country by ridiculing any of its ceremonies or affronting its votaries, has been ever deeply resented, you are to be particularly careful to restrain every officer and soldier from such imprudence and folly and to punish every instance of it. On the other hand, as far as lies in your power, you are to protect and support the free exercise of the religion of the country and the undisturbed enjoyment of the rights of conscience in religious matters with your utmost influence and authority." [20] Some of the officers and many of the soldiers offended the Catholic Canadians by their bigoted and thoughtless conduct and words. "Montgomery had from his birth been familiar

[18] *Ibid.*, Hist. U. S., VIII-177.
[19] Griffin, Caths. in Am. Rev., III-392.
[20] *Ibid.*, Caths. in Am. Rev., I-127.

with Catholics, but Wooster, a New England Calvinist, from a country town in Connecticut, cradled in the hatred of popery, irritated the feelings of the Canadian clergy who refused absolution to the friends of the Americans, and threatened them from the pulpits with eternal woe." [21] England had emancipated the Catholics and won the esteem of the Bishop and clergy while the invaders represented the Protestant colonies, inveterate enemies of their race and religion. The outburst of enthusiasm which greeted them on their arrival, soon gave way to resentment and opposition.

The weakness of the invading army and the lack of hard money, made the revolutionary cause unpopular. When Montgomery entered the province, the "ready assistance which they gave on all occasions by men, carriages and provisions, was remarkable.—But his most unfortunate fate added to the other incidents, has caused such a change in their disposition, that we no longer look upon them as friends but on the contrary, waiting an opportunity to join our enemies." [22] "The country was outraged by the arbitrariness of the military occupation; the peasantry had been forced to furnish wood and other articles at less than the market price or for promissory certificates." [23] Arnold was the worst offender; "regardless of Montgomery's solemn engagement with the citizens of Montreal, Arnold

[21] Bancroft, Hist. U. S., VIII-417.
[22] Washington, Writings, III-362.
[23] Bancroft, Hist. U. S., VIII-421.

so soon as he found himself free from immediate control, began systematically to plunder the inhabitants, seizing large amounts of goods without giving any account, and sending them to Ticonderoga." [24] These excesses were known and deplored by the American commanders; "I am convinced," wrote Washington to Sullivan, "that many of our misfortunes are to be attributed to a want of discipline and a proper regard to the conduct of our soldiers." General Schuyler ascribes the failure to the "scandalous licentiousness of our troops, the little care that has been taken to conciliate the affections of the Canadians." Treated as foes and ruthlessly plundered, the peasantry grew hostile, and all hope of uniting Canada to the thirteen colonies was lost.

The loyalty of Bishop Briand of Quebec materially aided England in preventing an alliance with the colonies. Following an interregnum of six years after the death of Bishop Pontbriand, he was consecrated only by the tacit consent of the English government which refused him the title of Bishop, reserving that honor for the Anglican prelate.[25] By the passage of the Quebec Act, the Catholic church was recognized and the rights of the clergy restored. "Religion is perfectly free," wrote Bishop Briand in 1775. "I can exercise my ministry without any restrictions." [26] True to his episcopal character, he was obedient to the established order and

[24] Griffin, Caths. in Am. Rev., III-393.
[25] Cath. Ency., Vol. XII.
[26] Ibid., Vol. XII.

kept the priests and people loyal to the King. When
Arnold and Montgomery invaded Canada, he issued a
"Mandement," denouncing the pernicious designs of
the invaders, praising the magnanimity and kindness
of the King, and urging the defence of homes and frontiers and religious interests against the Continental
troops.[27] He encouraged his flock to assist the Governor in expelling the Continentals and defending the
King's patrimony. "Carleton in his distress appealed to
the Catholic bishop. That prelate who was a stipendiary
of the British King sent a mandate to the several parishes to be read by the subordinate clergy after divine
service but the peasantry persisted in refusing to come
out." [28] The stipend referred to by Bancroft was a grant
of two hundred fifty pounds for his support, and one
hundred fifty pounds for his episcopal residence. Those
who joined the "Bostonnais" were excommunicated and
on repenting were forced to do public penance. "Eight
unfortunate Canadians had to do open penance, with
halters around their necks and beg pardon of God, the
Church and King George, for having helped the Americans." [29] The Canadian clergy were forbidden to have
intercourse with Father Carroll when he visited Montreal with the American Commissioners. Father Floquet,
the Jesuit, who entertained him, permitted him to say
Mass, and to hear the confessions of the American sym-

[27] Griffin, Caths. in Am. Rev., I-222.
[28] Bancroft, Hist. U. S., VIII-127.
[29] Lowell, Hessians in Am. Rev., 124-5.

pathizers, was suspended and sent to Quebec to answer the charges preferred against him. "I was complaisant to the Americans through human respect," he wrote to the Bishop.[30] Father Lotbiniere espoused the cause of America, was appointed Chaplain of Livingston's regiment by Arnold, accompanied the troops on retreat, and followed their fortunes until the end of the struggle. Father La Valiniere who also favored the invaders, was deported by Governor Haldimand and became an exile and a wanderer.[31] On the anniversary of the defeat of Montgomery, the Bishop ordered a *Te Deum* for the deliverance of Quebec and his majesty's dominions from the rebels. His loyalty is attested by the later Canadian hierarchy. Cardinal Begin of Quebec, writing to Archbishop Bruchesi of Montreal in 1900 pays a tribute to his patriotism: "If the Catholic emissaries of the United States, if the impassioned appeal of the French officers who served the cause of American independence could not triumph over the last revolt of the Canadian people, it is because the voice of the head of the church of Quebec, invoking the sacred principles of respect due to the ruling authority and stigmatizing with the name of 'rebels' those who allowed themselves to be allured, opposed to the revolution an insuperable barrier. And England, already deprived of the richest heritage in America, owed to a French Bishop, the conservation of

[30] De Coursey-Shea, Cath. Ch. in U. S., 47.
[31] Griffin, Caths. in Am. Rev., I-41.

the country of Canada,—one of the most precious jewels in the imperial crown." [32]

Some historians criticize the Bishop for his loyalty, forgetting that he was the ecclesiastical superior of another country, owing allegiance to its government and bound to support legitimate authority. Canada had no just cause to support the revolting colonies, the Quebec Act had restored their religious freedom and the colonies had protested against this just retribution. They attacked the religion of the Canadians as a menace to the free Protestant colonies and it was only when they needed help, that they solicited an alliance or neutrality. Bishop Briand as head of the church in Canada taught the old Catholic doctrine that resistance to lawful authority was resistance to the ordinances of God. He did his duty and Canada remained faithful to the Mother Country.

Although the Canadian people had no just cause for revolting, or joining the invading forces, they rendered substantial aid to the American cause. In his account of the Embassy to Canada, Father John Carroll relates, "from all the information I have been able to collect, concerning the state of Canada, it appears to me that the inhabitants of that country are nowise disposed to molest the united colonies or prevent their forces from taking and holding the strong places in that province, or to assist in any way the British arms. Now if it is pro-

[32] *Ibid.*, Caths. in Am. Rev., I-101.

posed that the Canadians should concur with the other colonies—than by such neutrality, I apprehend that it will not be in my power to advise them to it. They have not the same motives for taking up arms against England which renders the resistance of the other colonies so justifiable." The French peasantry sympathized with the invaders and were willing to assist them in reducing the country. Even in Canada—the spirit of liberty was so catching, that in spite of the direst penalties fulminated by the Bishop of Quebec, in spite of the hard things said in America about the Quebec Act, Canadians flocked to the cause of the colonies.[33] Arnold, Livingston and Schuyler testify to their friendly intentions to assist the patriots. "Find the inhabitants very friendly this way," said Arnold. "My best wishes and those of the Canadians attend you," reported Livingston. "The Canadians are friendly and join us in large numbers," was Schuyler's tribute.[34]

The names and services of some of those Canadian volunteers have been preserved in the revolutionary records. Christopher Pelissier, director of the iron works at Three Rivers, gave valuable information in regard to the defences of Quebec and the methods of reducing the fortifications and in his foundry made bombs and bullets to bombard the city and destroy the British army. He accompanied the Americans in the retreat

[33] O'Gorman, Cath. Ch. in U. S., 252.
[34] Griffin, Caths. in Am. Rev., III-338.

to Crown Point and was commissioned by Congress, an engineer. Captain Proudhomme Jeunesse urged Congress to send a special commission to promote the interests of the colonies, recruited many soldiers for the American regiments, and was exiled for his activities. Captain Clement Gosselin and Lieutenant John Goulet of Hazen's regiment were sent as secret agents and Ensign Amable and Privates Pierre Cadieux and Noel Belonge engaged in the same hazardous service. These men served in the southern campaigns and Gosselin was severely wounded at Yorktown.[35] Washington paid a tribute to their fidelity: "They behaved with stability to the United States and merit the esteem of all Americans."

So many recruits joined the invading army that Congress resolved to organize two regiments of Canadians. As the other units were under the jurisdiction of the different colonies, these new organizations were placed under the control of Congress and are known as "The Congress Own" regiments, and constituted the first regiments of the regular army of the future republic. The first unit was assigned to Colonel James Livingston of New York, a Canadian by birth. It aided in the capture of St. John's and Montreal and participated in the assault on Quebec. The second, commanded by Colonel Moses Hazen fought at Chambly and St. John's and several battalions accompanied Montgomery to Quebec.

[35] *Ibid.*, Caths. in Am. Rev., I-135.

Father Louis Lotbiniere was commissioned chaplain by Arnold. When the American army evacuated Canada these regiments accompanied it to New York although the expiration of many enlistments and the desertion of those displeased with the abandonment of the plan to reduce Canada, depleted their ranks. Recruits were sought in every colony and the regiments kept intact. The first regiment garrisoned the forts along the Hudson until the end of the war. It was Livingston's regiment which fired on the *Vulture*, thus causing Major Andre to attempt a land journey to New York, his subsequent capture near Tarrytown revealing the treason of Arnold. Hazen's command served at Brandywine and Germantown and was assigned to the projected invasion of Canada under Lafayette. At Yorktown it suffered severely losing many officers and men. Although consistent in their loyalty to their adopted country, these exiles were often unjustly treated by their comrades in arms, false charges preferred against them, and although acquitted by court marshals, many officers were forced to leave the service.[36] They were also true to their religion as Father Lotbiniere, exiled and suspended, accompanied Hazen's regiment through all its campaigns. Father Farmer visited Livingston's camp at Peekskill, baptizing children, blessing marriages. At the close of hostilities, Congress resolved "to reward the Canadian officers and men for their virtuous sufferings

[36] *Ibid.*, Caths. in Am. Rev., III-234.

in the cause of liberty." However, it was not until 1801, that grants of land were assigned them in the wilderness of central Ohio, "unsurveyed and uninhabited and of no known value." The Legislature of New York awarded them lands in Clinton County, where many of their descendants still dwell.

CHAPTER SIXTEEN

Changing Conditions

ALL the colonies, except Maryland, were founded under Protestant auspices. The Penal Laws of Elizabeth and the Stuarts were introduced, and in many instances, local enactments were framed to exclude or persecute Catholic settlers. The influx of Puritans and Episcopalians into Maryland, by the kindly invitation of the Lord Proprietor, brought intolerance to the province. Catholics were disfranchised, and obliged to pay double taxes. Pennsylvania alone, extended full religious freedom to the Catholics and they were never persecuted, although during the Seven Years War, the Assembly passed a law for disarming Roman Catholics.[1] The kindly Penn, "although he did not approve of all Catholic practises and certain doctrines, that he thought were Catholic" gave them civil and religious freedom, public worship was permitted and churches were erected.[2] Under William and Mary every official must abjure "Transubstantiation, the Mass, devotions to the Blessed Virgin and the Saints," so no Catholic could hold office,

[1] Cobb, Rise Relig. Lib. in Am., 450.
[2] Kirlin, Cath. in Phil., 83.

unless he denied the most sacred dogmas of his church. In every colony, the Dissenters hated "Popery and Prelacy"; the Anglicans abhorred "Dissenters and Papists," and both united to exclude Catholics from civil and religious freedom.

This hatred is clearly shown in the attitude of the colonists towards the French and Spanish settlers. England, France and Spain had been rivals on land and sea and the jealousy reappeared in the New World. Moreover France and Spain were the avowed champions of Catholicity, England the Protestant defender. The Carolinian colonists assailed and destroyed the missions of Santa Catalina, burned St. Augustine, plundered the chapels, and massacred several priests. "In the war with the Carolinas, the Christian Indians were nearly exterminated, only three hundred survivors gathered under the guns of the Fort at St. Augustine, remaining, to represent the once, numerous, happy towns of native converts." [3] Oglethorpe, the friend of the poor debtors of England, also attacked St. Augustine and wrought havoc among the converted tribes. The Canadian Catholics were likewise a source of anxiety to the English settlers, lest their intrigues with the savages, might bring them disaster or introduce popery. In the attacks on Canada, racial and religious hatred were intermingled, and Argall destroyed the infant settlement at Mount Desert, and carried off the priests as captives;

[3] Shea, Cath. Ch. in U. S., I-465.

New England troops plundered and desecrated the mission of Father Rale, murdered and mutilated the saintly Jesuit; English and colonial soldiers and sailors, deported the Catholic Acadians and scattered them among the English colonies; intolerant officials harassed the missionaries and destroyed their stations. "As the English colonies were constantly hounded on by their magistrates, and ministers against everything Catholic, laws, proclamations, newspapers, sermons and religious tracts all breathing the most uncharitable hatred of the church, its clergy and its faithful, the position of the missionaries in tribes along the frontier, of the French and English possessions, became one of continual danger, and they could continue their labors only by conforming to the wishes of the Canadian authorities, if they looked to them for protection or support." [4] To prevent the invasion of the English colonies, the Earl of Halifax proposed to colonize Nova Scotia with Protestants and invited Lutherans and Calvinists from the Continent, to settle in the British provinces of the Northeast. To resist Western encroachment, Virginia planned a colony west of Pennsylvania, in which, "no member of the church of Rome shall be able to hold any lands or real estate,—not to be allowed to be the owners of or have arms or ammunition,—nor shall any Mass or Popish chapels be allowed in this Province." [5] From

[4] *Ibid.*, Cath. Ch. in U. S., I-592.
[5] Griffin, Caths. in Am. Rev., I-5.

these enactments and plans, "one would suppose that the Roman Church was a constant and threatening foe to colonial institutions. The fact was far otherwise." [6]

Although England had persecuted the Catholics since Henry VIII's schism, "the troubles of the thirteen colonies led the Court of Great Britain to its first step in the emancipation of Catholics." [7] To placate the Canadians, the Quebec Act was passed conferring freedom of worship on the Roman Catholics, securing to her secular clergy their former dues or tithes, and extending its boundaries, to the Ohio and the Mississippi. "The Whigs, who secured the support of the Dissenters by posing as the Protestant party, had a hereditary claim to the popular cry, 'No Popery.' They denounced the bill as establishing popery while it merely permitted Protestantism." [8] While many parliamentary friends of America protested against the measure, Chatham declared "it was a breach of the reformation, the revolution, and of the King's coronation oath." [9] Colonel Barre warned the ministry, "if you are about to raise a papist army to serve in the colonies, from this time, all hope of peace in America will be destroyed." [10] The City of London protested against the bill, and crowds in the street saluted the King with cries of "No Pop-

[6] Cobb, Rise Rel. Lib. in Am., 451.
[7] Bancroft, Hist. U. S., VII-156.
[8] Hunt, Pol. Hist. of Eng., X-131.
[9] Ibid., Pol. Hist. of Eng., X-131.
[10] Griffin, Caths. in Am. Rev., I-9.

ery." [11] The Tories were determined to humble the patriots to their racial and religious foes; "in the belief, that the loyalty of its possessions had been promoted by the dread of the French settlements on their northern or western frontiers, Britain sought to create under its own auspices a distinct empire suited to coerce her original colonies and restrain them from aspiring to independence." [12] Anxious to conciliate the Irish Catholics and to unite the subjects of the King in Great Britain and Ireland, Lord North passed an act in 1774, "to enable His Majesty's subjects of whatever persuasion to testify their allegiance to him." [13] It became therefore a matter of policy to conciliate Ireland, in order to promote union at home, draw off the sympathy of the Irish for the Americans, and make the Irish more inclined to enlist in the regiments which it would be necessary to send across the Atlantic.[14] In 1778, the restrictions on Irish trade were partially relaxed, the penal laws modified, and Catholics, except converts, enabled to secure leases and to inherit lands as freely as Protestants.[15]

These concessions to the Canadian and Irish Catholics aroused the suspicions of the colonists. The extension of the boundaries of Quebec, convinced them that their

[11] Hunt, Pol. Hist. of Eng., X-131.
[12] Bancroft, Hist. of U. S., VII-156.
[13] Griffin, Caths. in Am. Rev., I-33.
[14] Amherst, Cath. Emanc., 52.
[15] Hunt, Pol. Hist. of Eng., X-201.

religion was endangered, that the King and Parliament planned to establish the Catholic faith among them and reduce the free Protestant colonists to religious slavery. The Continental Congress warned the people of Great Britain that the British Legislature had established "a Religion that has deluged your island in blood, and dispersed Impiety, Bigotry, Persecution, Murder and Rebellion through every part of the world." [16] They reminded the King "that his ancestors were seated on the throne to rescue and restore a pious and gallant nation from the Popery and Despotism of superstition and inexorable tyranny." [17] The leading American patriots joined their voices in the bigoted chorus, protesting against this flagrant attempt to establish Popery. "Consider your coronation oath, to protect the Protestant religion," said Thomas Paine, in Crisis Number One, addressing King George III. "Your lives, your property, your religion are at stake," Alexander Hamilton warned his countrymen. "Can a free government possibly exist with the Roman Catholic Religion?" wrote John Adams to Thomas Jefferson. The patriots of New York unfurled a banner inscribed, "No Popery." The Pope was burned in effigy in all the colonies from Massachusetts to Georgia. Bulletins were distributed in New York, exhorting the freeholders of the province "no placemen, pensioners, ministerial hirelings, popery not arbi-

[16] Griffin, Caths. in Am. Rev., I-16.
[17] *Ibid.*, Caths. in Am. Rev., I-16.

trary power." [18] This anti-Catholic spirit prevailed in every province, and sermons, addresses, pamphlets warned the patriots of the existing danger, exhorting them to defend their religion lest the King and Parliament establish the hated Catholic worship among them, as he had so lately done in Canada, and hordes of Jesuits endanger their liberties. "No King, No Popery," was the shibboleth of many of the patriots.

The outbreak of the Revolution, the invasion of Canada, the alliance with France, changed the attitude of the people in England and America. The British and Colonial Tories became the staunch defenders of Protestantism, the patriots were taunted as friends of Popery and enemies of the Established Church. Congress resolved to invade Canada, to secure her aid or neutrality, and Livingston, Paine and Jay, were constituted a committee to assure the Canadians: "We hold sacred the rights of conscience and shall never molest them in the free enjoyment of their religion." [19] Adams, Deane and Jay drew up a letter to the inhabitants of Canada, assuring them: "We perceive the fate of the Protestant and Catholic colonies to be strongly linked together." [20] Washington urged the Catholics to range themselves under the standard of general liberty,[21] warning the invading forces to respect the religion of the people, re-

[18] *Ibid.*, Caths. in Am. Rev., I-18.
[19] *Ibid.*, Caths. in Am. Rev., I-102.
[20] *Ibid.*, Caths. in Am. Rev., I-17.
[21] *Ibid.*, Caths. in Am. Rev., I-14.

buking his soldiers for indulging in the childish practice of burning the Pope in effigy. As the first expedition to Canada failed, another Commission was sent to negotiate with the northern Catholics, consisting of Chase, Franklin, both members of Congress, and Charles Carroll of Carrollton, and his cousin, the Reverend John Carroll, a member of the suppressed Society was requested to accompany them, to conciliate the Canadian clergy. Only a few months before, their religion had been reviled by the same Congress which now solicited their assistance or neutrality. The leader of the Maryland Catholics,—disfranchised and doubly-taxed, stigmatized as, "the patriot nursling of St. Omer's,"—"who did not enjoy the privileges of offering his puny vote at an election," and the banned and despised Jesuit, were beseeched to seal the good will or the neutrality of the people whom their fellow citizens had insulted so grossly during the controversy over the Quebec Act.[22] "England had treated them with justice and humanity, had with large minded policy, grappled the Canadians to her cause, by assuring to them their ancient rights and in respecting their religion." [23] The Bishop and his clergy remained loyal to constituted authority and neither the presence of the Catholic Carrolls, nor the belated promises of Congress, could swerve them from their attachment to England.

[22] Russell, Maryland, Land of Sanc., 479.
[23] Ibid., Maryland, Land of Sanc., 479.

The French alliance supplied the British adherents with further proofs that Congress had become "Papist" and that the success of the revolutionary movement meant the triumph of Popery.[24] While the Declaration of Independence had astonished and enraged the Tories at home and abroad, the alliance with Catholic France exasperated them beyond measure. "They could not see why Americans chose, 'instead of England, a faithful and loving mother,—even though at times a severe one,' to have France, 'a treacherous and cruel stepmother.' "[25] Rivington's Gazette, a New York Tory magazine, lamented the destruction of the reformed religion, and the seduction of its members to idolatrous practises and the loss of civil and religious freedom. "Since Dr. Franklin has ceded Canada and Florida to the French and Spaniards, it is to be hoped that he will give New England to the Pretender, and make the Pope Archbishop of North America and that the whole continent in the end may go to the devil."[26] Even the despised traitor Arnold, to justify his infamous conduct, warned the officers and soldiers of the Continental Army against the subservience of Congress towards the religion of their new allies: "Do you know that the eye which guides this pen, lately saw your mean and profligate Congress at Mass, for the soul of a Roman Catholic in Purgatory and participating in the rites of a church,

[24] Griffin, Am. Caths. His. Res., 1907-305.
[25] Van Tyne, Loy. in Am. Rev., 156.
[26] Ibid., Loy. in Am. Rev., 156.

against whose anti-Christian corruption your pious ancestors would have witnessed with their blood." [27] That Protestantism was doomed, that Catholicism would be fully established in the free Protestant colonies, was impressed on the patriots by the Tory journals. "But now the Congress are willing to make us the instruments of weakening the best friends and of strengthening the most powerful and ambitious enemies of the Reformation to such a degree as must do more than all the world besides could do, towards the universal reestablishment of Popery throughout all Christendom." [28] Rivingston's Gazette announced that a French fleet was sailing to convert the American Protestants, laden with "tons of holy water, and casks of consecrated oil, reliques, beads, crucifixes, rosaries, consecrated wafers, and Mass Books, as well as bales of indulgences." The French King planned to send priests, confessors, and mendicants to instruct the converts and hooks, wheels, pincers and firebrands, to torture the heretics. The venerable Franklin had been decorated by the Pope, with the Order of the Holy Cross of Jerusalem.[29] These persistent attacks encouraged the active Tories to greater zeal in the royal cause, and inspired the secret enemies to join the hostile party in defence of their persecuted Protestant brethren and to prevent the establishment of the French religion. Some patriots

[27] Griffin, Caths. in Am. Rev., I-307.
[28] Ibid., Caths. in Am. Rev., I-39.
[29] Van Tyne, Loy. in Am. Rev., 154.

yielded to the popular clamor, deserted the patriotic cause, and became zealous partizans of Britain. The ministry encouraged these charges, and even the friends of America in the English Parliament, looked with suspicion on the French alliance and the negotiations with Catholic Spain. The English newspapers copied these extracts from the colonial publications and spread them broadcast among the English people. The Whigs were accused of treason, an alliance with the American rebels. One of the most persistent rumors was the reported conversion of Sam Adams, his future ordination to the Catholic priesthood, and the desecration of the famous old Meeting Houses by changing them into Catholic cathedrals and convents. The French manners and customs, their national foibles, and the "Romish Mummery" of their worship, furnished ample materials for these sarcastic poems and ironical pamphlets. The ancient racial and religious rivalry of the two nations was revived, and every loyal Briton exhorted to defend his country and his religion. Even the leaders of the Congregationalists of New England and the Presbyterians of New Jersey and Pennsylvania, the bitterest foes of Catholicism, the consistent champions of freedom, were pictured as, "Papists" and "Jesuits."

The French army brought renewed hope to the patriots. Although Burgoyne's army had surrendered, Howe still occupied Philadelphia, and Washington's ill-clad, poorly armed, famished army was suffering at Valley Forge. While the assistance secretly given by France and the occasional gifts of Spain, had kept the American forces in the field, naval preponderance was necessary to achieve success, as England controlled the seas. French fleets and armies came to the American aid, and their active participation in the later years of the struggle, made freedom a certainty. Every ship, every regiment had its Catholic chaplains, and the hereditary distrust of Catholicism was materially decreased among the patriots by their coming. "The Catholic priests, hitherto seen in the colonies had been barely tolerated in the limited districts in which they labored; now came Catholic chaplains of foreign Embassies; army and navy chaplains celebrated Mass with pomp on the men-of-war, and in the camps and cities." [30] Religious intolerance still prevailed in certain localities and among certain individuals and occasional outbreaks occurred. The necessity and the value of the French alliance was recognized even by those who still secretly abhorred Catholicity and had denounced it in former years, so the religion of the allies was tolerated even if not respected. The Council of Massachusetts, ancient foe of the Catholic faith, had pillaged and destroyed the Indian villages and burned and desecrated the chapels, and murdered and mutilated their missionary, Father Rale. Yet, when the dusky allies proffered their aid to the patriotic cause, and petitioned the Council for a priest, an Au-

[30] Shea, Cath. Ch. in U. S., II-166.

gustinian, Father De La Motte, was sent to Machias in 1779. He had been imprisoned in New York for the crime of saying Mass without the permission of the General, and spent some months in the old sugar house on Crown Street.[31] In Pennsylvania, the change was even more notable. Catholics had always enjoyed religious freedom, were permitted to erect churches, and had organized several flourishing parishes in the city and the outlying districts. Philadelphia was the quasi-capital of the Confederacy, the seat of Congress, so the French Ambassadors, Gerard and Luzerne and the Spanish unofficial agent, Don Juan de Miralles, resided there. "Thus the first diplomatic circle at the American seat of government was Catholic, and openly so, for these envoys celebrated the great events either in their own countries or in the United States by the solemn services of the Catholic church, to which we find them inviting the members of the Continental Congress and the highest officers of the republic." [32] In 1777, General Du Coudray, a French artillery officer, serving as a volunteer, was accidentally drowned in the Schuylkill River. Mass was said in St. Mary's church, and the body interred in the adjoining cemetery. Congress voted that he be buried with all the honors of war, and attended the requiem in a body.[33] On July fourth, 1779, Gerard, the French Minister, invited the members of Congress,

[31] *Ibid.*, Cath. Ch. in U. S., II-180.
[32] *Ibid.*, Cath. Ch. in U. S., II-132.
[33] Griffin, Caths. in Am. Rev., I-295.

the President and Council of Pennsylvania and the prominent citizens to attend a *Te Deum,* the first Catholic celebration of the adoption of the Declaration of Independence. The President and many members of Congress and the Council were present, and Father Serapin Bandol the chaplain of the French Embassy preached a sermon which was printed and distributed by order of Congress.[34] In 1780, Don Juan de Miralles, the Spanish Agent, died at Washington's headquarters at Morristown. "His secretary, Francis Rendon,—set out for the camp with Father Bandol. After receiving the last sacraments, with great piety and contrition, from the hands of the Recollect priest, Senor Miralles expired.—The French chaplain recited the Catholic service at the grave and blessed it." [35] Luzerne, the new Ambassador, arranged a Requiem Mass at St. Mary's church and issued invitations to Congress and the prominent citizens to attend.[36] On November fourth, a Mass of Thanksgiving was celebrated in the parish church, and a *Te Deum* sung to commemorate the victory at Yorktown. Luzerne invited Congress and the Council of Pennsylvania to take part, and the Abbé Bandol preached an appropriate sermon.[37] The Tory papers furnished long and sarcastic accounts of these services, dwelling especially on the obsequious conduct

[34] *Ibid.,* Caths. in Am. Rev., I-316.
[35] Shea, Cath. Ch. in U. S., II-178.
[36] Griffin, Caths. in Am. Rev., I-298.
[37] *Ibid.,* Caths. in Am. Rev., I-312.

of Congress, taking holy water and kissing the crucifix. According to these reports, Congress had become "Papist" and the entire country gone over to idolatries and superstitions. It was at the requiem for Miralles, that the traitor, Arnold, saw "the mean and profligate Congress, praying for the soul of a Roman Catholic in Purgatory." [38] "The Tory papers held up to ridicule and scorn, the conduct of the Continental and State officials in approving by their presence, the worship and rights of the Roman Catholic Church." [39]

"That the times were changing, that a spirit of tolerance was coming over the nation, was proved, not only by the publicity and almost official recognition given to the solemn service of the church on certain occasions,—but much more by the constitutions adopted by the states immediately after declaring their independence of England." [40] The loyalty of Carroll, Barry, Moylan, Orono and Vigo, the patriotism of the Catholic clergy and laity, the assistance and sympathy of France and Spain, modified the former bigoted spirit and the principles of religious liberty and civil equality were recognized by the leaders of the revolutionary movement. "The time had not yet come for complete religious freedom which gained slowly; but progress was soon made." [41] Pennsylvania, Delaware, Maryland, and

[38] Van Tyne, Loy. in Am. Rev., 188.
[39] Shea, Cath. Ch. in U. S., II-168.
[40] O'Gorman, Cath. Ch. in U. S., 257.
[41] Shea, Cath. Ch. in U. S., II-166.

Virginia abolished the Penal Laws, Connecticut and Georgia placed no restrictions on Catholics, Rhode Island expunged from her statute books, the alleged discrimination against them. "Not all, it is true, inscribed on their charters, religious liberty at this time; bigotry dies not quickly." [42] Almost a century later, the last vestige of the old bias disappeared, showing that the people and their leaders had risen to the level of the Catholic Calvert." [43] Towards the close of his long and notable career, Charles Carroll of Carrollton declared that he had espoused the patriotic cause not only to secure independence but also to establish the toleration of all sects with equal rights for all. The wish of the Catholic statesman was literally fulfilled. "Happily, this wise and salutary measure has taken place for eradicating religious feuds and persecution and become a useful lesson for all governments." [44] The civil and religious principles enunciated by Calvert and Dongan were adopted and became the basis of the liberty and toleration and the source of the prosperity and greatness of the future nation.

[42] O'Gorman, Cath. Ch. in U. S., 257.
[43] Shea, Cath. Ch. in U. S., II-155.
[44] O'Gorman, Cath. Ch. in U. S., 257.

CHAPTER SEVENTEEN

Epilogue

THE treaty of Paris acknowledged the independence of the United States and inaugurated a new era for the persecuted Catholics. The Constitutional Convention of 1787 made only one reference to religion: "No religious test shall be required as a qualification to any office or public trust under the United States." Thomas FitzSimons of Pennsylvania and Daniel Carroll of Maryland were the Catholic delegates to the Convention. The famous Ordinance of 1787 extended toleration to the Northwestern Territory. "No person, demeaning himself in a peaceable and orderly manner shall ever be molested on account of his mode of worship or religious sentiments in the Territory." [1] From this great region the states of Ohio, Indiana, Illinois, Michigan, Wisconsin and part of Minnesota were formed, and the future settlers guaranteed protection from religious persecution.[2] The religious clause in the Constitution was warmly debated in the State Conventions called to approve or reject the measure. On one hand it was regarded as furnishing a sufficient guarantee

[1] Cobb, Rise of Rel. Lib. in Am., 499.
[2] McCarthy, Hist. of U. S., 219.

of religious freedom, and on the other it was feared, as giving entrance to a liberty which might endanger the Commonwealth. New York, New Hampshire, Virginia, and North Carolina insisted on a larger statement for religious liberty. The minority in Pennsylvania wished to reject the Constitution until much larger guarantees were incorporated.[3] The first Congress proposed ten Amendments recommended by the State Conventions, the first relating to religion. The jealousy and rivalry of the different sects precluded the establishment of a State Church so as in other disputed questions a compromise was effected by granting religious freedom to all sects: "Congress shall make no law respecting an establishment of religion or the free exercise thereof." Three Catholics were members of the First Federal Congress; Charles Carroll of Carrollton, Senator from Maryland, Daniel Carroll of Maryland and Thomas FitzSimons of Pennsylvania, representatives, Charles Carroll taking an active part in the discussion of the first amendment. "He thought it would tend more towards conciliating the minds of the people to the government than almost any other amendment he had heard proposed. He would not contend with gentlemen about the phraseology, his object was to secure the substance in such a manner as to satisfy the wishes of the honest part of the community."[4] Although the amend-

[3] Cobb, Rise of Rel. Lib. in Am., 508.
[4] Leonard, Chas. Car. of Carrl., 209.

ment was the result of a compromise, it was most welcome to Catholics. After a century and a half of intolerance, they were placed on the same religious footing as their Protestant brethren. Individual states might retain certain offensive enactments or formulate new ones, but the general government guaranteed freedom to all. "Thus from the beginning of national life, the United States ordained throughout all the land, as far as its constitutional power could reach, full liberty of mind, conscience and worship." [5]

The election of Washington to the Presidency of the new Republic was a source of gratification to the Catholic citizens. In March 1790, An Address from the Roman Catholics of America to George Washington Esq. President of the United States, signed by Rev. John Carroll in behalf of the clergy, Charles Carroll of Carrollton, Daniel Carroll, Dominic Lynch and Thomas FitzSimons was presented to the President. "Received an address from the Roman Catholics of the United States, presented by Mr. Carroll of the Senate, and Mr. Carroll and Mr. Fitzsimmons of the House of Representatives, and many other inhabitants of the State of New York," wrote Washington in his diary, March 15th, 1790.[6] After congratulating the President on his unanimous election the address petitioned that Catholics be allowed to participate in the benefits and the pros-

[5] Cobb, Rise of Rel. Lib. in Am., 509.
[6] Griffin, Am. Cath. Hist. Res., 1911-191.

perity accruing from the struggle for freedom. "Whilst our country preserves her freedom and independence, we shall have a well-founded title to claim from her justice, the equal rights of citizenship as the price of our blood, spilt under your eyes, and of our common exertions for her defence under your auspicious conduct, rights more dear to us than by the remembrance of former hardships." Washington responded fully acknowledging these claims: "I hope ever to see America among the foremost nations in examples of justice and liberality. And I presume your fellow-citizens will not forget the patriotic part which you took in the accomplishment of their revolution, or the important assistance which they received from a nation in which the Roman Catholic faith is professed." [7] It was a well merited tribute to the loyalty of Catholics during the titanic, revolutionary struggle, and a deserved recognition of the sympathy and aid of Catholic France, which made independence possible.

The American clergy and laity had been under the spiritual guidance of the Vicar-Apostolic of the London district but during the war he had ceased his relations with the rebellious colonies, and his American Vicar, Rev. John Lewis, governed the missions. [8] At the conclusion of the struggle, the American priests desired a local superior chosen from their own body. Foreign in-

[7] Russell, Maryland, Land of Sanc., 505.
[8] Shea, Cath. Ch. in U. S., II-204.

trigues to appoint a prelate were discovered, so a petition was dispatched to the Supreme Pontiff, asking for an American Superior and suggesting the Rev. John Lewis.[9] In 1784, the Secretary of the Congregation de Propaganda Fide, recommended the Rev. John Carroll; Pope Pius VI confirmed the choice, and issued a Bull naming him Superior of the Missions of the Thirteen Colonies.[10] The infant church was beset with many difficulties and dangers and a strong hand, clothed with sufficient authority was needed to guide her destinies. In 1789, Father Carroll was named Bishop with Baltimore as his See, and the entire Republic as his diocese. He was consecrated at Lulworth Castle, England, on August 15th, 1790, by the Rt. Rev. Charles Walmsley, Bishop of Rama, and Senior Vicar-General of England, a learned and zealous Benedictine. From that historic function dates the establishment of the American Church. Secular and Regular priests came from Europe, a steady tide of immigration from Catholic countries began. St. Mary's Seminary, Baltimore, provided native-born priests. Georgetown College and the Visitation Academy furnished training for Catholic youth. The formative period was ended, the constructive period had begun.

[9] Ibid., Cath. Ch. in U. S., II-218.
[10] Ibid., Cath. Ch. in U. S., II-223.

BIBLIOGRAPHY

AMHERST. *Catholic Emancipation.*

BAILEY. *A Sketch of the Catholic Church on Manhattan Island.*

BANCROFT. *The History of the United States.* 10 Vols.

BANCROFT. *The Formation of the Constitution of the United States.* 2 Vols.

BENNETT. *Catholic Footsteps in Old New York.*

BOOTH. *A History of the City of New York.*

BOUGHTON. *A History of the Ancient Peoples.*

BOURNE. *Spain in America.*

BREASTED. *A History of Egypt.*

BROWN. *Maryland, the History of a Palatinate.*

BURNS. *The Catholic School System in the United States.*

CAMPBELL. *Pioneer Priests of North America.* 3 Vols.

CHANNING. *The United States of America.*

COBB. *The Rise of Religious Liberty in America.*

COOKE. *Virginia.*

D'ALTON. *A History of Ireland.* 8 Vols.

DECOSTA. *Pre-Columbian Discoveries.*

DE COURSEY-SHEA. *History of the Catholic Church in the United States.*

DOWLING. *A History of the Diocese of Providence.*

FINEN. *A History of the Diocese of Manchester.*

FISKE. *The American Revolution.* 2 Vols.

FISKE. *The Discovery of America.* 2 Vols.

FISKE. *The Dutch and Quaker Colonies in America.* 2 Vols.

FISKE. *Old Virginia and Her Neighbors.* 2 Vols.

FLYNN. *A History of the Catholic Church in New Jersey.*

GRIFFIN. *Catholic American Historical Researches.* 1905-1911.

GRIFFIN. *Catholics in the American Revolution.* 3 Vols.

GRIFFIN. *The Life of John Barry.*

GRIFFIN. *The Life of Stephen Moylan.*

GUILDAY. *The Life and Times of John Carroll.*

GUILDAY. *The Life and Times of John England.*

GURN. *Charles Carroll of Carrollton.*

GURN. *Commodore John Barry.*

HALTIGAN. *The Irish in the American Revolution.*

HENNING. *Statutes At-Large of Virginia.*

HOWARD. *The Beginnings of the Revolution.*

HUGHES. *The Society of Jesus in North America.*

HUNT. *The Political History of England.* Vol. X.

IRVING. *The Life of Columbus.*

KINGSBOROUGH. *Mexican Antiquities.*

KIRLIN. *Catholicity in Philadelphia.*

LEAHEY. *A History of the Diocese of Boston.*

LEONARD. *Charles Carroll of Carrollton.*

LODGE. *The Story of the American Revolution.*

LOSSING. *A History of the City of New York.*

LOWELL. *Hessians in the American Revolution.*

MAGINISS. *The Irish Contribution to American Independence.*

MICHAUD. *The History of the Diocese of Burlington.*

MULHALL. *Explorers in the New World.*

MURRAY. *Catholic Pioneers in America.*

MUZZEY. *Life of Thomas Jefferson.*

McCARTHY. *History of the United States.*

McCARTHY. *Columbus and His Predecessors.*

McCOY. *A History of the Diocese of Springfield.*

McGEE. *The Irish Settlers in America.*

McSHERRY. *The History of Maryland.*

New York, Documentary History of. 4 Vols.

New York, Ecclesiastical Records of. 8 Vols.

O'BRIEN. *A Hidden Phase of American History.*

O'DONNELL. *A History of the Diocese of Hartford.*

O'GORMAN. *History of the Catholic Church in the United States.*

OLSON. *Northmen, Columbus and Cabot.*

PERKINS. *France in the American Revolution.*

PHELPS. *Louisiana.*

PINKERTON. *The History of Scotland.*

PRESCOTT. *The History of Ferdinand and Isabella.*

ROBERTS. *New York.* 2 Vols.

ROSENGARTEN. *American History from German Archives.*

ROSENGARTEN. *The German Soldiers in the Wars of the United States.*

ROSENGARTEN. *German Allied Armies in the North American Revolution.*

RUSSELL. *Maryland, the Land of Sanctuary.*

SCHROEDER-LOSSING. *Life and Times of Washington.*

SCHUYLER. *The Transition of Government in Illinois.*

SHAHAN. *The Middle Ages.*

SHEA. *History of the Catholic Church in the United States.* 4 Vols.

SHEA. *History of the Missions Among the Indian Tribes of the United States.*

SMITH, J. T. *History of the Catholic Church in New York.* 2 Vols.

SMITH, T. K. *The Commonwealth of Pennsylvania.*

SMITH, W. *History of New York.* Vol. I.

SOUTTAR. *History of the Ancient Peoples.*

THWAITES. *France in America.*

VAN RENSSELAER. *History of the City of New York in the Seventeenth Century.* 2 Vols.

VAN TYNE. *The American Revolution.*

VAN TYNE. *Loyalists in the American Revolution.*

WALSH, J. J. *The Thirteenth, the Greatest of Centuries.*

WALSH, J. J. *The Century of Columbus.*
WALSH, W. T. *Isabella of Spain.*
Washington, The Diary of.
Washington, The Letters of.
WINSOR. *Aboriginal America.* 2 Vols.
WINSOR. *The History of America.* 8 Vols.
YOUNG. *A History of the Diocese of Portland.*
ZWIERLEIN. *Religion in New Netherland.*

INDEX

Academy, Visitation, 280.

Acadians: In New York, 78; in Massachusetts, 123; in New Hampshire, 125; in Rhode Island, 126; in Connecticut, 127; in Virginia, 151; in North Carolina, 152; in South Carolina, 152; in Georgia, 152.

Albany: Fort Near, 63; Charter of, 69.

Albertus Magnus: Sphericity of the earth, xvii.

Albion, New: Plowden's grant, 90.

Aleutian Island, 3-4.

Allefonce Voyage, 62.

Altham, Father, S.J.: In Maryland, 44-55.

Andros, Sir Edmond: Governor of New York, 64; summoned home, 65; relieved, 65; Union of Colonies, 69; succeeds Dongan, 69.

Anhalt-Zerbst, Prince of, 238.

Anne, Queen: Kind to Maryland Catholics, 53; the statutes of Pennsylvania, 91.

Anspach-Bayreuth: Margrave of, 238.

Aquinas, St. Thomas: Configuration of the earth, see pp. 291-xvi-xvii.

Arnold, Benedict: Reasons for treason, 242; lauds Canadians, 247; conduct in Canada, 251.

Assembly, General: In New York, 66; its acts, 66-67.

Atilla: Seven Cities, xv.

Atlantis: Location, xv; Tables concerning, xv.

Azore Islands: Prince Henry, xviii.

Bacon, Roger: Distance to India, xvii.

Balboa: Discovers Pacific Ocean, 28.

Bandol, Abbe: Preaches, 216.

Barre, Col. John: His views, 263.

Barry, Captain John: Family, 183; enlists, 183; Trenton and Princeton, 183; Alliance, 184; America, 184; Father of the navy, 184; private life, 185.

Baxter, Jervis: In New York, 70-76.

Baxter, John: In navy, 190.

Beaumarchais: American friend, 209-210.

Bede, The Venerable, Saint, xvi; shape of the earth, xvi.

Begin, Cardinal: On Bishop Briand, 254.

Behring's Straits: 3-4.

Bellamont, Earl of: Law against priests, 77.

Berkeley, Lord: Grant in New Jersey, 105-106.

Blanco, Florida: His policy, 218-219.

Bok, Landnama: Norse work, 7.

Boston: Massacre, 117; Tea Party, 117.

Braddock, Gen. James: Defeat, 94-98.

Brazil: Island of, xv; voyages to, xvi.

Brendan, Saint: Island of, 8; voyages of, 8-9.

Brent, George: His grant in Virginia, 149; his religion, 149.

Bressani, Father, S.J.: His rescue, 74.

Briand, Bishop: His attitude to Colonies, 253-254.

Brockholles, Anthony: Deputy Governor, 65; in New York, 76.

Brooke, Robert, S.J.: At Newtown, 60.

Brunswick, Duke of: Sends Soldiers to America, 238.

Buddhist Priests: In America, 3-4.